To our parents,
Anna and Samuel Davidman
and
Winifred and Clarance Terry,
who started the ball rolling
and kept it on track

TEACHING
WITH A
MULTICULTURAL
PERSPECTIVE

TEACHING
WITH A
MULTICULTURAL
PERSPECTIVE
A PRACTICAL GUIDE

Leonard Davidman with Patricia T. Davidman
California Polytechnic State University, San Luis Obispo

Longman
New York & London

Teaching with a Multicultural Perspective: A Practical Guide

Longman, 10 Bank Street, White Plains, N.Y. 10606

Associated companies:
Longman Group Ltd., London
Longman Cheshire Pty., Melbourne
Longman Paul Pty., Auckland
Copp Clark Pitman, Toronto

Acquisitions editor: Stuart B. Miller
Sponsoring editor: Raymond T. O'Connell
Development editor: Virginia L. Blanford
Production editor: Victoria Mifsud
Text design adaptation: Betty Sokol
Cover design: LCI Design
Text art: Fine Line, Inc.
Production supervisor: Richard C. Bretan

Library of Congress Cataloging-in-Publication Data

Davidman, Leonard.
    Teaching with a multicultural perspective : a practical guide / by
Leonard Davidman with Patricia T. Davidman.
      p. cm.
    Includes bibliographical references.
ISBN 0-8013-0835-6
1. Intercultural education—United States. 2. Intercultural
education—United States—Curricula—Case studies. I. Davidman,
Patricia T. II. Title.
LC1099.3.D39   1993
370.19'6'0973—dc20   92-38387
                                          CIP

2 3 4 5 6 7 8 9 10 - CRS - 98 97 96 95 94

Contents

Preface

We began writing this text for elementary and middle-school teachers in the late 1980s and were deeply influenced by the spirit of educational reform that characterized that decade. Report after report showed clearly that teacher education programs would have to improve their preparation of prospective and veteran teachers for the various types of diversity that were fast becoming a pervasive part of America's classrooms. In the 1990s classroom teachers routinely face increased diversity in students' ethnicity, linguistic and cultural backgrounds, family structures, socioeconomic status, learning styles, and degree of learning handicap. More diversity, rather than less, appears to be predictable as increased numbers of immigrants from around the world join the American drama and teachers work with families suffering the consequences of new levels of economic deprivation.

In this setting, the challenge to teacher educators is at least fourfold, and this text is organized to meet these challenges. First, in a manner that encourages open-minded inquiry, we must stimulate in teachers a more positive attitude toward diversity. Second, we must motivate teachers to review their beliefs about multiculturalism in general and their own ethnocultural identity in particular. In addition, we must help teachers identify information and tools they can use to transform the complex elements of diversity into an illuminating classroom and community database. Finally, we must ignite in our teachers a desire to study their students in the students' full cultural context, to see them clearly as individuals whose school behavior is influenced by the family, community, and ethnocultural groups of which they are part. Our teachers will need to understand that to treat their students respectfully as individuals, they will need to learn about the relevant social groups in their students' lives, in both the community and the classroom. This more sophisticated perspective on individuality is an integral part of the multicultural education we espouse and a key element in the implementation process we call "teaching with a multicultural perspective."

To help achieve these goals, the text provides a number of tools. These include a practical model for multicultural education, a set of key multicultural planning questions, and a set of curriculum case studies that illustrate how the planning questions contribute to the multiculturalization of lesson plans and units. In addition, the text provides instruments and observation guides to help put multicultual teacher education into practice. Included here are the Classroom Demographic Profile, the Typology of Multicultural Teaching, the Specially Designed Academic Instruction in English Observation Form, and the Ethnic and Cultural Self-disclosure Inventory. Finally, to help prospective and veteran teachers shape their own perspective on multicultural education, teacher educators will find a well-rounded introduction to the various conceptions of multicultural education, several sets of field-tested discussion questions and experiential activities, and an annotated bibliography for equity-oriented teaching resources.

The text has been designed for flexible use in courses in which professors are integrating multicultural education and analysis into traditional content areas such as language arts, social studies, bilingual education, and models of instruction. It will also be useful in courses in which the instructor is emphasizing both the understanding and practice of multicultural education.

In different ways all five chapters contribute to this understanding and practice. For example, chapter 1 provides the conceptual underpinning for the text by clarifying the definition and model of multicultural education espoused by the authors; the postscript provides a brief review and extension of the ideas introduced in chapter 1. In addition, although all chapters contain traditional textlike conceptual material, chapters 2 through 5 offer experiential field-based activities and the opportunity to reflect on these excursions in the form of a journal entry. Chapter 2 also provides a deeper exploration of educational equity and the strategies teachers can employ to promote equity in their classrooms. In chapters 3 and 4 we use planning questions and curriculum case studies to engage prospective and veteran teachers in a reality-based dialogue about the creation of multicultural education across the K–8 curriculum. Finally, in chapter 5 we take the reader one step further as we show how multicultural education can be productively linked to other important curriculum emphases such as citizenship education, global education, and environmental education.

Regarding sequence, except for chapter 1, the chapters in this text are organized for individual and nonsequential use. The best use of this text and its individual chapters will be determined by professors as they create their own multiculturally informed courses. We look forward to hearing from those who adopt this text and would appreciate their completing and returning to us the evaluation form in appendix 7 after using the book in their classes. Finally, we ask that readers be tolerant of two stylistic conventions that are employed at different points in this text. First, in discussing teachers in general, we alternate our use of "he" or "she" because we find that using "he/she" is awkward. Second, when referring to certain ethnocultural groups we sometimes vary the label. For example, although we most often use the label African American, we sometimes use Black American out of respect for the diversity of opinion that still prevails in the African-American community over the most appropriate group label. With another group label we employ,

Native American, there seems to be a movement back toward American Indian. We hope that you will respond positively to our attempt to maintain a flexible, open-minded approach to group labels.

ACKNOWLEDGMENTS

Although the content of this text is ultimately the responsibility of the authors, many persons have contributed in various ways to its successful production. To the many pre-service candidates and classroom teachers whose questions and ideas gave us deeper insight into this project we are deeply indebted. To the reviewers whose critiques and thoughtful suggestions made the text more readable and practical we are especially grateful; these reviewers include

> David Berman, University of Pittsburgh
> Jesus Cortez, University of California, Chico
> M. Eugene Gilliom, Ohio State University
> Phyllis Goldblatt, Northeastern Illinois University
> Ellen Kronowitz, California State University, San Bernadino
> Natalie Kuhlman, San Diego State University
> Valerie Ooka Pang, San Diego State University
> Thomasine Sellers, San Francisco State University
> Rodolfo Vilaro, Northeastern Illinois University

In addition, we wish to thank our exemplary teachers for their inspirational teaching.

We also express our gratitude to colleagues at California Polytechnic State University, San Luis Obispo, for their interest, advice, and support. Richard Warren, our former department head, nurtured the project from its very beginnings, and Anita Smith, Veda Marie Flores, Ilene Rockman, David Sanchez, Mary Lou Brady, Patricia Mulligan, Bernie Troy, Donald Cheek, Mary Lud Baldwin, Howard Drucker, Susan McBride, and Robert Levison all helped in various ways.

In addition to those who inspired or enhanced the content of the text, we also wish to thank those who contributed to the production of the original manuscript and the revised draft that ultimately became *Teaching with a Multicultural Perspective: A Practical Guide*. Special thanks go to Connie Rogalla who helped with the typing of the first draft, and to Kelly Zimmerman and Nancy Vilkitis who worked on the final draft. Of course, the text itself would not have been possible without the outstanding efforts of the editorial and production staff at Longman, most notably Susan Alkana, Ken Clinton, and Victoria Mifsud. We appreciate their support and expertise in making our vision a reality.

Finally, we thank our children, Rachel and Josef, for the support and encouragement they provided as we, on too many occasions, disappeared into our respective offices to work on this project.

Leonard Davidman
Patricia T. Davidman

CHAPTER **1**

The Idea of Multicultural Education: Past, Present, and Future Possibilities

CHAPTER OVERVIEW

This chapter has three major objectives. First, it will provide veteran and prospective teachers with a practical goal-focused model of multicultural education. Second, it will demonstrate the model's flexibility by highlighting the work of five exemplary educators. Third, it will provide background material regarding the conceptions of multicultural education that are currently shaping the field; this, in turn, should help teachers develop a deeper understanding of the evolution in multicultural thinking that has occurred over the past two decades. We hope this insight will encourage teachers to develop their own practical approach "to teaching with a multicultural perspective."

With these objectives in mind, we will begin with introductory remarks regarding the significance of multicultural education, and then introduce our synthesis conception of multicultural education, a conception that will be particularly helpful for elementary and middle-school teachers. This section will be followed by an introduction to the work of five exemplary multicultural educators, leading into the multicultural education definitions that have emerged in the United States over the past 25 years. These definitions will reveal the diversity and complexity that surround the term *multicultural education*, and will help you understand why multicultural education is both controversial and critically important. We will close with questions designed to encourage critical and creative thinking about multicultural education.

INTRODUCTION

This chapter embodies a major premise of the book—that teachers in the United States, and various other nations in an ever-shrinking world, will have to be more insightful practitioners of multicultural education if they are to meet the multiple challenges that confront citizens in the fast-paced, extremely fluid, highly unequal societies of the information era. To become such practitioners, educators will need full comprehension of the various meanings of multicultural education, along with the awareness that there is no precise, "right" definition for this term. What we have are various valuable meanings, some more suitable than others for specific grade levels, school settings, and cultures. Equally important is the awareness that classroom teachers who consciously try to create a multicultural curriculum typically work with an eclectic conception of multicultural education, one that emphasizes equity and intergroup harmony. To help establish knowledge of these multiple meanings, we will turn first to a conception of multicultural education that we have synthesized specifically for teachers who work in elementary and middle-school settings.

MULTICULTURAL EDUCATION: A SYNTHESIS CONCEPTION

The conception of multicultural education that we recommend is defined by six major goals and integrates elements from several other thoughtful conceptions, most notably those articulated by James Banks, Carl Grant and Christine Sleeter, and H. Prentice Baptiste, Jr., and Mira Baptiste; because of these multiple sources we call it a synthesis conception. Although you will see in the latter part of the chapter that several theoreticians of multicultural education have sought to strengthen multicultural education by integrating it with other important curriculum areas such as multiethnic education, social reconstructionism, and global education, we will use a simpler, goal-oriented conception, one that will serve as a useful point of departure for K–8 educators seeking to learn more ways to create multicultural education in their respective grades.

We define *multicultural education* as a multifaceted, change-oriented strategy that is aimed at six interrelated but distinct goals. These goals are (1) educational equity; (2) empowerment of students and their parents; (3) cultural pluralism in society; (4) intercultural/interethnic/intergroup understanding and harmony in the classroom, school, and community; (5) an expanded knowledge of various cultural and ethnic groups; and (6) the development of students, parents, and practitioners (teachers, nurses, counselors, principals, curriculum coordinators, etc.) whose thoughts and actions are guided by an informed and inquisitive multicultural perspective. (See figure 1.1 for a visual summary.) At the classroom level of operation this set of goals can be achieved by a wide range of teaching strategies, some of which are included in figure 1.2. A more detailed list of these is provided in appendix 1, The Typology of Multicultural Teaching, a tool created by us, first, to familiarize teachers with the large number of approaches that can be used to promote

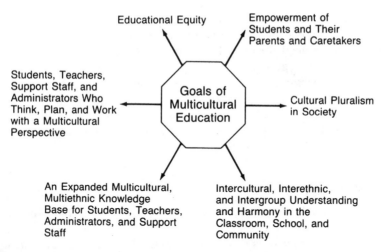

FIGURE 1.1   Examples of Goals

FIGURE 1.2   Examples of Strategies

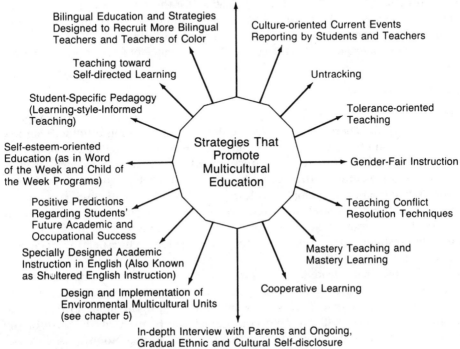

multicultural education, and second, to help educators perceive that many teachers already engage in some form of multicultural education, although they may label it otherwise (see appendix 1 for more information on the typology).

Although the typology will help you get your arms around a set of teaching strategies that can promote multicultural education, some remarks regarding the meaning of *educational equity, cultural pluralism, empowerment, intergroup/intragroup harmony, multicultural/multiethnic knowledge,* and the idea of teaching with a multicultural perspective will help you get your minds around the full meaning of the goals in our conception.

Educational Equity

We define *educational equity* in terms of three types of observable conditions: (1) physical and financial conditions, (2) the opportunity to learn, and (3) educational outcomes for both individuals and groups. For example, when teachers and administrators try to create educational equity in a classroom or school, they will strive to make roughly equivalent (exact equality is a social and bureaucratic impossibility) (a) the physical conditions under which children learn; (b) the quality and experience of teachers and administrators; (c) the opportunity for various types of learners to learn; and (d) the educational achievement of various groups of learners within the class, school, and school district (e.g., boys and girls; Blacks, Whites, and Hispanics; monolingual and bilingual learners; the economically impoverished and those who are more fortunate). It is the heightened concern with equity that, in our view, most distinguishes multicultural education; for this reason we shall discuss the topic in greater depth in chapter 2. At present, suffice it to say that when most teachers contemplate equity, they think about this basic ethical question: Is my class a *fair* learning environment for the (typically) wide range of learners in my charge?

Cultural Pluralism

Cultural pluralism, although related to educational equity, is a different type of educational goal. Whereas educational equity focuses attention on modifying key educational conditions to promote equitable learning, cultural pluralism is concerned with attitudes. It directs educators toward curriculum experiences designed to create positive cultural attitudes in the minds of teachers, students, and administrators. When teachers contemplate cultural pluralism they ask themselves this question: How can I help my students develop respect, appreciation, and/or tolerance for individuals and groups that are culturally and/or physically different from themselves? Interestingly, for decades educators have created such respect, appreciation, and tolerance among *different* learners by helping them discover what they have in common as they participate in developing a supportive classroom community. Furthermore, when teachers have developed in their students an orientation toward tolerance, it is likely that there will be better intergroup harmony in their classrooms. This, in turn, will promote educational equity, primarily because of the increased ease in establishing effective cooperative learning groups in such classrooms. It is in this way that cultural pluralism is potentially related to educational equity.

Empowerment

When we discuss empowerment as a goal of multicultural education, we think primarily about the empowerment of students, but we also include the empowerment of parents, teachers, and other school practitioners. The empowerment process we advocate would leave students better prepared in terms of attitude and skill for a variety of tasks such as

1. becoming self-directed learners, students who want to grow educationally and gradually take more responsibility for the shape and content of their educational growth;
2. taking an active role in improving the quality of the various communities they inhabit (classroom, school, local, national, and world);
3. learning how to work independently and interdependently to accomplish these tasks.

Parents are a part of the triangle of empowerment because research showed that when parents are involved in their children's education, student learning proceeds more smoothly.[1] Also, logic and experience suggest that students will develop a stronger belief in their ability to shape their world when they see their parents, and other community representatives playing an influential role in school site governance councils, school district committees and boards, and similar bodies. Thus, teachers and administrators should find ways to increase the level of meaningful parent participation in the operation of schools. This is even more true in communities that have been historically, and remain, disempowered because of racism and/or impoverished economic conditions. An effective model for developing such participation is briefly discussed later in the chapter when we review the work of James P. Comer.

Although other writers have emphasized the importance of teacher empowerment for the overall improvement of schools,[2] we include teachers in the triangle of empowerment because it is hard to imagine passive, unempowered teachers creating empowerment conditions for their students. Thus, when we plan for multicultural staff development, opportunities to engage in policy-making that extends beyond teachers' own classes is pertinent. For example, finding ways to meaningfully involve teacher and parent representatives in the selection of school and district level administrators would be a step forward for multicultural education. This more inclusive process could lead to the selection of educational leaders more in touch with community and teacher aspirations. Furthermore, parents and teachers involved in such decisions should be more knowledgeable when they set out to create empowerment conditions for their children and students.

Other multicultural education goals play an important role in the empowerment process. Although intergroup/intragroup harmony and multicultural/multiethnic knowledge are quite significant by themselves, each goal contributes in an important way to the empowerment of students.

Intergroup/Intragroup Harmony

To accomplish the goal of intergroup/intragroup harmony teachers provide knowledge, skill training, and a classroom environment that leaves individual students better prepared to live and work with members of their own social group as well as members of different cultural and ethnic groups. Because of the increasing tide of cultural and ethnic conflict in our nation and around the world, more teachers are aware that their students would benefit from a curriculum that places greater emphasis on developing positive intergroup and intragroup relationships.

Parenthetically, when we speak of cultural and ethnic groups, we have in mind general cultural groups like men and women, heterosexuals and homosexuals, and immigrants and nonimmigrants, as well as umbrella groups that are more commonly associated with ethnicity such as African Americans, European Americans, Asian Americans, Hispanic Americans, and American Indians; also included are the specific ethnic and cultural groups that are a part of these larger groups such as West Indians (Jamaicans, Barbajans, Haitians, etc.), Mexican Americans, Cuban Americans, Korean Americans, Japanese Americans, Jewish Americans, Italian Americans, Navajo Americans, and hybrid cultural groups (ethnocultural groups) like Mormon Americans who have taken on some ethnic characteristics.

As race- and sex-based crimes continue to increase,[3] it is timely indeed for educators to create curriculum experiences designed to promote intergroup tolerance and harmony. These types of experiences contribute to empowerment because they increase the range of individuals a student can work with to achieve selected goals. At the same time they also develop skills and attitudes that will help students survive in communities where drug-influenced crime and violence compete on a daily basis with the social order. Knowledge of self and the cultural, ethnic, and racial group(s) that contribute to "self" identity is a vital ingredient in the development of the positive survival attitudes alluded to above, and the multicultural/multiethnic knowledge we discuss below.

Multicultural/Multiethnic Knowledge

Each year that students are in school their knowledge regarding the history of their own ethnocultural roots should increase, along with their knowledge and appreciation of other cultural groups. Such knowledge should increase children's sense of self-worth and their belief that they and their friends have a chance for a successful future. It may also play a positive role vis-à-vis prejudice reduction. Ultimately, such knowledge lays the groundwork for the empowerment process, the development of cultural pluralism and intergroup harmony, and the ability to think, plan, and work with a multicultural perspective.

Teaching with a Multicultural Perspective

The goal of thinking, planning, and teaching with a multicultural perspective is similar to the goal of cultural pluralism in that it is strongly influenced by the beliefs and attitudes an individual holds, but it is also a much broader, inclusive goal. We can gain greater insight into this goal by addressing a basic question: What is a multicultural perspective?

A *multicultural perspective* is a state of mind, a way of seeing and learning that is shaped by beliefs about multiculturalism in American history and culture, or Canadian or British history depending on the nation the teacher is working in. This belief system helps teachers see (a) that culture, race, gender, religion, socioeconomic status (SES), and exceptionality, in complex ways, are potentially powerful variables in the learning process of individuals and groups, and (b) that useful ideas about teaching and living can be gained from studying the cultural systems and educational organizations of various nations such as New Zealand, Japan, and Germany, as well as the various co-cultures that are part of the national culture. Educators who work with a multicultural perspective will selectively utilize data related to the previously mentioned variables and knowledge base as they strive to maximize the learning experience of *each* individual student and group in their classrooms. In addition, a multicultural perspective will lead curriculum developers and teachers to select content that shows students that the art, music, language(s), history, ethics, science, mathematics, and politics of American culture have been decisively influenced by a wide range of individuals, cultures, and ethnic groups. Beyond helping teachers focus on the major objectives or goals of multicultural education, a multicultural perspective will encourage them to examine new challenges and curriculum ideas from a much broader point of view. For example, at a workshop where a principal was introducing a new assertive approach for helping parents meet their school-defined societal responsibilities vis-à-vis homework, reading aloud to children, and monitoring TV watching, a multicultural perspective would prompt teachers to wonder out loud whether assertiveness—across the board—was a culturally logical strategy given the range of parents they were communicating with in their local community. An assertive approach to enlist the active involvement of tradition-oriented Vietnamese-American parents, whose culture did not support the idea of volunteering in community agencies, or closely collaborating with teachers in the education of their children, might stem from an ethnocentric rather than a multicultural perspective.[4]

You should also realize that your point of view regarding multiculturalism will influence major dimensions of your teaching. The teacher who works with a multicultural perspective will want to be culturally sensitive to students and their families and, therefore, will become adept at collecting, interpreting, and making instructional and management decisions based on sociocultural data. This educator will also know the meaning of "cultural continuity" between home and school and will understand how to minimize or maximize this continuity tactfully depending on the circumstances. In addition, this educator will know how to teach an accurate "pluralist" American history rather than an ethnocentric, monoculturalist history. A negative example here may be illuminating. In 1987 during a week devoted to highlighting women's contributions to American society, Mrs. White (a pseudonym), a fourth-grade teacher in our community, asked her students to conduct independent research on famous American women. She gave the students a list to help them get started. All eighteenth-, nineteenth-, and twentieth-century women on this list were White and the list included such notables as Ma Barker, a female American criminal of dubious fame. This teacher probably did not realize that her list was biased. Fortunately, given the resources now available from the National Women's History Project (NWHP), it is much easier to provide multicultural, multiracial lists (see appendix 6 for more specific information regarding the NWHP). In a similar but more significant example of exclusion, the editorial board of *The Great Books of the Western World*, a 37,000-page, 60-volume compilation of classic texts, selected the work of 130 authors, including William Faulkner and Ernest Hemingway. Not one African-American author was included, even though the works of Ralph Ellison, James Baldwin, and W. E. B. Du Bois, to name a few, are to many authorities clearly on par with those of Faulkner and Hemingway in terms of their intellectual contributions to the Western world.[5]

Creating a Multicultural Setting

Of all the new things a teacher will see with a multicultural perspective, the three most important are the following: (1) effective teaching is *directly* linked to multicultural education, (2) every classroom and school has the potential to be a multicultural setting, and (3) a classroom becomes a *multicultural setting* when the students in that room experience a multicultural curriculum. In our eyes, the *multiculturalness* of a setting is not determined by the type of students in the class; it is created by the perspective and knowledge base the teacher works with. Mrs. White's class was filled mainly with White-American children, but it could have been mostly Black and Hispanic Americans, or it could have been in a Catholic girls' school where all the students were Asian Americans of one kind or another. Whatever the color, religion, ethnicity, or gender of her students, Mrs. White was delivering a biased, monocultural unit on famous American women, and in so doing was creating a monocultural curriculum *and* setting in her classroom, a curriculum that could have the effect of perpetuating racism.

This point is worthy of elaboration because it is counterintuitive to many educators' notion of what the term *multicultural setting* should mean. It is understandable for educators to want to distinguish between a classroom that is one-fifth Hispanic American, one-fifth African American, one-fifth Asian American, one-fifth White American, and one-fifth multiethnic American, and a classroom that is, let us say, 100 percent White American or 100 percent African American by considering the former to be multicultural. However, we prefer to describe such a class as multiethnic and the latter as possibly but not necessarily monoethnic. We wish to emphasize that the average public school classroom is inevitably multicultural in terms of the groups and cultures that are found in any public school classroom. There are the girls, and then the boys with their respective "cultures"; then there are the children of various socioeconomic groups, religions, and family types, and quite likely a number of ethnic, biethnic, and/or mainstreamed students who bring their own cultural baggage to the classroom. Then there is the teacher, who, among other things, is a representative of the "professional education" culture. Because public school settings are inevitably multicultural in terms of the groups that interact in the classroom, the most significant multicultural question to ask is whether the students in the classroom are receiving a multicultural curriculum. If they are not, then the setting is not multicultural in the critical educational sense of the term. In short, every classroom in the United States will be more or less multicultural in terms of ethnic and cultural groups (demography), but not all of these classrooms will provide a multicultural setting. The latter depends on the type of *curriculum* the teacher is implementing, and as we have indicated, the multicultural nature and quality of the curriculum will be a function of the beliefs and values of curriculum coordinators, principals, and, most decisively, classroom teachers.

We have talked about these values and beliefs and given some examples of what a teacher who works with a multicultural perspective will see and do; we hope we have stirred some thoughts and questions in your mind. It is time now to sharpen and extend your understanding of what it means to think, plan, and teach with a multicultural perspective by providing some examples of teachers who have taught, and continue to teach and lead, with a multicultural perspective.

EXAMPLES OF MULTICULTURAL TEACHING

The five educators we have selected—Phillip Uri Treisman, James P. Comer, Bruce C. Davis, Jaime Escalante, and Susan K. Sherwood—allow us to illustrate what can be accomplished when imaginative and energetic educators accept the challenge of working creatively with a multicultural perspective in their program, school, or classroom. Although Treisman, Comer, and Davis each worked as a school site or program leader as they applied their multicultural perspective, the lessons and inspiration provided by their work, and the work of classroom teachers Escalante and Sherwood, can easily be translated into individual classroom practice.

Phillip Uri Treisman: Mathematics Educator

Our first exemplar, Phillip Uri Treisman, a professor at the University of Texas, Austin, and formerly a mathematics educator at the University of California at Berkeley (UCB), is an example of a teacher and researcher who dramatically improved the academic achievement of an assortment of individual students after analyzing and studying the differential mathematics achievement of two different American ethnic groups.

In 1975 while Treisman was working with teaching assistants at UCB, he learned that 60 percent of the African-American students at the university were failing freshman calculus while the failure rate for Chinese students was only 12 percent. His search for the explanation of this huge difference led to a doctoral inquiry wherein he employed a wide range of methods. When traditional survey and hypothesis-directed research did not yield clues, Treisman arranged to observe and videotape 20 Black students and 20 Chinese students in their dorms and other settings as they worked on their mathematics assignments.

After 18 months of observation and interviewing, he discovered that the key to the differential pattern of success was the way students interacted with each other at the university. The vast majority of the Black-American students (18 out of 20) never studied with other students and attributed their success in getting to UCB to knowing how to separate studying from socializing. Treisman's discovery and description of the support-oriented pattern of study adopted by many Chinese students (13 out of 20) suggested that the isolated and individualistic pattern of study adopted by the Black-American students made it quite difficult for them to discover what was going on in the course and at the university.

From the "cultural" facts uncovered in his dissertation inquiry, Treisman, from 1978 to 1989, developed and refined a workshop strategy that allows students to study mathematics under the guidance of a skilled teacher and within a community of peers. In a recent interview,[6] Treisman noted the failure rate of Black students in calculus has dropped from 60 percent to 4 percent, and that for the last 10 years the minority students in the workshop program have done much better than other students. In the same interview, Treisman reported that about 30 colleges and universities are experimenting with his workshop strategy in courses such as physics, chemistry, engineering, and mathematics.

If Treisman had perceived his calculus students only as individual Americans and not as members of ethnic groups (Chinese Americans and Black Americans) and had examined the failure and success of individual students only, he probably would never have developed the educational equity workshop strategy that proved to be so successful. Treisman had to see color and ethnicity and then discover the effects of ethnic culture on study habits before he could pilot and evaluate an equity-oriented strategy. He did more than just compare the success and failure rates of one group of students against another. By not accepting the status quo, by not accepting and rationalizing the tremendous failure rate of the Black-American students as somehow linked to their lack of preparation, weaker motivation, or intellectual capacity, Treisman, unknowingly and in an embryonic manner, was beginning to work with a multicultural perspective. When he began his doctoral inquiry, in his own way, Treisman was saying "no" to dramatically unequal outcomes, at least at the level that was manifest in the UCB calculus program. And then, when his doctoral inquiry did not yield useful answers to his research problem, Treisman continued to work with a multicultural perspective, using participant observation to learn whether culturally influenced behavioral norms and patterns of behaviors were somehow linked to the differential patterns of achievement in the calculus classes. Finally, he developed a teaching strategy that has dramatically improved the success rate of Black-American students and produced positive results for other targeted ethnic groups.

Uri Treisman was working with a multicultural perspective when he attacked the problem of unequal success (educational equity), and he was using a multicultural perspective (knowledge of the family and cultural background of his students) when he developed a solution. At no point did he directly teach about the significant cultural or ethnic characteristics of a specific group, but this was not necessary. Teachers do not have to aim simultaneously at all six goals of multicultural education to teach with a multicultural perspective, but in the course of a year, they should aim for as many as are possible and logical, given their specific course and instructional context.

James P. Comer: Child Psychiatrist and School Reform Leader

With our next example we examine another success story involving Black-American students, and in this instance, a creative Black-American educator as well. This story began in 1968 at Katherine Brennan and Martin Luther King, Jr. Elementary Schools, two predominantly (99 percent) Black-American schools in New Haven, Connecticut. In 1968 these two schools were ranked near the bottom of New Haven's 33 elementary schools in achievement and attendance, and teachers were leaving the school at the rate of 25 percent per year. The parents were described as "dejected, distrustful, angry and alienated."[7] At this point an educator with the right instincts, assumptions, methodology, personal history, and historical perspective entered the history of these two schools and became the hero of a drama that is still unfolding in the 1990s as more and more schools across the nation adopt what is being called the "Comer Plan." The protagonist in this story is Dr. James P. Comer, professor of Clinical Psychiatry at Yale University and director of the Yale University School Development Program, a component of Yale's Child Study Center. Within the space of seven years—by 1975—Comer and his Yale colleagues, and the schools' parents, administrators, teachers, and mental health specialists had developed a plan that had essentially turned these two schools around. As evidence Comer has written: "By 1975 the program was clearly having an effect. Behavioral problems had declined, relations between parents and staff had improved and the intelligence of the children had become manifest."[8] He adds that by 1979, the students who had once ranked lowest in achievement among the 33 elementary schools in the city had caught up to their grade level by the fourth grade, and that by 1984 "pupils in the fourth grade in the two schools ranked third and fourth highest on the Iowa Test of Basic Skills."[9]

For our purposes, three elements in this story are crucial: first, two perceptive realizations that lie at the core of the Comer plan; second, several of the key components in the Comer plan; and finally, the manner in which a dualistic and multicultural perspective was brought to bear in Comer's problem analysis and solution.

Comer and his colleagues realized that the essence of the problem at Katherine Brennan and Martin Luther King, Jr. schools was not the low achievement, low morale, and low attendance; it was the schools' failure to pay attention to the psychological development of their students and the lack of positive relationships between the schools and the schools' parents. These perceptions, along with other insights, led to the development of carefully structured governance and management teams that included all major stakeholders at each school site. The teams consisted of the principal, teacher representatives, parent representatives, and a member of the school's mental health unit, and operated under some very interesting guidelines.

Team members would recognize the authority of the principal, but the principal would not push through decisions without weighing the concerns of team members, and remarkably, decisions made by this governance team would be by consensus rather than vote. As a result of the consensus strategy, most of the decisions made by the governance team resulted in ownership and buy-in by team members rather than winning or losing. At these schools the principals shared real power with teachers, mental health professionals, and most significantly—in these disenfranchised, alienated, economically poor communities where 70 percent of the families received Aid to Families with Dependent Children—with parents.

The creation of a school governance team and a mental health team, and development of a comprehensive school plan based on input from all adult stakeholders were major elements in Comer's problem solution. But in what ways did a dualistic and multicultural perspective contribute to this solution? Let us begin with what might not be so obvious. Comer saw ethnicity (African Americans), saw poverty, and recognized a distinct and unique ethnic and cultural group (African Americans) whose children were failing as students in large numbers in American schools. Comer did not choose to study several of these children or several families, a decision that would have been intellectually and ethically defensible. He and the team he led chose to study and become intimately involved over 12 years with the real day-to-day life of an entire school. Comer's team studied the interactions between the school and the African-American students and families who lived in an economically poor community—in Comer's words "out of the mainstream." Comer's solutions, if they were achieved, would be for poor African Americans as a group, as well as other American ethnic groups with overlapping characteristics.

Beyond selecting low socioeconomic status (SES) African-American families and their low-achieving schools as the focus for long-term study, Comer, like many social scientists and educators, brought a specific belief system or mind-set to this inquiry. His own life as a Black American and his academic preparation had produced a belief system that said, in effect, that culture, and race, and SES, and ethnicity, and self-esteem could all be powerful variables in the learning process of individuals and groups. It was this set of beliefs, functioning as a multicultural perspective, that led Comer to see the problems at King and Brennan Schools as cultural in nature. In Comer's own words, "our analyses of interactions among parents, staff, and students revealed a basic problem underlying the schools' dismal academic and disciplinary record: the sociocultural misalignment between home and school."[10] In anthropological terms, Comer and his colleagues discovered that there was cultural discontinuity between the home and school; this discontinuity created conflict between the schools and the families in the community, and further, the children, parents, teachers, and administrators were all victims of this heretofore invisible clash of culture. It was Comer's ability to see the *cultural* nature of the problem that allowed him to design a powerful, schoolwide approach to psychological, social, and academic development, an approach that attended to differences between the home and school culture as well as any problems that might arise because of ethnic or racial differences between teachers and students.

Bruce C. Davis: Elementary School Principal

Our third example centers on the work of Bruce C. Davis, a principal who has helped create a unique parent involvement program over a nine-year period at Emerson Elementary School in Rosemead, California. Because our conception of multicultural education has as a major objective the establishment of a strong, empowering, culturally informed relationship between the home and school, almost any parent involvement program that is implemented in a culturally sensitive manner will provide an example of an educator working with a multicultural perspective. Davis's efforts are worthy of recognition because of the special demographic characteristics of his school and the unique aspects of his personal effort to create a dynamic parent participation program at Emerson.[11]

In 1989–1990 Emerson Elementary had 650 students; 44 percent of these students were limited English proficient and 38 percent of the school's families were on welfare. In addition, the school's families spoke 19 different languages or dialects, creating an atypical and challenging circumstance for a principal interested in parent involvement. Languages used for oral and written communication included Cambodian, French, Tagalog, Thai, Burmese, German, Italian, Zapotec (Native Mexicans from Mexico), Spanish, Vietnamese, Cantonese, Mandarin, Chiu Chao, Fukinese (a Chinese dialect), and English. Since 1980 Davis and his staff have met their multilingual challenge in a number of ways. One of these is the Emerson School parent participation program, which includes the following:

1. Each week one student from each class receives a blue ribbon for being the "student of the week" and one student receives a red ribbon for being "super reader of the week"; these ribbons (1,470 per year), which are donated by the Parent–Teacher Association, are presented to the students every Friday during morning assembly.

2. Each teacher completes two "reason slips" per week, listing the reasons the selected students received their ribbons. Later, the principal and two home/school coordinators call the parents of each selected child; referring to the reason slips, the callers tell the parents why their child was awarded the ribbon and emphasize how proud the teacher and school are of their child.

3. School meetings that involve parents are conducted in six languages, and letters are sent home in four languages.

4. The school constantly sends home thank-you notes and letters of praise to both parents and students.

5. The school learns about parents' special skills and encourages the parents to use them at the school.

Because of these and other program elements, Emerson Elementary School has received a California Distinguished School Award. Once again, in a complex setting, we see a school staff joining together to involve parents in the school program. These examples from Connecticut and California should convince you that parents will support the school program when educators find creative, meaningful, and culturally informed ways to involve them.

Jaime Escalante: High School Calculus Teacher

Our fourth example reviews the strategies and accomplishments of Jaime Escalante, the remarkable and highly acclaimed mathematics educator whose work was vividly portrayed in the film *Stand and Deliver.* Our focus is on Escalante's efforts specifically, even though we are aware that Garfield's successful advanced placement program in mathematics and other content areas was the creation of a team of dedicated educators, most notably Benjamin Jimenez who worked with Escalante in mathematics. When Escalante began teaching in Los Angeles' Garfield High School in 1974 the school was predominantly Latino American (95 percent); approximately 75 percent of the student body was eligible for free or reduced-cost lunches if they chose to apply. By American standards Garfield High School served a low-SES community in 1974, and the same held true in 1987. However, one important statistic did change in the 13-year period between 1974 and 1987: the number of Garfield students who were taking and passing the advanced placement calculus exam.

It took Escalante, a Bolivian immigrant, a few years just to discover what the advanced placement examinations were all about, but when he understood the nature and rationale for the exam, he realized that the advanced placement (AP) exam in calculus could become a powerful motivational force for the entire mathematics program at Garfield. In 1977, the idea of linking the AP calculus test with Latino-American students from a low-SES high school that had almost lost its accreditation in 1975 was a bold thought, but bold is an understatement when discussing the drive, imagination, and single-mindedness of Jaime Escalante. In 1978, four out of seven of his students passed the exam. This number grew each year until in 1987 129 of the students taught by Escalante and Jimenez took the exam and 89 passed (66 percent). In 1987 there was no comparable high school in the United States that performed nearly as well, and Garfield students scored much better than students at most middle- and upper-class high schools in the United States. What led to this tremendous change at Garfield, and how does it relate to teaching with a multicultural perspective?

The story of Escalante's success with students taking advanced mathematics at Garfield (algebra, trigonometry, analytic geometry, and calculus) has been spelled out in detail by Jay Matthews in his book *Escalante, The Best Teacher in America,*[12] and much of what we relate here is based on our interpretation of material in the Matthews book. In terms of our model of multicultural education, the goals Escalante addressed were educational equity and the creation of collaborative, empowering relationships among parents, teachers, and students.

From the very beginning Escalante "wanted to prove that Mexican-American children with fathers who were fourth-grade dropouts could match the best seniors at Beverly Hills High School."[13] This is what equity meant to Escalante. His was not an expansive view that consciously included Blacks, Asians, and other minorities, but it encompassed the Latino cultures Escalante could identify with, and the largely

Mexican-American student population at Garfield. For Escalante, equity meant that relatively poor Latin-American students would perform as well as, or better than, the children of wealthy White Americans in what he considered the most difficult of all high school subjects. In a sense, calculus became a metaphor for success, a vehicle for showing Latin-American students at Garfield, and every school, what they could accomplish if they worked hard and believed in themselves, and Escalante. Of course, Escalante worked just as hard with the Asian-American, Black-American, and White-American students who enrolled in his classes, largely as a result of Garfield's special magnet program related to computers.

Escalante also sought to establish a special collaborative relationship with and between his students. He cared about the students he worked with and gave of himself in a manner that few would or could emulate. The amount of time he invested in this program shows his dedication. Escalante and his close collaborator Jimenez were available to answer student questions before school, at lunch time, and after school—often until 5:00 P.M. For many students and teachers the day ended between 2:00 P.M. and 3:30 P.M. Escalante was also not shy about contacting parents, enlisting their support, and sometimes challenging them. At the beginning of the year he would call the parents of all of his algebra II students, introduce himself, and exchange pleasantries. The parents of his calculus students (starting in 1981) received another message in the form of a contract, which he asked, and expected, all students and parents to sign. With their signatures, both parents and students agreed that the student would return to Escalante's room at 2:00 P.M. for more lectures and exercises, which often lasted until 5:00 P.M. For these hours, Mr. Escalante received no extra pay. In Japan such after-school education to prepare for special exams takes place in private schools and is called *juku*. The educators who provide it are paid well. At Garfield, Escalante and Jiminez, and others who strongly identified with their students' academic success, received a different type of reward, although they would surely have been delighted to accept extra remuneration if it had been available.

Escalante and Jiminez would sometimes speak with parents about matters that related to cultural conflict and cultural pluralism. An example that involved one of Jiminez's students is particularly revealing. The student was having difficulty keeping up with trigonometry homework because she had to work as a cashier three nights a week at her parents' restaurant, which was a one-and-a-half hour bus ride from her home. When she had stopped handing in homework, Jiminez decided to visit the girl's parents, accompanied by his more experienced colleague and department head Escalante. After Escalante explained to the parents that their daughter was bright enough to be an engineer or physicist or teacher, the father informed them that they had "the wrong picture. Women are just here to get married and have kids and that's all. She has to work."[14] Escalante informed his father that *he* had the wrong picture, that he could not force his child to work, and that Escalante might have to call the authorities. The bluff led to a compromise. The student would work two nights a week, and her parents would buy her a desk to help her do her homework. The student later passed the advanced placement calculus test and went to Princeton before returning to California State University, Los Angeles, to pursue an engineering degree. In this instance Jiminez and Escalante took a couple of extra hours to speak with a traditional Latino male about the new Hispanic-American culture they wanted his daughter to be a part of, a culture in which both men and women could aspire to be professionals.

In the course of his Garfield career, which ended in 1991 when he joined the faculty of Hiram Johnson High School in Sacramento, California, Jaime Escalante confronted and challenged administrators, teachers, counselors, and students. But with his students, in particular, he did it in a manner that endeared him to them. For his students he played many roles and used many tactics, but the persona that comes through most strongly in Matthews's book is Escalante as the inspirational and demanding coach of the calculus team. For him the AP exam each spring was the Olympics. He would get his team ready, and his students would behave like teammates; the fast would help the slower, and all would move forward together. His classes would have a pep rally at the beginning and receive occasional pep talks during the period as needed. At the beginning of the year he told them: "You want to make your parents proud. You want to make your school proud. Think how good it will feel to go to college and know that you did the Calculus A.P."[15] His calculus team had special jackets, a special sweatshirt, and a special affinity for hard work and winning. Like many successful athletic coaches Escalante intuitively understood the power of a winning team and a winning tradition, together with the utility of a mystique and reputation for the coach.

Susan K. Sherwood: Primary Grade Teacher

For our final example we'll travel to Hansen Elementary School in Cedar Falls, Iowa, to describe the work of veteran first-grade teacher, Susan K. Sherwood. Hansen Elementary, located in what is commonly perceived as America's heartland, has the student population most Americans would stereotypically expect. In 1988 with about 480 students Hansen Elementary had fewer than five African-American students, a few Asian, American-Indian, and Hispanic students, and a large (95 percent plus) population of White-American students of varying socioeconomic status and religious background. However, along with the abundance of White students, there was a great deal of diversity for teachers to manage, and Sherwood's first-grade classroom was no exception. In her eighteenth year of teaching first grade at Hansen Elementary, this is the way Sherwood described the diversity in her classroom in an article entitled "Portrait of an Integration: A Child with Severe Multiple Disabilities Integrated into a Regular First Grade Classroom."[16]

> As a teacher of young children, my perspective on this integration process was different. Every class has a wide range of abilities and problems. This particular group of twenty-one students was no different. The intelligence range as measured by the Cognitive Abilities Test was 137–168. Shane was reading at the eighth grade level; Tom was diagnosed as learning disabled; Jane was medically diagnosed as hyperactive; Micah was adept at mathematics problem solving; Erica was a six year old in puberty; Jennifer, Ryan, and Samantha were at-risk because of their home environments and past experiences. (All the students' names are pseudonyms.)

Sherwood, like many contemporary K–8 educators, accepted the responsibility of creating a caring, supportive, environment for the wide range of learners she described. These students, like the others in her class, needed a special kind of caring environment, and at this point in her career, Sherwood was very well prepared in terms of philosophy and skills to create such a climate. In discussing the needs of this group of first graders, she wrote:

> *All* needed to belong to our classroom community and to accept their own strengths and limitations before they could freely accept others. To develop confidence, instill love of learning, and enhance self-concept, the teacher builds on each child's uniqueness—creating a motivating and challenging environment where all children are free to work cooperatively, learn from mistakes, take risks and rejoice in accomplishments. Such a classroom community is a support system for each of its members.[17]

Clearly, this is an educator who is attending to the equity, self-esteem, and intergroup harmony needs of her students, and in so doing is creating a strong foundation for a wide-ranging multicultural curriculum. With her commitment to, and competence in, meeting the diverse academic and social needs of her students, Susan Sherwood provides a fine example of teaching with a multicultural perspective. But she was more than a fine example, and it was her willingness to work with Ann, her twenty-first student—on a full time basis—that transformed this teacher into an exemplary and inspiring model for future and veteran educators.

At six years of age Ann was a child with severe multiple disabilities. She had suffered birth trauma, was head injured, had moderate to severe mental disabilities, had no right field vision, and possessed a small amount of left-peripheral and central vision. She had hemiplegia to the right side of her body but was ambulatory and was verbal. She was a child who, in the past and in many schools in the present, would have spent all or a good portion of her day in a "special day class" taught by a "special" educator, a teacher who had received special training to work with severely handicapped (or challenged) learners like Ann.

Jeni Moravec, the special educator at Hansen Elementary, felt that for Ann the "least restrictive environment" stipulated by federal law might be a full-time integration placement in Susan Sherwood's first-grade classroom, and she asked Sherwood to accept such a placement. Although she had no formal preparation in special education, Sherwood's belief in free public education for all students and her understanding of Public Law 94-142 (the Education for All Handicapped Children Act of 1975) suggested to her that if her classroom might be the one most likely to allow for maximum social and academic growth for Ann, then she ought to agree to the request and do her very best to make her classroom the least restrictive environment. After reaching this decision, she soon discovered, to her surprise, that she was something of a pioneer in Iowa, at least in 1988. Although PL 94-142 had mandated full implementation of its provisions by 1980, Susan soon learned that in 1988 she was one of the few public school educators in Iowa working with a severely challenged student on a full-day basis in a regular education classroom. Several years later, Ann, the student Sherwood worked with, had completed her third year in a regular education environment, and in 1990 all the severely challenged students at Hansen Elementary were learning in regular education classrooms.

Creating Equity for Ann.   Several factors combined to make Susan Sherwood's classroom work for Ann and the other children in her class. First, Jeni Moravec, the special educator, on most days spent at least one hour in Sherwood's class working with Ann as well as other students and simultaneously providing Sherwood with the technical and emotional support she needed, particularly at the beginning of the year. A second factor stemmed from Susan Sherwood's realization that she needed to create a team of adults to make this type of integration work. Her classroom team consisted of herself, the special educator, a parent volunteer, and a graduate student from a nearby university. In addition, the building principal and two professors served as resource people for the team, and the members of this team had to function in a special way, as she explains:

> Before working in my classroom, each [team member] had to agree to assume the role as a "facilitator of learning." Their primary purpose may have been to facilitate integration; however, any child in need was to be supported when the adult was not directly involved with Ann. In this way, children did not perceive Ann as having a special helper. Additionally because the support person was not always immediately available for anticipating and intervening prior to the natural flow of actions and consequences, Ann had to develop independence and responsibility. At times it was difficult to step back and allow Ann the opportunity to fail. Like other students she needed the freedom to fail in order to learn through trial and error.[18]

It is noteworthy that the nonhandicapped students in the class were also a significant part of the classroom team. The students served as role models for appropriate behavior, and several served in more direct facilitative roles, sometimes gathering materials for Ann and other times encouraging her to complete the task in an unemotional but firm manner.

A third critical factor, from our perspective, pertains to class size. The school district in this instance created an environment where educators could take action regarding equity because they were working in a classroom with the appropriate number of students. The debate about the "educational significance" of class size goes on and on, but not in our minds. Given the diversity in Sherwood's first-grade classroom, 21 students is quite ample; 30 or more students, in our opinion, would make failure for such efforts almost inevitable.

While other factors could be mentioned, the most critical one was Susan Sherwood and her belief system. She did not have to accept Ann and could easily have worked out a compromise with the special educator—"I'll take Ann in the morning, and you keep her the rest of the day." Indeed, a half-day assignment by itself would have been quite challenging. But it would not have been the test Moravec wanted, nor the chance Sherwood wanted Ann to have. Sherwood was willing to risk failure, to go beyond past practice, to accept change and continue learning. Although much of her success could be attributed to employing the correct set of strategies (the team of adults, cooperative learning, full as well as parallel participation in classroom activities), it was her belief in Ann's right to have a full-time opportunity to live and learn in a regular classroom that set the stage for success with integration and prepared the way for what will likely be Ann's later successes in living a fruitful life in an integrated world filled with people of varying strengths and disabilities. Because of their experiences with Ann, and Sherwood's modeling, all of the 21 learners in Ann's first-grade classroom will be better prepared to live with her in this integrated world, a world where the academic, employment, and general citizenship rights of disabled citizens are increasingly well protected.[19] Although Susan Sherwood was a modern-day pioneer in Iowa in 1988, she was also part of a slow national movement toward greater classroom integration of students with severe handicaps. In 1987 the Severely Handicapped Branch of the Federal Office of Special Education funded five states (California, Colorado, Kentucky, Virginia, and Illinois) to undertake "systems changes projects," and since then has approved projects in 11 other states. In these 16 projects the main goal has been to increase significantly the number of students with severe disabilities who were being educated in integrated learning environments—the so-called regular classroom environment.[20]

Each of these five educators—Phillip Uri Treisman, James P. Comer, Bruce C. Smith, Jaime Escalante, and Susan K. Sherwood—with their special projects and successes, remind us that educators can pursue selected goals within our model with different strategies. Our model of multicultural education has six goals, and each can be pursued in a variety of ways. Furthermore, although the goals in our conception will likely remain the same, the methods to achieve them will change as the educational context changes and the teacher's multicultural perspective matures and evolves. Some of this evolution in perspective will likely arise from exposure to other conceptions of multicultural education, and with such potential growth in mind we next review the definitions that have shaped the dialogue in the field of multicultural education over the past 25 years.

MULTICULTURAL EDUCATION: AN EVOLVING CONCEPT

Definitions or interpretations of multicultural education can be categorized into at least four broad, overlapping categories. First, there are definitions in which *cultural pluralism* is the dominant defining characteristic. A second type defines multicultural education in terms of *educational equity,* while a third type links multicultural education to the reduction of racism, sexism, and other -isms. Finally, there are definitions that integrate multicultural education with other philosophical movements or approaches to education such as social reconstructionism, multiethnic education, global education, and Afrocentric education. We will examine several cultural-pluralism definitions first.

Definitions Involving Cultural Pluralism

In 1977 several examples of cultural-pluralism-type definitions were disseminated in *Multicultural Education: Commitments, Issues, and Applications,* a document edited by Carl Grant and published by the influential Association for Supervision and

Curriculum Development (ASCD).[21] The following are located in the "definition" section of this document:

1. In educational terms, the recognition of cultural pluralism has been labeled "multicultural education."
2. Multicultural education, as interpreted by ASCD, is a humanistic concept based on the strength of diversity, human rights, social justice, and alternative life choices for all people.

Elaborating on these statements the ASCD authors wrote that

> the essential goals of multicultural education embrace: (a) recognizing and prizing diversity; (b) developing greater understanding of other cultural patterns; (c) respecting individuals of all cultures; and (d) developing positive and productive interaction among people and among experiences of diverse cultural groups.

Another definition that revolved around cultural pluralism appeared in the work of Mira L. Baptiste and H. Prentice Baptiste, Jr.[22] The Baptistes, whose definition was part of a competency-based approach to multicultural teacher education, wrote: "Conceptually, multicultural education is that which recognizes and respects the cultural pluralistic nature of our society in the United States." While these pluralism-oriented definitions were being articulated in the late 1970s, another view that emphasized equity was being formulated, and to this type we now turn.

Definitions Involving Equity

The following are illustrative of the equity-oriented definitions. The first comes from James Banks[23] and the second from Gollnick and Chinn.[24]

> Multicultural education [is] an educational reform movement that is concerned with increasing educational equity for a range of cultural and ethnic groups.

> Multicultural education is the educational strategy in which the student's cultural background is viewed as positive and essential in developing classroom instruction and a desirable school environment. It is designed to support and extend the concepts of culture, cultural pluralism, and equity into the formal school setting.

Gollnick and Chinn's definition embraces cultural pluralism as well as equity; both theirs and Banks's, like the Baptistes', suggests that for multicultural education to become a reality, the total school environment will need to reflect a commitment to multicultural education. In this vein, Banks has recently described multicultural education as an institutional change process that requires changes in the total environment.[25] Although the definitions in this section present a substantial challenge for educators, some multicultural advocates feel they are incomplete because they do not focus on racism. Examples of definitions that explicitly mention racism follow.

Definitions Involving Racism

The first two definitions in this section emerged from the work of educators brought together to carve out guiding definitions for influential organizations; the final definition appeared in a survey disseminated by Eugene Kim of California State University, Sacramento. The first one below is extrapolated from Standard 2.1 of the standards employed by the National Council for the Accreditation of Teacher Education (NCATE) during the years 1979–1986; the second is from *Excellence in Professional Education,* a document created and disseminated by the Office of the Chancellor of the California State University system.

> Multicultural education is preparation for the social, political, and economic realities that individuals experience in culturally diverse and complex human encounters. . . . Multicultural education could include but not be limited to experiences which: 1) Promote analytical and evaluative abilities to confront issues such as participatory democracy, racism and sexism, and the parity of power; 2) Develop skills for values clarification including the study of the manifest and latent transmission of values; 3) Examine the dynamics of diverse cultures and the implications for developing teaching strategies; 4) Examine linguistic variations and diverse learning styles as a basis for the development of appropriate teaching strategies.[26]

> Multicultural education is viewed as a methodology to encounter racism and prejudice based on ethnic identification and to promote positive attitudes about human diversity.[27]

Finally, Kim, in a 1987 survey pertaining to multicultural education, offered this definition:

> Multicultural education is a deliberate educational attempt to help students understand facts, generalizations, attitudes, and behaviors derived from their own ethnic roots (origins) as well as others. In this educational process students will unlearn racism (ethnocentrism) and recognize the interdependent fabric of our human society, giving due acknowledgment for contributions made by various ethnic groups throughout the world.[28]

Although these definitions clearly address racism and integrate this focus with cultural pluralism, it is noteworthy that within this set the issue of equity is not mentioned at all, and each of the definitions stops short of actively preparing students to restructure society significantly. To find this more radical conception we will need to examine our final and most complex type of multicultural definition.

Multicultural-Education-Plus Definitions

The fourth type of multicultural education definition derives from the work of Carl Grant and Christine Sleeter, James Banks, Asa Hilliard III, and Christine Bennett, among others. Both Banks and Grant, and to a lesser extent Hilliard and Bennett, have been leaders in defining and redefining the field of multicultural education. For example, in this chapter we see Grant associated with the 1977 ASCD document that almost equated multicultural education with cultural pluralism, and find Banks disseminating a definition that tightly linked multicultural education to educational equity. It is noteworthy, therefore, that in their writings in the 1970s and 1980s both of these African-American educators connected multicultural education to a broader orientation to education to make it, in their eyes, a more complete and meaningful approach. Perhaps this was because their own ethnic perspective and experience persuaded them that multicultural education was only a partial response to the curriculum needs of students of color, particularly those who have experienced the greatest amount of oppression. In Banks's case it was *multiethnic education,* and for Grant and his collaborator, Sleeter, it was *social reconstructionism.* Other educators such as Hilliard and Bennett also forged new connections; for Hilliard it was Afrocentric education and for Bennett it was global education. Below we discuss Grant's integrated conception of education that is multicultural and social reconstructionist, Banks's view of multicultural/multiethnic education, and last, the idea of Afrocentric education.

Multicultural Education Plus Reconstructionism. Sleeter and Grant in their book *Making Choices for Multicultural Education: Five Approaches to Race, Class, and Gender*[29] describe multicultural education as an approach that seeks to "reform the entire process of schooling for all children,"[30] "improve society for all,"[31] and "develop skills and a knowledge base that will support multiculturalism."[32] In contrasting multicultural education with education that is multicultural and social reconstructionist, Sleeter and Grant write that the latter "deals more directly than the other approaches have with oppression and social structural inequality based on race, social class, gender, and disability . . . [and] prepares future citizens to reconstruct society so that it better serves the interests of all groups of people and especially those who are of color, poor, female, and/or disabled."[33]

Multicultural/Multiethnic Education. Although Banks would find much to agree with in Sleeter and Grant's words, his reaction to multicultural education suggests that he would want to add a multiethnic component. Banks has provided a lucid equity-oriented definition of multicultural education, but he always believed that multicultural education needed to be complemented and strengthened by multiethnic education. His 1981 remarks suggest that he would have a similar concern about education that is multicultural and social reconstructionist:

> A generic focus within a school reform effort, such as multicultural education, can make a substantial contribution to the liberal education of students. However, school reform efforts should go beyond the level of generic multicultural education and focus on the unique problems that women, Blacks, youth and other cultural groups experience in American society. Many of the problems these groups have are unique and require specialized analyses and strategies. . . . Multicultural education is a politically popular concept because it is often interpreted to mean lumping the problems of ethnic minorities, women, and other groups together. Public and school policies that are based primarily on lumping the problems of diverse groups together will prove ineffective and perhaps detrimental to all of the groups con-

cerned. Because of the unique problems some ethnic and racial groups have in American society, school districts should implement *multiethnic* education to complement and strengthen *multicultural* education. These concepts are complementary but not interchangeable.[34]

Geneva Gay, another leading advocate of multiethnic education, in discussing what she believes should be the central focus of multicultural education, notes that socioeconomic status, gender, and religion are legitimate areas of study and clearly intertwined with ethnicity. However, she cautions that "including them under the conceptual rubric of multiethnic or multicultural education may tend to divert attention away from ethnicity."[35] Thus, we see that for Banks and Gay the conception of multicultural education that asks teachers to consider ethnicity along with other variables as they work to achieve educational equity is problematical; they fear that such an effort will dilute efforts to create and deliver multiethnic education.

Afrocentric Education.   The problems of some U.S. school districts in the early 1990s are so severe that the debate between multicultural and multiethnic advocates in these settings is no longer a critical issue. Indeed, in some large urban districts, demographic trends, such as hypersegregation, and the economic and social problems of the isolated urban poor have combined to create a need for what might be called a monoethnic curriculum. Because the dropout rate, prison rate, and death rate have reached such alarming proportions in some urban centers, we are seeing public school boards and administrators develop total school programs that resemble the nineteenth- and twentieth-century private school "solutions" of selected ethnic and cultural groups, that is, Catholic schools and military academies. For instance, in 1991 in Milwaukee, Wisconsin, two African-American immersion public schools, Dr. Martin Luther King Jr. African-American Immersion Elementary School and Robert L. Fulton Middle School, were opened. An initial major focus for these schools was the education and human development (survival) of Black males; however, meeting the needs of young African-American women is also a major priority in these coeducational schools.[36] In other settings—most notably the Portland Oregon Public Schools but also in other large districts such as Atlanta, Georgia—school districts have developed a curriculum that integrates multicultural and multiethnic education in a manner that strongly links it to *Afrocentric education,* a model of education that places African history, knowledge, and values at the center of the curriculum. The result is a curriculum that systematically incorporates and emphasizes the accomplishments and importance of Africans and African Americans throughout history. The Portland School curriculum is guided by the following pluralism-oriented definition:

> Multicultural/multiethnic education is education that prepares the student to live, learn, and work in a pluralistic world by fostering appreciation, respect, and tolerance for people of other ethnic and cultural backgrounds.[37]

To further guide the implementation of this curriculum by teachers, counselors, administrators, and other staff, the developers of this curriculum noted that multicultural/multiethnic education provides three critical components:

1. Specific content that provides a balance of information about the history, culture, and contributions of six identified geocultural groups (i.e., African American, Asian American, European American, Hispanic American, Indian American, and Pacific Island American)
2. A structured process designed to foster understanding, acceptance, and constructive relations among people of different cultural and ethnic backgrounds
3. A perspective (a philosophy and educational attitude) that guides one in the selection and infusion of information and challenges one to deliver "education that is multicultural" or other school-related services in a manner that promotes access and equity

Because it links multicultural/multiethnic education to a specific model and philosophy of education, namely, Afrocentric education, the Portland Schools conception can be viewed as another type of "multicultural education plus" definition.[38] The direction of this conception and its supporting curriculum materials can also contribute to our understanding of multicultural education as a controversial concept, an idea we shall explore in the following section.

MULTICULTURAL EDUCATION: THE ONGOING CONTROVERSY

The diverse set of conceptions delineated above should help to explain why multicultural education specifically and the broader idea of multiculturalism in society remain so controversial. Furthermore, because prior reading of material critical to multicultural education may negatively influence your initial perception of material in this document, a few words of explanation may prove helpful. What is it about multicultural education that provokes so much heated discussion?

At least six factors contribute to the controversy. First, leading advocates of multicultural education have continually stressed that it was and is a reform movement. From the emergence of multicultural education as a curriculum movement, its advocates have set out to shake the status quo at all levels of school district and university operation. As a curriculum movement, multicultural education has always been quite comfortable with a revisionist approach to American and world history. Thus, it has been accurately associated with historical research and opinion that tends to puncture theories and myths dearly held by individuals comfortable with the way things are.

Second, advocates of multicultural education have articulated a new vision of what it means to be an American. As opposed to the melted down, assimilated, unidimensional Anglo-Saxon model of the true American, multiculturalists have developed a multidimensional, pluralist, rainbow image of the model American. Multiculturalists advocate an America where differences as well as the common ground can be celebrated. In contrast, some of their opponents want to shape an America where cultural differences are reduced and the common ground expanded and emphasized. The rainbow image, because it embraces bilingualism and other cultural maintenance strategies, frightens some Americans who believe that the celebration of cultural differences could lead to a more divisive and vulnerable America.

In addition, multicultural education poses a challenge to some individuals who have a strong, negative reaction against the idea of emphasizing the logic and morality of actually seeing and positively reacting to the cultural, ethnic, racial, and gender diversity in our schools and world. Students have told us that continued attention to all the labels that highlight differences will ultimately create a more divided, racist, sexist, and economically segregated world. These students plan to continue to see the world through a monocultural monochromatic lens for, as they say, the sake of humankind. Multicultural education threatens such individuals because it explicitly suggests that their inflexible, universalistic, one world, one people way of seeing the world is problematical.

In turn, these individuals threaten multiculturalism. In refusing to see the color, culture, ethnicity, and gender of others, humanitarian monoculturalists diminish the right of others to define themselves. This stand, which refuses to acknowledge the existence of people as they are and want to become, tends to make some individuals and groups more invisible than they already are (e.g., the gay community). This act of rendering people invisible might make them, during a crisis, more vulnerable or disposable.

To sum up, multicultural education is controversial because it challenges the way some individuals want to see and name the world, and themselves in relation to the world; it cuts deeply into one dimension of their value system as it prods them to see and partially accept the peoples of the world in their rich complexity.

A fourth area of controversy stems from multicultural education's emphasis on equity. Fundamentally, educational equity costs money. Equity, for example, means that school and transportation facilities will be transformed to provide access for the physically challenged, and new training programs will be developed for teachers who work with second language learners. The idea that all Americans should have a real and fair opportunity to learn in American schools has always met resistance from educational administrators and taxpayers, who saw this equalitarian emphasis reducing the amount of money available for other important programs, such as programs for the gifted and talented.

Beyond equity-oriented education lies multicultural education in which antiracism education is emphasized. Because antiracism curricula often produces dialogue marked by guilt, anger, and blame, educating Americans directly about racism has always been difficult.[39] Because of this, antiracism education often takes place in an indirect manner. Nevertheless, when well-intentioned educators, under the auspices of multicultural education, try to use class time to reduce the racist impulses of their students, multicultural education becomes controversial. And the same could be said, to a lesser extent, for antisexism education.[40]

Last, multicultural education is controversial because it is a multifaceted concept. Several diverse conceptions are associated with multicultural education, and sometimes advocates of one kind of multicultural education argue with advocates of another. One leader prefers a type that unifies rather than divides; another describes fear of division as exaggeration designed to prevent authentic multiculturalism from emerging. For you, who may be new to multicultural education, the key point to remember is that multicultural education is not a monolithic entity. When you encounter praise or criticism of multicultural education, you should ascertain which conception of multicultural education the critic is comfortable with, if any.

Finally, there is tension between multicultural education and multiethnic education, and now Afrocentric education, and this tension is symptomatic of a larger problem. Advocates for cultural pluralism, multicultural education, multiethnic education, bilingual education, special education, gender-fair instruction, and instruction for "at-risk" children have not been able to define a common ground philosophy that would allow these disparate advocates and reform movements to unify on a theoretical and organizational basis. This inability has made it difficult for these advocates to support each other in various forums that influence the real world of education. However, a positive step forward was taken in February 1991, when a new and potentially unifying organization, the National Association for Multicultural Education (NAME), held its first annual conference.[41] Although this organization is clearly worthy of attention, teachers working in their classrooms can forge their own unified approach by adapting the synthesis conception described earlier in the chapter. This model links instructional issues to curriculum issues and equity concerns to intergroup relationship skills, emphasizing that multicultural education is for every child *and* every classroom. It is not the only model that prospective and veteran teachers should study, but it is a valuable point of departure for teachers preparing to meet the challenges of this decade and the upcoming millennium.

DISCUSSION QUESTIONS

1. The conception of multicultural education recommended in this chapter includes educational equity as one of its significant goals. In aiming at this goal, teachers are encouraged to examine the participation and achievement of their students from a dual perspective. Essentially, this means that teachers would monitor the participation and achievement rates and interaction styles of both individuals and socially relevant groups in their classroom; these groups include African Americans, Latino Americans, American Indians, and girls and boys. In your opinion, should this dual observation be the responsibility of classroom teachers or should their observational and evaluative focus remain exclusively on individual students? What are the pros and cons of dual assessment at the classroom, school site, and school district level of operation?

2. When we assert that classroom instruction to be considered effective must occur within the context of a multicultural curriculum, we are really saying that classroom teachers (and by implication entire schools) who do not actively pursue several of the goals of multicultural education should not be considered effective even if their students are making good progress in learning how to write, compute, read, draw, and carry out science experiments. In your opinion, is our assertion logical, or do you think we have gone too far in advocating the importance of multicultural education? Provide several reasons for your response, and if time permits, argue both sides of the question.

3. We make the following assumption: At the classroom level of operation, multicultural education can and should be implemented in different ways and with different emphases at the elementary, middle school, high school, and other levels of education. Assuming

that this is a valid idea, at approximately what grade level would it be appropriate to read and discuss literature (fiction and nonfiction) that explicitly discusses racism and sexism in American culture? In other nations? Provide one or two reasons to explain your choices, and if possible identify specific curriculum materials that would help to introduce these concepts for a specific age group.

4. We believe that it is wise to distinguish multicultural education from other related curriculum topics such as citizenship education, global education, futures education, and environmental education. Do you think that any of these related curriculum topics should be considered an integral component of multicultural education? If yes, please identify the curriculum topic(s) and your reasons.

5. We believe that the goals of multicultural education are closely related to the goals of citizenship education. Based on your growing knowledge of multicultural and citizenship education, where do you see the overlap between these two important areas of education?

6. Why might it be appropriate to conceptualize and discuss global education, environmental education, futures education, and citizenship education as content areas in which educators can teach with a multicultural perspective, as opposed to conceptualizing one or more of these curriculum areas as a major goal of multicultural education?

7. We assert that our conception of multicultural education provides an integrated conception of curriculum and instruction, and that such integrated models are valuable places for prospective educators to begin their study of effective schools and instruction. What is the difference between a model of instruction and an integrated model of curriculum and instruction? Can you give some examples of the former? If yes, contrast the elements of one with the other.

8. In our conception of multicultural education and effective teaching we underline the importance of establishing positive, collaborative relationships among parents, teachers, and students. In terms of achieving other goals of multicultural education—educational equity and positive intergroup relations, for example—what programs and research suggest that such collaboration is a sound idea? In responding to this question, the following resources should prove helpful:
   a. Amy R. Anson, Thomas D. Cook, et al., "The Comer School Development Program: A Theoretical Analysis," *Urban Education* 26, no. 1 (April 1991): 56–82.
   b. James P. Comer, "Educating Poor Minority Children," *Scientific American* 259, no. 5 (November 1988): 42–48; and James P. Comer, *School Power* (New York: Free Press, 1980).
   c. J. Epstein, "Parent Involvement: What Research Says to Administrators," *Education and Urban Society* 19, no. 2 (February 1987): 119–136.
   d. Charles Payne, "The Comer Intervention Model and School Reform in Chicago: Implications of Two Models of Change," *Urban Education* 26, no. 1 (April 1991): 8–24.
   e. C. Snow, W. S. Barnes, J. Chandler, I. Goodman, and L. Hemphill. *Families and Schools: Effects on Literacy* (Cambridge, Mass.: Harvard University Press, 1989).
   f. The October 1989 (vol. 47, no. 2) issue of *Educational Leadership* entitled "Strengthening Partnerships with Parents and Community."

9. What do you think were the three most important points made in this chapter? Why were these your choices?

10. In your opinion, what specific beliefs will change in the minds of educators as they make the shift from a monocultural to a multicultural perspective?

11. Which idea or ideas in this chapter appear to be questionable?

12. If our conception of multicultural education differs from the one you brought to class, how does it differ?

13. We believe that children at any grade level and that content from any part of the curriculum can be taught with a multicultural perspective. In your opinion how would this apply to mathematics? As you respond consider (a) the specific contributions that mathematicians working in various non-Western cultures have made throughout history and (b) the contributions of outstanding mathematics educators such as Jaime Escalante, Uri Treisman, and Abdulalim Shabazz of Clark Atlanta University. For information about Shabazz and more regarding Jaime Escalante, see "Do We Have the Will to Educate All Children," by Asa Hilliard III in the September 1991 issue of *Educational Leadership* (vol. 49, no. 1).

14. We suggest that teachers who work with a multicultural perspective will be inclined to study and consider the ideas of educators (and philosophers, management experts, etc.) who work in cultures other than their own. What are some of the positive attributes and potential pitfalls in such an inherently practical approach to professional growth? As you develop or refine your point of view, consider reading one or more of the following essays or books:

   a. Janice E. Hale-Benson, *Black Children: Their Roots, Culture, and Learning Styles* (Baltimore: Johns Hopkins University Press, 1982).

   b. Jerry L. Milligan, "Learning to Read in New Zealand," *Teaching K–8* 21, no. 1 (August/September 1990): 62–65.

   c. Gay Su Pinnell, Mary D. Fried, and Rose Mary Estice, "Reading Recovery: Learning How to Make a Difference," *The Reading Teacher* 43, no. 4 (January 1990): 282–295.

   d. James W. Stigler and Harold W. Stevenson, "How Asian Teachers Polish Each Lesson to Perfection," *American Educator* 15, no. 1 (Spring, 1991): 12–20, 43–47.

15. We believe our conception of multicultural education is conservative. Why do you think we have this perception, and do you agree with our assessment? Why? Why not?

16. In this chapter we discuss the perspective of a "humanitarian monoculturalist." What part of this vision contains wisdom? Do you share any part of this perspective, and if so, please describe? Also, can you see a way to integrate this perspective with the multicultural perspective recommended in this text? If so, please elaborate with as much specificity as possible.

17. What questions would you like to ask us? Try to answer one of these yourself.

NOTES

1. Joyce Epstein, "Parent Involvement: What Research Says to Administrators," *Education and Urban Society* 19, no. 2 (February 1987): 119–136.
2. Gene I. Maeroff, "A Blueprint for Empowering Teachers," *Phi Delta Kappan* 69, no. 7 (March 1988): 473.
3. Richard Vega, "Hate Crimes on the Rise," *USA Weekend* (January 8–10, 1993): 5.
4. Imogene C. Brown, "Counseling Vietnamese", in *Counseling American Minorities: A Cross-Cultural Perspective,* ed. Donald R. Atkinson, George Morton, and Derald Wing Sue (Dubuque, Iowa: Brown, 1983), 110.
5. Michele McCalope, "Blacks Furious over Exclusion from New Great Books of the Western World," *Jet Magazine,* December 1990, 14–18.
6. Beverly T. Watkins, "Many Campuses Now Challenging Minority Students to Excel in Math and Science," and "Berkeley Mathematician Strives to Help People Get Moving," *Chronicle of Higher Education* 35, no. 40 (June 1989): A-13.
7. James P. Comer, "Educating Poor Minority Children," *Scientific American* 259, no. 5 (November 1988): 44.

8. Ibid., 48.

9. Ibid.

10. Ibid., 44.

11. Bruce C. Davis, "A Successful Parent Involvement Program," *Educational Leadership* 47, no. 2 (October 1989): 21–23.

12. Jay Matthews, *Escalante, the Best Teacher in America* (New York: Holt, Rinehart and Winston, 1988).

13. Ibid., 13.

14. Ibid., 130.

15. Ibid., 14.

16. Susan K. Sherwood, "Portrait of an Integration: A Child with Severe Multiple Disabilities Integrated into a Regular First Grade Classroom." Unpublished manuscript. Ms. Sherwood is now a professor and teacher educator at Wartburg College in Waverly, Iowa.

17. Susan K. Sherwood, "A Circle of Friends in a First Grade Classroom," *Educational Leadership* 48, no. 3 (November 1990): 41. This article is a brief version of the manuscript cited above.

18. Sherwood, "Portrait of an Integration," 8.

19. See the provisions of P.L. 101-336—the Americans with Disabilities Act of 1990—an act that gives civil rights protection to individuals with disabilities in private sector employment, all public services, public accommodations, transportation, and telecommunications.

20. The following resources will prove helpful for teachers interested in learning more about the full inclusion of students with severe disabilities:

    a. A bulletin entitled *Strategies* is published by the California Research Institute—the latter is funded by the U.S. Department of Education to carry out research and technical assistance activities regarding the integration of students with severe disabilities. *Strategies* appears as an insert in the TASH (The Association for Persons with Severe Handicaps) newsletter on a quarterly basis. The fall 1991 issue of *Strategies* contains a bibliography of current articles and resources pertaining to full inclusion. For more information about this bulletin call Patricia Karasoff, the editor at (415) 338-1162, or write California Research Institute, 14 Tapia Drive, San Francisco, CA 94132.

    b. A. Halvorsen and W. Sailor, "Integration of Students with Severe and Profound Disabilities: A Review of Research," in R. Gaylord-Ross, ed., *Issues and Research in Special Education* (New York: Teachers College Press, 1990), 110–172.

21. Carl A. Grant, ed., *Multicultural Education: Commitments, Issues, and Applications* (Washington, D.C.: Association for Supervision and Curriculum Development, 1977), 2.

22. Mira L. Baptiste and H. Prentice Baptiste, "Competencies toward Multiculturalism," in *Multicultural Teacher Education: Preparing Educators to Provide Educational Equity,* Vol. 1 (Washington, D.C.: American Association of Colleges of Teacher Education, 1979), 44.

23. James Banks, *Multiethnic Education: Theory and Practice* (Boston: Allyn & Bacon, 1981), 32.

24. Donna M. Gollnick and Phillip C. Chinn, *Multicultural Education in a Pluralistic Society,* 2d ed. (Columbus, Ohio: Merrill, 1986), 5.

25. James Banks, "Multicultural Education: Characteristics and Goals," chap. 1 in *Multicultural Education: Issues and Perspectives,* ed. James Banks and Cherry McGee Banks (Boston: Allyn & Bacon, 1989), 3.

26. Standard 2.1 is included in its totality on pp. 1–2 "Multicultural Teacher Education: Case Studies of Thirteen Programs," Volume II, a document printed and disseminated by the American Association of Colleges for Teacher Education (Washington, D.C., 1980). It is

noteworthy that in the new Standards of the National Council for the Accreditation of Teacher Education (NCATE), which were disseminated in 1986, the glossary includes *multicultural perspective* but not *multicultural education.*

27. Ann Morey, ed. *Excellence in Professional Education* (Long Beach: Office of the Chancellor, California State University System, 1983), 85–86.
28. This definition appears in a survey entitled *Questionnaire on Multicultural Teacher Education* that was disseminated by Eugene Kim in 1987. For further information contact Professor Kim at the School of Education, California State University, Sacramento, 6000 J Street, Sacramento, CA 95819.
29. Christine E. Sleeter and Carl A. Grant, *Making Choices for Multicultural Education: Five Approaches to Race, Class, and Gender* (Columbus, Ohio: Merrill, 1988), 137–173.
30. Ibid., 153.
31. Ibid.
32. Ibid.
33. Ibid., 176.
34. Banks, *Multiethnic Education: Theory and Practice,* 52–53.
35. Geneva Gay, "Multiethnic Education: Historical Development and Future Prospects," *Phi Delta Kappan* 65, no. 8 (April 1983), 560–563.
36. Donald Leake and Brenda Leake, "African-American Immersion Schools in Milwaukee: A View from the Inside," *Phi Delta Kappan* 73, no. 10 (June 1992): 783–785; Carole Ascher, "School Programs for African-American Males . . . and Females," *Phi Delta Kappan* 73, no. 10 (June 1992): 777–782.
37. *African-American Base Line Essays* (Portland, Ore.: Portland Public Schools, 1987), vi. The address is Portland Public Schools, 501 N. Dixon St., Portland, OR 97227.
38. John O'Neil, "On the Portland Plan: A Conversation with Matthew Prophet," *Educational Leadership,* 49, no. 4 (December 1991/January 1992): 24–27.
39. Beverly D. Tatum, "Talking about Race, Learning about Racism: The Application of Racial Identity Development Theory in the Classroom," *Harvard Educational Review* 62, no. 1 (Spring 1992): 1–24.
40. A helpful resource supporting the need for gender-fair instruction is the report entitled "How Schools Shortchange Girls: The AAUW Report," from the American Association of University Women. A summary of the report is available from the AAUW sales office (800-225-9998).
41. For more information about the National Association for Multicultural Education, contact Priscilla Walton, California Commission on Teacher Credentialing, 1812 9th Street, Sacramento, CA (916-324-2450), or Dr. Rose Duhon-Sells, Office of the Dean, Southern University, P. O. Box 9983, Baton Rouge, LA 70813-2092 (504-771-2290).

CHAPTER **2**

Creating Equity Conditions in School Settings

CHAPTER OVERVIEW

The march toward educational equity and related political and economic rights for disenfranchised groups has been a centuries-long struggle in the United States. In this effort the *Brown v. Board of Education* (1954) Supreme Court decision was a major victory and turning point. This decision created a climate of opinion and possibility that led other ethnic and cultural groups to use the courts more vigorously to seek redress for limitations on their educational and civil rights. The *Serrano v. Priest* case is one such example. In this case the plaintiffs sought to create more equality of opportunity in the schools by arguing that the school funding procedures prevailing up to 1971 created a pattern of rich and poor school districts and that this pattern in effect denied equal educational opportunity for significant numbers of California students.

The struggle to create equality of opportunity or at least some form of tolerable equivalency in America's schools continues. Since 1954 there have been prominent legal victories and notable setbacks, but the most significant reality for current and future educators is that dramatic inequality of educational opportunity still prevails in many school districts and states. As a result of this persistent, and in some areas increasing, inequality, the language used to focus and direct the continuing equity struggle has changed. In the 1990s, as in much of the past decade, the thoughts and voices of equity advocates carry a much stronger emphasis on *equality of results,* now coupled with equality of opportunity.

The new emphasis on equality of results derives from a variety of sources and conditions. These include (a) the realization that extensive, enduring, de facto segregation caused by housing patterns and middle-class flight from inner cities has made equality of opportunity in schools through integration virtually impossible for millions of minority students (who are now part of the majority, "students of color" population in the inner cities) and (b) the belief that at various levels of American society there is more support for inequality than for equality of opportunity. Thus, in the 1990s in those schools and school districts where students are so racially and ethnically isolated as to make integration nonfeasible, advocates of equity have created their own version of separate but equal, and it has much to do with equality of resources, equality of results, and curricula geared to the psychosocial and political needs of children of color.

When creating equitable conditions in schools, administrators, counselors, parents, students, politicians, private corporations, and teachers all have a role to play, but their responsibilities for the most part are different. In this chapter we will focus on strategies that teachers can use to start off the school year positively in terms of educational equity. Strategies that you can employ, which we will discuss below, include the following:

1. visits to the surrounding community;
2. examination of student files and portfolios, if available;
3. development of a plan for communicating with, and involving, parents (introductory letters, parent interviews, class newsletters);
4. selection of multicultural content;
5. creation of a collaborative learning environment through class- and team-building activities;
6. utilization of a typology of multicultural teaching.

INTRODUCTION

In chapter 1 we attempted to illuminate the idea of teaching with a multicultural perspective by describing and discussing the work of five distinguished educators, and we hope that you now have a clearer grasp of the type of teaching and research that is congruent with this approach to education. In this chapter we will further clarify the meaning of teaching with a multicultural perspective and the meaning of educational equity, the latter being the preeminent goal in our conception of multicultural education. To accomplish this end, the chapter begins with remarks about the contemporary meaning of educational equity and then progresses to a discussion of teaching with a multicultural perspective, seen from the point of view of in-service and student teachers. The material in these sections will show how strategies associated with a multicultural teaching perspective combine to create equitable learning conditions and will demonstrate that this comprehensive approach to effective teaching is feasible for both experienced teachers and student teachers. However, before turning to the strategies, we will review historical information that provides a useful context for understanding the current debate regarding educational equity.

EDUCATIONAL EQUITY:
A CONTEMPORARY PERSPECTIVE

Summarizing the history of public education in the United States between 1926 and 1976, historian R. Freeman Butts discussed this 50-year period in terms of the search for equality and the search for community.[1] These quests, which together can be viewed as part of the ongoing struggle to create a more complete American democracy, have modified the face of public education in the United States, and the shift has led to changes in the basic responsibilities of public school teachers.

This struggle, and the protests, law suits, and legislation that figured prominently in the century-long battle against segregation, poverty, and unequal access to learning, created the legal conditions under which teachers all over the United States were increasingly expected to teach students who were in one way or another different from the teachers themselves.[2] More specifically, as a result of *Brown v. Board of Education* (1954) and the persistence of the Supreme Court and civil rights organizations in later decisions such as *Cooper v. Aaron*[3] and *Alexander et al. v. Holmes County (Mississippi) School Board,*[4] White and Black teachers in the South, North, East, and West were assigned to teach students whom the states and federal government perceived to be racially different from the teachers. No longer would White teachers be restricted to White students and Black teachers to Black students.

Quite significantly, the success of the Reverend Oliver Brown and a dozen other Black parents in *Brown v. Board of Education* encouraged other educationally disenfranchised groups to seek or continue to seek "equal protection of the laws" as guaranteed by the Fourteenth Amendment to the U.S. Constitution. For example, in 1970 a federal judge ruled that Corpus Christi, Texas, was operating a dual school system for Mexican Americans and ordered the board of education to submit a plan for desegregation as provided in the Brown case.[5] In 1971 in a related case argued on behalf of Mexican-American children in east Los Angeles, the California Supreme Court in *Serrano v. Priest* ruled that the state's system of financing public schools exclusively through local property taxes invidiously discriminated against poor children; the court held that this system made the quality of education provided in local schools dependent upon the wealth of the school district in which students happened to live.[6]

The parallel in language between the Brown case of 1954 and the Serrano case is revealing. In 1954, expressing the unanimous decision of the U.S. Supreme Court, Chief Justice Earl Warren wrote:

> In these days, it is doubtful that any child may reasonably be expected to succeed in life if he is denied the opportunity of an education. Such an opportunity, where the state has undertaken to provide it, is a right which must be made available to all on equal terms.[7]

Utilizing a similar theme 17 years later in the Serrano decision, the California Supreme Court said:

By our holding today we further the cherished idea of American education that in a democratic society free public schools shall make available to all children equally the abundant gifts of learning. This was the credo of Horace Mann, which has been the heritage and the inspiration of this country.[8]

The underlying belief that equality of educational opportunity should prevail for all students in public schools has led to a number of other important decisions. In 1973 in *Lau v. Nichols,* a class-action suit on behalf of Chinese-speaking students who attended the San Francisco schools, the U.S. Supreme Court ruled that schools must provide special language programs for students who do not understand or speak English.[9] In 1975, in a decision that affected every school and school district in the nation, Congress created more equal educational opportunity, this time for the physically and mentally handicapped. The occasion was passage of Public Law P.L. 94-142, the Education for All Handicapped Children Act.[10] This law stipulated that handicapped children must be educated in the environment that is least restrictive to their learning. Thus, handicapped students would be educated in regular classrooms (mainstreamed), in special classes, or some combination thereof, and it would be the responsibility of the school site administrator to ensure that an individual educational plan (IEP) was written and followed for such students. In addition, other acts of Congress in 1965,[11] 1972,[12] 1973,[13] and 1974[14] were directly aimed at creating more educational opportunity for children of low-income families, for Native Americans, and for women. A final illustration that the quest for equality is still a major transformational factor in American education is the June 1989 case, *Rose v. Council for Better Education, Inc.* (a consortium of 60 Kentucky school districts). The Kentucky State Supreme Court declared the *entire* school system of Kentucky to be unconstitutional and ordered sweeping changes to ensure financial and educational equity for the state's 176 school districts.[15] It is instructive that Kentucky Chief Justice Robert Stephens, in the majority opinion that declared the public school system unconstitutional, described the Brown decision cited above as "the polestar of this opinion."[16]

Separate but Equal Revisited

The direction was not always forward, and one can easily point to contemporary public school realities across the nation that suggest the legal victories of the 1950s, 1960s, and 1970s fell severely short of the mark in creating equal educational opportunity for millions of students.[17] It is important, however, to note that the quest for greater and fairer access to learning continues, and that today there is much more emphasis on equality of results as opposed to equality of opportunity. This new emphasis puts the spotlight on both "at-risk" students, wherever they may be, and outcome results. This approach arises from a number of factors; significant among them is the projection that by the year 2020 White students will be a minority or close to a minority in the nation's schools.[18] In the 1990s and possibly beyond, vast numbers of Black and Hispanic youth and youth from other minority ethnic groups, concentrated in large urban centers, will inevitably receive a form of de facto segregated schooling because of housing patterns, immigration patterns,

White flight, and the conservative nature of the U.S. Supreme Court,[19] among other factors.

Meaningful face-to-face integration, as it was conceived and defined in the 1950s, 1960s, and 1970s, seems no longer to be a viable strategy for attempting to equalize education for millions of students of color. Thus the emphasis in the late 1980s and early 1990s on children at risk and equality of outcomes is understandable even though "equality of outcomes" does not have the legislative and constitutional support that equality of opportunity has in the nation's creed and constitution.[20] With close to 13 percent of the nation's youth not completing high school (1989 data), with dropout percentages reaching 50 percent in some of the nation's urban centers, and with widespread attention paid to other national problems such as drug abuse and declining industrial productivity, politicians and educational leaders have increasingly turned to the classroom teacher and school site administrator for answers to the equity puzzle.

When Chief Justice Earl Warren concluded in 1954 that "in the field of public education 'separate but equal' has no place," no one could foresee that educational leaders and politicians in the 1980s, faced with the harsh realities of de facto segregation, would revisit the idea of separate but equal. These leaders realized, first, that large numbers of American children would continue to be educated in settings that were quite unequal in degree of Black/White integration, dollars spent per child, school morale, age of school facilities, safety, amount of support provided by school volunteers, and so on; second, the leaders were helpless to change this de facto reality. Thus, they opted for the next best thing: to aim for equality of outcomes in settings that were far from integrated. An example of this new reality-based approach to educational equity (an approach that rejects busing as a solution) is evident in the San Diego desegregation case, *Carlin v. San Diego Unified School District*, decided in 1977. Judge Lewis Welsh, the presiding judge in this case, ordered the San Diego City School District to devise a program that would raise achievement test scores in the minority schools identified by the court. Specifically, he required 50 percent of the students in grades K–11 to achieve at or above the national norm on the California Test of Basic Skills (CTBS) Total Reading, Language, and Mathematics subtests within five years.[21]

The new logic seemed to go like this: if it is inevitable that large numbers of students will study in quasi-segregated and unequal facilities, then by all means needed let us assure that the education these students receive will be powerful enough to propel large numbers of them through high school and into postsecondary institutions. In this new era and interpretation of equity, where de facto segregation is a persistent reality, the emphasis is on empowered teachers and parents, highly motivated administrators, restructured and decentralized schools, and financial equity for school districts. In addition, we hear about vouchers and competition between schools and other arrangements unknown only a few years ago. But, in the midst of all of the empowerment rhetoric, the goal of equity remains an ambiguous ideal. No social scientist, educational administrator, or politician has clearly defined what equity consists of so that educators can know when a state, school district, school, or nation has attained it. Furthermore, in the absence of national standards and exams, such clarity will be very hard to achieve. Thus, when one examines the complex conditions and conflicting ideas associated with educational equity, the silence and ambiguity surrounding the concept become somewhat understandable. Nevertheless, one finds in the 1990s various well-intentioned educators, including the authors, asserting that there can be no excellence in education without equity. What are we to understand this political and value-laden statement to mean? It is clear that we must come to grips with the complex idea of equity before we can meaningfully specify strategies that aim at achieving it.

It is helpful to remember that most words in the English language have more than one meaning, and so it is with equity. Furthermore, the meaning of educational equity will vary somewhat with the level of education under discussion. When one asks whether educational equity exists at the national, state, school district, school site, or classroom level of operation, different types of evidence will come into play. In an attempt to create a discussion that relates directly to the responsibilities and concerns of classroom teachers, we will confine ourselves in this chapter to the school district level of operation, even though this level of analysis will allow for only partial insight into educational equity.[22]

Educational Equity: The School District Level

Educational equity, as a characteristic of a school district, will exist when certain conditions are met. In this section we discuss three types of equity conditions: physical and financial conditions, educational outcomes, and opportunity to learn. With regard to facilities and funds, for a district to be equitable the students in the district should have the opportunity to study in schools that are roughly equivalent in terms of physical dimensions, attractiveness, educational equipment, and safety. Inevitably, school districts will have newer and older schools; to keep the older schools as attractive and safe as the newer ones it is likely that more money will have to be spent on the older buildings. Further, the students in each elementary and middle school in the district should have an equivalent amount of money spent on their education. If school district policy allows veteran teachers, typically the more expensive and experienced teachers, to gravitate to one set of schools—the middle- and higher-socioeconomic schools in a district—and assigns newer teachers to staff the more challenging lower-socioeconomic schools, then in terms of dollars and experience the district is not providing equitable conditions for its students.

The second window on educational equity pertains to educational outcomes. With this variable we examine educational results in terms of pertinent culturally defined social groups and get closer to phenomena that classroom teachers can influence directly or indirectly. To illustrate the relationship between excellence and equity we can look at one critical outcome variable: rates of graduation from high school. Let us consider a hypothetical district, the APT Unified School District, in which 60 percent of all students who start in the district at kindergarten continue through to the high school years, 20 percent transfer into the district during the junior high school years, and another 20 percent come in during the high school years. How many of the students who started kindergarten in the district would need to graduate—70 percent, 80 percent, 90 percent, 95 percent, or 98 percent—for *you* to consider this district excellent? Let us assume that both you and the school district's parents, school board, and administrators believe that 90 percent is a suitable criterion for excellence. Because we want to live in a society that is equitable in terms of educational outcomes, we can also assume that both you and the school board want pertinent social groups—girls and boys; Hispanics, Asians, Native Americans, Whites, and Blacks; and low-, medium-, and high-SES students—all to achieve a 90 percent graduation rate. Finally, if one or two of these groups had a graduation rate of 50 percent when other groups were achieving 90 to 100 percent, and the lower achieving groups were those who on the whole earn less money per family than the other groups, it is quite likely that neither you nor the school board would want to describe APT Unified as excellent.

This group-oriented, quantitative outcomes basis for assessing quality is what educators have in mind when they say there can be no excellence in education without equity. Increasingly since the 1970s, educational equity and educational excellence have become intertwined concepts. Because of this integration of meaning, when we evaluate the quality of a K–12 educational organization, we no longer look only at overall graduation rates, overall admittance to community colleges, overall anything; excellence is now strongly related to the organization's relative success with the varied ethnic and cultural groups that make up its total student body. Educational leaders are becoming aware that it will be the members of these varied groups—people of color and women—who will constitute a significant part of the labor force of the twenty-first century. One recent article reported that in 1990 60 percent of the net additions to the American work force were women, 25 percent were minorities, and 15 percent were white males; the author speculated that 66 percent of American workers by 2020 will be female and minority.[23] Another research report estimated that in the year 2000 nearly one of every three new workers will be of minority origin.[24] The fate of America rests with all students, but it is clear that the educational success of students of color and women of all colors has assumed a new economic importance in the minds of political and educational leaders as the 1990s unfold.

The third window on educational equity pertains to equal opportunity to learn at the classroom level of operation, and it is through this window that teachers and principals will see the equity condition they can influence most directly. For educational equity to exist at this level, in every classroom in the district each student and each culturally pertinent group of students must have the following:

1. open and ample access to learning;
2. the opportunity and resources for all students to grow, academically and emotionally, to their fullest potential;
3. a successful experience in learning.

These conditions can be translated into equity-oriented questions that all teachers can address. As we outline these possibilities, we will move from the goals and outcomes associated with educational equity to specific behaviors that you can manifest if you choose to achieve the goals of multicultural education.

First Steps toward Educational Equity

Like others who believe they have articulated a more complete theory of effective teaching and say, "Behold we have a good and logical thing," we have the additional responsibility of addressing some basic operational questions about that theory—in this case multicultural education: If I teach with a multicultural perspective, what do I do that is different? Or more fundamentally, how do I begin? We will address these questions by enumerating and discussing decisions that can be made during the early phases of the school year or the student teaching assignment. Before we begin our discussion, however, it is important to note several things. First, what we discuss here is just one interpretation of how classroom teachers can apply a multicultural perspective in student teaching or at the beginning of a first year of teaching. There is no one exact recipe that specifies how all teachers at all grade levels in all settings should implement multicultural education, but there is one common ingredient— the six goals of multicultural education—that provides a framework for thinking about multicultural education. Although we must ultimately discuss a variety of teaching decisions and strategies to familiarize you with potential building blocks for multicultural education, there is one best response to the question, "What do I do that's different?" That is, when you work with a multicultural perspective, you persistently aim at all, or most, of the goals of multicultural education. Your strategies will change from grade level to grade level and decade to decade, but your goals, for the most part, will remain the same. We say "for the most part" here because it is logical to assume that educational conditions or personal philosophy will point some of you toward new goals or heightened versions of the ones we include. For example, teachers who are convinced that the political and social structure of a state or nation oppresses their students should engage in some form of liberation or emancipatory education. The form such education will take will be influenced by the nature and degree of oppression. It is, to be sure, a long way from Soweto, South Africa, to Detroit, Michigan, and emancipation education in Havana, Cuba, will certainly be handled differently from such education in Mexico City or Los Angeles, if only for reasons of job security and teacher safety.

Multicultural Planning Questions

To help you weave these goals into your short- and long-term planning, we have developed a preliminary set of goal-focused planning questions:

1. Do the lesson content and strategies promote educational equity? For example, does the lesson content help to create an inclusive curriculum, one that attempts to maximize student participation in the everyday and overall class curriculum?
2. Do the lesson content and strategies make use of, or help to develop, collaborative empowering relationships among parents, students, and teacher?
3. Do the lesson content and strategies promote cultural pluralism in society or intergroup harmony in the classroom?
4. Does the lesson content help to increase the students' knowledge regarding various cultural and ethnic groups, including their own?

5. Do the lesson content and strategies increase students' proclivity and ability to see and think with a multicultural perspective?
6. Does the lesson content help to correct distortions in the historical, literary, or scientific record that may be linked to historical racism or to other forces related to the oppression and exploitation of specific ethnic and cultural groups? Does it present material in a manner that suggests that racism-related distortions are or may be part of the historical and scientific record the students are studying?

To illustrate further the kinds of teacher decisions and behaviors that will logically result from planning and teaching with a multicultural perspective, we will identify several decisions teachers can make before the beginning of the school year, and then several that can be made during the first months of the term. Together these decisions will establish a strong foundation for multicultural teaching through-out the entire term. Following this discussion we will address related questions from the unique perspective of the student teacher.

BEFORE THE SCHOOL YEAR BEGINS

Prior to the beginning of the school year, you can begin to develop an equity-oriented learning environment by striving to discover as much as possible about your students, their families, and the communities they reside in. This can be accomplished by visiting the local community to learn about its special resources and characteristics, speaking with your school principal and counselor, and most important, by reading your students' files and portfolios. The purpose of this is to learn about students' health problems, past academic performance, and attendance, and to discover pertinent family and student-related data such as the following:

1. Was the learner ever in a "special learner" category (learning disabled, learning handicapped, limited English proficient), and is the student still in one of these categories?
2. Who is the child's primary caretaker?
3. Is English or Spanish or some other language spoken at home (to place you in a better position to communicate orally or in writing with your students' parents/caretakers)?
4. Does it appear, from the child's name, such as Nguyen Hung Dung, that the student is a member of an ethnic, immigrant, or refugee group with which you are relatively unfamiliar?

Examination of Student Records

As we move through the 1990s it is predictable that more elementary and middle schools—where teachers have fewer students to interact with and stay with the same set of students across the school year—will begin to augment the school file. Traditionally this has contained health, attendance, and test score data and in some cases a record of parent–teacher conferences; in many schools it will be expanded to include a student portfolio that will allow representative student work in writing and art, for example, to be passed on to all of the student's new teachers so they can examine concrete examples of student progress during the last six or twelve months. This augmented information will place you in a better position to develop trust, respect, and rapport with your students and parents at the beginning of the school year. In a variety of settings during the first days of school you can allude to your examination of students' prior work as you spell out and predict the type of progress you know students will make in your class that year. This subtle display of professional knowledge gained from files and portfolios ought to be reassuring and encouraging to parents and students.

You will probably discover or already know of experienced teaches who do not look at files until the second or third *month* of the school year so they can form their *own* opinions about each student without being influenced by the opinions of past teachers and past academic performance. We strongly encourage you to examine the files and portfolios beforehand so that you can begin to see the students in their full family, community, and developmental context, and thus be better prepared to develop knowledgeably your own tentative and emergent views regarding your students. We consider the examination of these files to be the professional responsibility of a multicultural educator and encourage you to pay attention to the information shared by your colleagues as well as your own professional instincts about this data base. Teachers need to know as much as possible about their clients as decisions and recommendations are made concerning educational growth and development. This was true a decade ago but is even more important today when so many of our students' parents are pressed hard just taking care of their family's health and economic needs.

Developing a Collaborative Plan

We believe you should decide to have a professional, and therefore respectful and collaborative, relationship with your clients—your students and their parents. This means that you and they will have rights and responsibilities vis-à-vis the learning process that you both will initiate and participate in within the confines of the *public* school classroom. We emphasize the word *public* to stress that the class you will teach is not exclusively your class, or the students', or even the local community's. It belongs to the larger public, and in a broader sense to the American people and their culture. Although you work or will soon be hired to work in one of America's 15,000-plus school districts, in a very real sense you are there as a representative and transmitter of American history and culture, helping to build continuity between America's past and present, and justice in its future. This is a significant moral responsibility and one quite worthy of your consideration as you carry out your civic responsibilities as a teacher.[25] Equally significant is the fact that you will play out this general cultural transmission role in a specific concrete community, one that may have its own concept of what your classroom curriculum should look like and what its responsibilities for the education of its students ought to involve. These concepts will vary across regions and ethnic communities, and you will need to learn the specific cultural facts about your local community, particularly if it is one where school boards or state legislatures have increased parental influence over the governance of local schools.

To fulfill this responsibility and to prepare yourself to go beyond the data in the student files, you should develop a plan for implementing ongoing two-way communication between yourself and your students' parents. If you are new to this idea or new to a particular school, you should have an early discussion about parent communication and parent involvement with your principal to learn (a) what already exists in the school program, (b) what your minimal responsibilities in this area are, and (c) if some of the things you would like to try seem reasonable given school and district written and unofficial policies regarding parent involvement and the cultural climate in the community. To assist you in developing your own ideas regarding parent communication and parent involvement in your classroom, several resources are briefly described in appendix 6. Research demonstrates that many different approaches to parent involvement work,[26] but it is also clear that some, such as the one initiated by Madeline Hunter in her UCLA Lab School in the 1970s, will make a greater contribution than others to multicultural education. Among other things, parents at the Lab School were asked to share their special expertise regarding the culture of a particular country, people, or region, and they were invited to do this as part of a small cadre of parents.[27] We will return to this use of parents' expertise in the next section when we discuss other strategies that should be employed at the beginning of the school year.

Planning to Use Cooperative Learning

With equity and collaboration in mind, it is our opinion, based on research, that you should decide as early as possible that (a) cooperative learning will play an important role in the instructional and organizational format you will employ, and (b) you will develop a plan for introducing and utilizing cooperative learning groups in your classroom. Because cooperative learning is a major teaching strategy for multicultural education, we recommend that you carefully lay out the ideas you will use to introduce it and then deliver your remarks extemporaneously. For example, in a third-grade or eighth-grade class, you might say something like this:

> Although I will be the main teacher in this class, I want you to know that we will all be teachers and learners in this classroom, and we'll be responsible for helping each other teach and learn. Furthermore, we'll fulfill our responsibilities as a community of learners in a variety of ways. For example, we will also engage in several different forms of cooperative learning. Raise your hand if you have had some experience in cooperative learning. Good. Let's hear about some of those experiences, and then you'll all have a chance to share some of your thoughts about cooperative learning in writing.

You may well be wondering, what is so special about cooperative learning? If the goals of multicultural education are so preeminently important, why is cooperative learning singled out as a major strategy?

Although it is true that the goals are preeminent, it is also true that cooperative learning has earned a special position in the universe of possible strategies. Research data accumulated over two decades suggest strongly that cooperative learning is a powerful cross-content, cross-grade-level strategy for accomplishing simultaneously several of the goals of multicultural education—namely, educational equity, intergroup understanding and harmony, and the establishment of positive collaborative empowering relationships among students, teachers, and parents. In a well-researched article Robert Slavin provided evidence that supports this thesis.[28] However, in commenting on the cross-grade-level appropriateness of cooperative learning, Slavin noted that although there is ample evidence that cooperative methods are instructionally effective in grades two through nine, there are "relatively few studies [that] examine grades ten through twelve," and that "more research is needed in this area."[29] Slavin concluded this research overview by noting that "what we know already is more than enough to justify expanded use of cooperative learning as a routine and central feature of instruction."[30] We hope soon to see evidence that clarifies the utility of cooperative group learning in grades 10 through 12. A strategy that has been demonstrated to be clearly appropriate for eighth and ninth graders all over the United States should be equally effective for students who are only one or two years older.

Beyond the research results summarized by Slavin, there is another vital contribution that cooperative learning makes when the groups that are formed are heterogeneous in terms of ethnicity, gender, *and* current academic performance. In working with such classes teachers and schools are making a critical move away from the deleterious effects of tracking and ability grouping, which Jeannie Oakes and others have persuasively documented.[31] Overall, for K–8 equity-oriented instructors, an extensive literature suggests that they ought to become expert users of cooperative learning. To facilitate your planning in this area, a list of resources is included in appendix 6, and an activity at the end of the chapter provides you with guidelines for observing and interviewing a teacher who makes effective use of cooperative learning.

Planning a Curriculum of Inclusion

Now that you have chosen to study your community, students, and parents, and have begun to think about the ways in which you will incorporate cooperative learning into your curriculum, it would be appropriate to identify and review the content you will be teaching during the first months of school to make sure you thoroughly understand the concepts you will be teaching. When this review is completed, you will be ready to carry out a critical task pertaining to educational equity. More specifically, after examining the content you will be teaching, you should be able to list ways this content can be used to demonstrate the following:

1. the art, music, language, history, ethics, politics, sports, literature, and technology of our nation has been positively influenced by a wide range of individuals, cultures, and ethnic groups; and
2. in contemporary American society women and men of all colors and ethnic groups are succeeding in a wide range of occupations.

Thus, no matter what your grade level or content area, you should be well prepared to show your students, from day one, that people of all colors, ethnic backgrounds, and gender have created and are continuing to create America. In your class, students should learn that there is opportunity for all to succeed throughout American society, even if this opportunity is unequally distributed. Whatever your personal beliefs are about the distribution of opportunity in American society (or Canadian society, etc.), it is your responsibility to give your students convincing reasons to believe that they will be able to use their education—both to succeed in American society as it exists and to help transform it into a more equitable society. Every teacher must become a part of the effort to reduce the tremendous dropout rate that saps the strength of American education, and helping students see the long- and short-term practical benefits of their education is an important element in this struggle. If in doing this you can let your students know that there is a challenging future for them in the field of education, you will also be serving the profession well. In addition, if you pointed out that your school district and the nation has a great need for teachers of color and bilingual teachers, you would also be making a positive contribution to educational equity and excellence. By the year 2000, if current trends continue, 19 out of 20 teachers in America will be White, and 40 to 60 percent of students will be of color. This statistic is counterproductive to educational equity. Classroom teachers, with their enthusiasm for teaching and the teaching profession, can help to encourage more of their students to choose teaching as a career and thus be instrumental in creating a more diverse teaching faculty for the twenty-first century.

THE FIRST FOUR WEEKS AND BEYOND

Cross-Cultural Parent–Teacher Communication

In the initial month of the school year you should activate your plan to communicate with parents. Your career in teaching will be more successful if you and as many parents as possible are working together toward common goals. We, therefore, recommend that you make a strong, culturally sensitive, attempt to communicate with 100 percent of your parents. Setting this goal implies that you will use multiple means of communication, and your repertoire of strategies will probably extend beyond your school's planned events.

Some of your students and their families may be recent arrivals who have been in the United States fewer than five years. They may be immigrants who chose to come or refugees who were forced from their homeland. Many of these families may have come from a culture with no tradition of parents' playing an active role in their children's education.[32] When you attempt to communicate and establish collaborative relationships with these parents you will need to modify goals, expectations, and strategies; you may also need to change some of your face-to-face communication patterns as well. Communicating with immigrant parents and some nonimmigrant parents, particularly the parents who constitute the "poor" in America, is truly a cross-cultural experience. You may need translators. It is helpful to assume that there are pertinent differences between the culture of your school and the culture and language of the home. We suggest that these differences, when they exist, should influence the way you engage in verbal and nonverbal communication with parents, students, and instructional aides.

Research has demonstrated that cultural differences do exist and that they are significant.[33] Vietnamese parents, Punjabi Sikh parents (from the Punjab in Northwestern India) and Hmong parents form Laos, when they arrive in America, are unfamiliar with the idea of being active, collaborative parents who visit school on several occasions a year. If their child is well behaved and doing well in school, they see no reason to visit. Traditional Vietnamese parents are made uncomfortable by a teacher who consistently tries to look them in the eye while talking, is loud and informal, and is noncognizant of the superior position of the male in the Vietnamese family structure. Also, traditional Vietnamese and Punjabi Sikh as well as some American parents will likely be made uncomfortable if asked to discuss the relationships they have with their children at home. (An example of such a question might be, How do you discipline your child at home?) In their mind and prior culture, home is home business, and school is the teacher's business; they have not yet learned or simply do not value the American propensity, embodied in our national television and radio talk show hosts, to ask relative strangers the most intimate questions, and to do so in public settings.

Establishing collaborative relationships with parents, teachers, and students will likely prove difficult when the home culture that values education does not value collaboration or has a centuries-old, and different, conception of collaboration between teachers and parents.

In addition, the likelihood for cultural discontinuity and conflict, or at least misunderstanding, is heightened when immigrant or minority cultures do not value *equal* educational opportunity, or results, for males and females, as we understand these terms in America. This is the case with many Punjabi Sikhs who want their young men to go to four-year colleges but their young women to agree to arranged marriages before decisions about advanced education are made. Typically, in this immigrant culture the husband's approval or disapproval about further education at a four-year college will be decisive. In such situations where there is a discontinuity or clash between an important and basic value of the home culture—arranged marriages help to ensure the continuity and survival of traditional Sikh culture in the United States—and an important value of the school culture, like gender equity, the teacher working within a framework of multicultural education will have to make personal choices between various goals in the model. For example, for the teacher working with Punjabi Sikh students, it will be challenging to model cultural pluralism (appreciating, valuing, and understanding the internal logic of many cultures) and simultaneously present the choices and promise of American culture, which includes equal opportunity for men and women. Teachers should be aware that in subtly advocating equal opportunity and independence for Sikh students, they are inviting the Sikh student to separate from the Sikh family and culture. And they should also remember that some Punjabi Sikh-American families may have already begun to value equal opportunity for men and women. In such contexts multicultural education can become very complicated, particularly if the teacher attempts to create a multicultural curriculum in the absence of family knowledge.

Interviewing School Leaders

Even with the incomplete knowledge of the various cultures one is working with, however, it is possible to (a) attempt to establish educational equity and a collaborative parent–teacher relationship and (b) teach students to appreciate, understand, and value the internal logic of specific cultures and the commonalities and differences between disparate cultures like the Sikh and mainstream American culture. To achieve this delicate balance teachers will benefit from dialogue with the principal, the school psychologist, and other knowledgeable educators. Such dialogue will help teachers gain insight into the "local wisdom of practitioners" as they develop their own perspective on appropriate multicultural teaching while teaching in settings where the interacting cultures have divergent core values. Questions that might prove helpful when discussing this issue with the principal or school psychologist include the following:

1. In terms of explicit (verbal) and implicit (nonverbal) patterns of communication, will students from this particular culture or ethnic group tend to communicate in a manner that (a) is different from standard mainstream American patterns of communication or (b) conflicts with the standard operating procedure of most schools' or teachers' general expectations for appropriate student behavior?
2. In terms of explicit and implicit communication for this group, are there patterns of communication that teachers should utilize or avoid when communicating with students or parents?
3. In terms of sex-role socialization in this particular cultural group, are there "cultural facts" I should know as I
   a. implement my curriculum in general?
   b. form heterogeneous cooperative learning groups?
   c. carry out physical education (P.E.) activities?
4. Regarding the (name of group) _____ students in my class, are there generalizations about their learning style or the teaching style of teachers in their former country that would be useful to know as background knowledge?
5. Are you aware of books, articles, and videotapes that would provide me with useful background knowledge about _____ culture and language, recommended teaching strategies, or other information?

We have focused here on cultural differences between immigrant parents and teachers, but teachers should be aware that socioeconomic differences between parents and teachers can also lead to communication breakdowns that are cultural in nature. This situation is likely to occur when the parents are a part of the group considered to be the "poor" in America. The children of these parents have much to gain from parent involvement in the schools. With this in mind teachers are strongly encouraged to examine the parent–teacher communication resources listed in appendix 6, as well as the resources pertaining to selected immigrant and language minority groups.

Special Communication Strategies

Now that you are somewhat better prepared for cross-cultural encounters, it is helpful to examine the planned events referenced earlier; for example, your school will probably organize a Back-to-School night within the first four to six weeks of school, and parent–teacher conferences, especially in the elementary grades, may follow. However, if you rely on these events alone to meet your parents, you may well fall short of your goal of communicating with all of them, and second, you will certainly fail to make contact with a high percentage of the parents whose children would benefit most from an ongoing parent–teacher dialogue.

Knowing this and keeping the goal of equity in mind, you will need to be proactive. You should begin the school year ready to implement a set of communication strategies; some teachers even begin their communication with parents and future students several weeks before the beginning of school. To facilitate your work in this area we have listed some recommended strategies that K–8 teachers can adapt to their specific circumstances.

1. During the first week of school send home a polite and positive letter to parents in the appropriate languages. We developed the letter below as a model for elementary teachers who had begun to send home abrupt, culturally uninformed letters to parents after attending a brief workshop in "Assertive Discipline." Teachers should adopt a professional and respectful tone when addressing parents. It is within your province of responsibility to request, encourage, and invite parents to get involved in their child's education, but you cannot demand it. Something as reasonable to you as expecting parents to check their child's homework each night and sign off on it can prove stressful to some parents who do not want to sign off on material they do not understand; it can be burdensome to a single parent who comes home late and has several children and may be confusing to some immigrant parents who come from cultures where teachers do not ask parents to do the teacher's work. However, an invitation to check homework periodically for neatness and legibility, expressed in language that dignifies and empowers parents, can be constructive for all concerned. If your principal agrees, he, a mentor teacher, or possibly a teacher aide who is also a parent in the community could check your letters for content and tone before you send them out. Below we have included two letters (see figures 2.1 and 2.2); the first, which has been employed in our region and which a number of our pre-service candidates like, is too rigid and assertive for us. The second letter is one we composed to illustrate the possibility of discussing rules with parents in a positive tone and spirit.
2. Follow up this first letter with a call inviting parents to visit with you during Back-to-School night; prepare your material carefully for that evening. If your school has facilities to generate computer-assisted automatic phone messages, use this technique to extend invitations to parents who are hard to reach. At the same time be aware that some new immigrant parents will be unfamiliar with telephones, and that something as culturally logical to an

Dear Parents:

In order to guarantee your child, and all the students in my classroom, the excellent learning climate they deserve, I am utilizing the following discipline plan as of September 9, 1991.

MY PHILOSOPHY

I believe all my students can behave appropriately in my classroom. I will tolerate no student stopping me from teaching and/or any student from learning.

CLASS RULES

1. Students will stay in seats unless given permission to get up.
2. Students will raise hands for help, questions, or group participation.
3. Students will keep hands, feet, and objects to self.
4. There will be no teasing of others.
5. All students will follow directions.
6. Students will walk in the class quietly and sit appropriately.

IF A STUDENT CHOOSES TO BREAK A RULE

1st Consequence—Verbal Warning
2nd Consequence—Name on the Board
3rd Consequence—Writing Assignment in the "You Blew It Book"
4th Consequence—Notice Sent Home
5th Consequence—Phone Call Home or Parent Conference
Severe Disruption—Sent to Principal or Immediate Jump to Consequence #3

STUDENTS WHO BEHAVE WILL EARN

Stars for the "Star Chart," Special Cooking Activities, Special Lunch, Walking Field Trips, Class Awards, School Awards, Other Special Activities, and Lots of Positive Reinforcement

It is in your child's best interest that we work together on his/her schooling. I will thus be in close contact with you regarding your child's progress in my classroom. Please sign the tear-off sheet below and have your child bring it with him/her to school tomorrow. If you have any questions or comments, please feel free to call, come by the classroom, or write me a note. I will be discussing this discipline plan during the upcoming Back-to-School night in October (date to be announced).

Sincerely,

I have read and understand the discipline plan for your classroom.

(Signature of Parent or Guardian) _____

FIGURE 2.1   Letter #1 (A Bit Too Assertive)

Dear Parents:

Welcome to a new school year. I have been getting to know your child this week and thus have a good reason to be excited about the coming school year.

In order to promote an enjoyable as well as academically productive year, I would like to share some ideas about my approach to classroom discipline. This year I will combine elements from several successful approaches to discipline to create an orderly classroom environment wherein your child can safely learn valuable content and simultaneously have the opportunity to grow in self-discipline, self-direction, and self-esteem.

During the first week of class, I will introduce several important rules and then, with the class's help, a rationale and set of consequences will be developed for each rule. Some of the rules and a preliminary rationale (in parentheses) follow:

1. Students will raise their hand when they wish to ask a question or share information. (Calling out is disruptive and discourteous.)
2. Students will walk, not run, jump, or skip in the classroom. (We want our classroom to be a safe learning environment.)
3. Problems will be discussed and analyzed during classroom meetings. (Trying to solve problems by fighting is disruptive, nonproductive, and dangerous.)
4. Students will be polite with each other and their teachers. (Polite students avoid problems better than impolite students and are quite pleasant to work with.)

By or before mid-October, I hope the class will be ready to share a document that lists its rules along with a rationale and list of consequences for each rule. The rules and consequences will be applied sensitively and flexibly and will be periodically reviewed.

This letter is written to you because you are part of our classroom community. I believe the letter will place you in a better position to speak knowledgeably about this program with your child. If you have any comments or questions, please share them in a note or at our upcoming parent–teacher conference.

Join with me, then, in a year that promises excitement and academic achievement for us all.

Yours truly,

FIGURE 2.2 Letter #2 (A More Positive Tone)

American as an invitation by phone may be perceived as frustrating and intrusive by some of these parents.

3. Prior to Back-to-School night arrange to have a 20- to 45-minute interview with the parents of each of your students. If you schedule meetings two to three afternoons a week, you should be able to meet with many of them within the first six weeks. Although some teachers prefer to meet parents in their homes or some other setting in which parents are comfortable, we recommend that you attempt to meet them in your classroom where you can use your charts, wall space, and other teaching tools to help answer questions and make a good impression. If it proves impossible for parents to meet you at the school, however, by all means arrange to meet them at their home, a nearby restaurant, the library, or a skating rink. Let the parents know that it would be very helpful to you if you could ask them a few questions about their concerns, the child's recent health history, and interests at home. Here are a few of the questions that elementary teachers in our region have found useful in initiating a culturally informed collaborative relationship with parents and their children.

   a. Could you tell me how old Marquis is, and if he has any special interests or hobbies I can make use of as I'm working with him?

   b. Does Marquis have any special chores or responsibilities at home, and if so, what are they?

   c. A follow-up question could be, How long has he been taking trumpet lessons?

   d. Are there rules at home that Marquis is expected to follow, and if so, what are they?

   e. If Marquis doesn't follow family rules, what kinds of discipline do you use?

   f. Do your disciplinary techniques generally work?

   g. What are your expectations for Marquis at school?

   h. What kind of letter grades would you like him to get?

   i. As Marquis's parents, do you have any special concerns, requests, or expectations that you'd like to share with me?

   j. What has been Marquis's strongest area in school? Has he had any weak areas?

   k. How does he get along with other children? Brothers and sisters?

   l. Has Marquis had any recent health problems—over the summer?

   m. Is he currently taking medication for any reason, and if so, for what purpose?

   n. Do you think Marquis would be interested in tutoring younger children?

   o. What does Marquis do on weekends?

   p. There are many ways parents can help out in my classroom for an hour a week or more. Would you be interested in serving in my class, or in the school, as a volunteer? You can try this for a period of two or three weeks to see whether you like it.

   q. In the area of homework, have you worked with Marquis in earlier grades?

r. Are you comfortable with the idea of checking Marquis's homework on a weekly or daily basis for neatness?

s. Is there something else you'd like to discuss that I haven't addressed with my questions?

Please note that prior to asking question p above you should make some brief remarks that tell parents they can play a variety of supportive roles in your classroom. They can serve as part of an audience for the culminating presentation of a unit of instruction, or they can be a tutor, presenter on a topic of special interest, fellow traveler on a field trip, volunteer aide to generate supplies for craft activities, or play many other roles. Your message is that there are dozens of ways to support your classroom and school; if the parents cannot come to the school, there are ways to support the school program in their own home. Some handouts with simple ideas regarding homework support would be helpful here. Always, however, you should remember that some new immigrant as well as nonimmigrant parents may be unaccustomed to playing the supportive role you are describing. Checking homework at home may be something they have never been asked to do before, and the idea of sharing their concerns and expectations with their child's teacher may be a wholly new experience.

Finally, in this one-to-one meeting with parents, which occurs before the large group Back-to-School night presentations, you can raise questions sensitively about concerns of your own, perhaps stemming from your analysis of student record cards. For example, the attendance pattern of individual students can fundamentally affect educational equity, and if your review of the cumulative file reveals that a student has had an uneven, or poor, rate of attendance during the past two years (over 25 absences per year), you could take several steps:

1. inquire further to learn whether other siblings have similar rates of attendance and absence;
2. wait two months to see whether the pattern of absences is continuing;
3. share the attendance data with the student's parents and ask them why Marquis had missed school at this rate in the past two years;
4. mention to the parents that by working together as a team you could definitely improve Marquis's attendance.

If handled well, such questioning might lead to a productive, problem-solving dialogue between you and the parents. In this situation, handling it well means that you are careful not to throw the parents on the defensive but are able to take a proactive posture with a student who may be at risk because of a poor pattern of school attendance.

Class-building Activities

Another major activity that begins during the first month of the year is class building. As a multiculturally oriented educator, one of your primary goals will be to create a total curriculum and environment that promotes intercultural, interethnic, and intergroup understanding and harmony. Your work will be greatly facilitated if your students perceive and identify with the idea that they are part of a community of learners, a group that cares about each other's feelings, academic progress, and social development. Classroom teachers need to understand that increasing numbers of students are coming to school ill prepared to care, share, and help each other. Many factors have combined to create this dilemma, and schools cannot avoid filling what Spencer Kagan calls a "socialization void."[34] Your students will either become more competitive and individualistic or more cooperative and caring in your classroom, and the way you choose to structure the learning process will be the decisive factor. You can help to fill the socialization void by building a "we're in this together" class norm, and you can promote a collaborative class identity by

1. providing class time for the students to get acquainted at the beginning of the school year;
2. identifying a class project to which all individuals, through cooperative learning groups or other ways, will contribute—examples include a mural, a monthly or quarterly newsletter, a play, a beautification project for the class or the school, the development of a class song or logo, a partner system to help each other with homework, or an upper-grade-class teaching or tutoring project for a lower grade;
3. holding classroom meetings to develop and refine the rules and consequences (the justice system) for the class;
4. providing one activity per week during the first month wherein students will simultaneously discover more about each other and learn to be accepting of each other's personal opinions and values;
5. providing each student with a partner to facilitate learning both within and outside the classroom; and
6. telling your students that
   a. you expect to learn a lot about and from each student,
   b. that you and they will both be teachers and learners in this classroom.

In his compilation of resources for cooperative learning, Kagan describes a structure entitled "Corners" that is quite suitable for providing students with the opportunity to learn more about each other's commonalities and develop an appreciation for their own point of view and the views of others.[35] In this activity the teacher picks an item that students will have different opinions about or preferences for. It could be four different foods, television shows, forms of entertainment, music, professions, approaches to solving inflation, seasons, sports, characters in a novel, or pets. Students will be given some time to make their choice and decide the reasons for this choice. After proceeding to the corner of the room designated for their chosen item, students will

1. share the reasons for their preference with a partner; and
2. form groups of approximately four where each student will paraphrase the reasons their partner just presented.

Then, a spokesperson from each corner will summarize all the reasons that were presented in that corner. After each spokesperson presents his group's reasons, the original pairs of partners will collaboratively paraphrase each spokesperson's ideas; when all spokespersons have been heard, the corner groups will come together as one group or in groups of four to make certain that everyone can identify reasons for each of the possible choices. This type of class-building activity can also lead to a creative writing activity or some other content-related lesson. A corner's session on seasons, for example, could serve as an introduction to a poetry writing activity or a science unit on weather, and one on sports could serve as a lead into the introduction of a new physical education activity or as a piece of literature related to sports.

Team-building Activities

In addition to class-building activities, equity-oriented teachers will engage in team-building activities after they have learned more about the special strengths and growth areas of individual students. They will structure the small groups so that over the course of the year each student will work closely with students of different ethnic and cultural backgrounds, academic achievement potential, and gender.

Unless you inherit a group of students almost intact from a previous grade in which they have already had a number of team-building experiences, at the beginning of the year you should engage in a series of team-building activities. As Kagan has noted, "Teambuilding creates enthusiasm, trust, and mutual support which in the long run leads to more efficient academic work."[36] Team-building activities follow the same logic as class-building activities, so after forming your teams you will provide them with activities that (a) allow them to get acquainted, (b) develop the team's identity and cohesiveness, (c) allow team members to experience mutual support, and (d) provide opportunities to value the unique personalities and perspectives of individual team members. Below are some examples of team-building activities:

1. For Getting Acquainted: As a part of a class-building exercise each student can develop a personal web (see figure 2.3) that could contain some or all of the following information: hobbies; names of family members; favorite food, TV shows, sports, singers, songs, colors, athletes, and books. The students, working in pairs, could orally share their webs with their partners, and then each partner could introduce her partner to the class, selecting one or two facts from each major category, using the visual web as a frame of reference if needed. After additional information was added to each category, or a new category to the web, the web could be used for the same purpose when the first teams are formed in the class. In this setting the partners would introduce each other to the other pair of their four-student team; next would be a team interview in which each member asks at least one question. The partner being introduced can answer, pass, or invite the introducer to take a shot at the question. The expanded webs can be used again when teams are restructured, and each team, using the same rules for selecting a team name can select a new category to be added to the personal web.

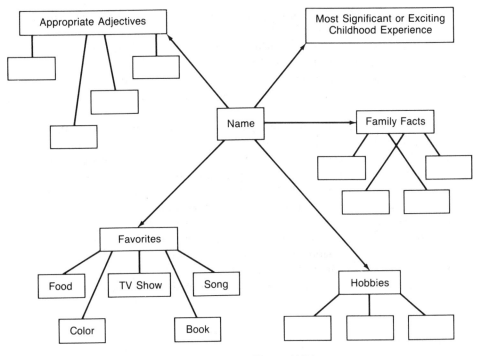

FIGURE 2.3 My Personal Web

2. For Team Identity Building: Having students select names for their groups is a very basic and enjoyable team-building activity, provided certain basic rules are followed. Kagan identifies three rules to facilitate this process: (a) each team member must have a say, (b) no decision can be made unless everyone consents, and (c) no member consents to the group decision if he or she has a serious objection.[37] With a multicultural perspective in mind I would suggest a fourth rule: (d) team names should be positive in nature. The names should contribute to the class-building and team-building process and should not be exclusive in nature (Four White Dudes) or self-derogatory (the Four Jerks or the Three Idiots) or suggestive of ill will (the Klan, or the name of any gang in the community). If you do not establish ground rules for your team names, you should be prepared to accept anything, and "anything" could easily undermine the goals you are attempting to achieve through multicultural and cooperative education. Collaborative art projects such as designing and creating a team mural or team banner are also excellent vehicles for building team identity.

3. For Appreciating Individual Differences: One approach would be to establish brainstorming rules, such as everyone participates, all ideas accepted (*No Put Downs*), zany ideas welcome, connections encouraged—one idea building on a previous idea or connecting two other ideas. Then each team could use the brainstorming process to generate ideas for improving one area of the total school community (the classroom, lunchroom, playground, li-

brary). After each team has delineated and copied a long list of possibilities, each team member will

a. pick the two ideas he considers the most important (the criterion could be practicality rather than importance);
b. write down one or two reasons for each choice; and
c. share his first choice and reasons with the group.

After each team member has presented her idea and reason to the group, on a quasi-voluntary basis the other team members can comment on why they liked the idea and reasons. The encourager in the group will make sure that everyone receives some positive feedback, and after the first round, team members can share their second choice and reasons. As the culminating step, the team, using a consensus process, can submit its six best ideas to the teacher or entire class; all team members will pick one of their own ideas for this list, and the student's name will be listed next to the idea. This particular activity could end with the submission of that list, or it could be developed into a group project with the students conducting research and then submitting their proposals for improvement to the appropriate individuals in the school.

Selection of Content

In the previous section we suggested that the way you communicate with parents and the way you structure your class for learning can promote educational equity to a greater or lesser degree. The main idea in this section is that the same premise holds true for curriculum content. Curriculum content is not neutral. What you choose to teach in history, current events, language arts, English, music, art, mathematics, science, physical education, and foreign languages can

1. contribute to individual self-esteem and thereby contribute to educational equity and related goals such as interethnic and intercultural harmony;
2. provide examples of individuals from disparate cultural and ethnic groups who are harmoniously working together in normal as well as trying circumstances and thereby contribute to the goal of intergroup understanding and harmony;
3. allow students to see that people just like themselves have contributed, and are contributing, to American and world civilization in all its facets, and thereby contribute to educational equity by increasing the students' ethnic and cultural pride and belief that their education can lead to attainable, interesting careers;
4. provide students with intriguing accurate information about specific cultural and ethnic groups at home and abroad and thereby increase the students' multicultural/multiethnic knowledge base, their ability to think from a multicultural perspective, and perhaps their potential for successful interaction with individuals of varying ethnic and cultural background;
5. create opportunities for students to articulate and consider the various points of view surrounding general as well as culturally laden issues and

thereby contribute to the students' ability to think from a multicultural perspective, and perhaps interact with individuals of varying cultural backgrounds;

6. help students see history and current events through the eyes of the conquered as well as the conqueror, the slave as well as the plantation owner, the soldier as well as the general, the poor as well as the rich. Thus, with your content choices you have the potential to uncover and share a multiperspective or monoperspective (ethnocentric) view of American and world history, and your responsibility—with multicultural education in mind—is to the former.

The list of curriculum possibilities should encourage you to keep the goals of multicultural education clearly in mind as you choose your content or decide what to emphasize in content you are required to teach. In chapters 3, 4, and 5 we will return to the issue of curriculum content as we present and discuss lessons, lesson sequences, and units of instruction that in various ways—methods and content—incorporate a multicultural perspective. This material will illustrate how teachers can teach with a multicultural perspective throughout the school year and across the school curriculum.

Now that we have examined the manner in which in-service teachers can incorporate a multicultural perspective in their planning and teaching at the beginning of the school year, we will delineate strategies that student teachers can adapt, in their respective situations, so that they too can begin to plan and teach with a multicultural perspective. In-service teachers who serve as master teachers will benefit from this discussion, particularly the parts that deal with the Demographic Profile and the Typology of Multicultural Teaching.

TEACHING WITH A MULTICULTURAL PERSPECTIVE DURING STUDENT TEACHING

It is critically important for the prospective teacher to realize that student teaching is not just something to get through. Student teaching provides a series of experiences that will deeply influence your first years of teaching. Ideas that you try out and evaluate during student teaching you will likely try again in modified form early in your teaching career. Ideas that you read about during your methods courses but elect not to try because they do not exactly fit your student teaching assignment may well remain untried during your first teaching years. Some of those ideas might make a world of difference in helping you decide whether to remain a teacher. Thus we encourage you to try out a variety of teaching strategies during your student teaching assignment and to give the ideas discussed below serious consideration during that time. Although they range in complexity, all of these tactics and strategies have been successfully implemented by student teachers in a variety of teaching programs.

Please note that even though you are working in someone else's classroom, there are many ways for you to incorporate a multicultural perspective into your student teaching. Furthermore, in addition to your actual planning and teaching of lessons and lesson sequences, there are several important research activities that can help you to aim your student teaching at the six goals in our conception of multicultural education. We will discuss a few of these student teaching possibilities under the following headings: parent–teacher communication; interviewing and observing students, teachers, and community; developing and extending a classroom demographic profile; and using the Typology of Multicultural Teaching as you develop lessons, lesson sequences, units of instruction, and your total class curriculum.

Parent–Teacher Communication

How does parent–teacher communication contribute to multicultural education, and more specifically, educational equity? Clearly, effective culturally sensitive communication can lead to greater cooperation and collaboration between parents, students, and teachers, a development that in turn can promote equity by creating more access to learning for your students. Schoolwork and homework become more rewarding and illuminating when parents adopt strategies that support school goals. Furthermore, if you ask the right questions parent–teacher communication can also provide you with additional insight into your students' interests, personalities, and cultural background, and this knowledge can create more opportunity for learning and culturally sensitive instruction in your classroom. In addition, by sending home introductory letters in the appropriate languages, by using interpreters when necessary, by showing interest in family concerns, and by providing culturally appropriate communication when interacting with students and parents, you are modeling a positive pluralistic attitude; in so doing you are teaching cultural pluralism in a most meaningful and convincing manner.

However, although you ought to be an active communicator with parents, you should appreciate that typically in student teaching you are not trying to develop a full-blown collaborative relationship with parents (that is your master teacher's responsibility). You are simply practicing parent–teacher communication, and a logical place to begin is with a letter introducing yourself to the parents of your students. Please note that most parents will hear about you regardless of whether you choose to send a letter, but what they hear may not be accurate. For example, students in a primary grade may announce that they have a "new" teacher, leading some parents to wonder what happened to their old teacher. For this and other reasons we believe that it is polite and professional for you as a student teacher to let parents know exactly who you are. The letter you write should be checked by your master teacher and your principal, if your master teacher considers this appropriate. There is no one correct formula for an introductory letter. However, there are some recommended ingredients; these include your name, the length of your stay, the name of the program you are a part of, a statement about your personal goals, a special project you are planning such as a unit of instruction, and a closing positive statement. A brief example is presented in figure 2.4.

If you will be teaching a unit of instruction during your student teaching, it would be appropriate to send home to parents a newsletter that describes the content of the unit and special activities their child would be involved in and invites the parents to participate as guests during a culminating unit activity, as a helper on a

Dear Parents

This letter is to inform you that for the next _____ weeks I will be working in your child's classroom. My name is Melinda Mendoza, and I am a student teacher in the Bowling Green Teacher Education Program. This is my second student teaching assignment, and I look forward to beginning my career in teaching this September.

I am grateful for the opportunity to teach and learn in Mrs. Chiarelott's class and for the chance to work with all of her students. Among other things this semester, I will be teaching a unit on American inventors and will be sending you more information about this unit later in the semester. In the meantime, if you are in or near the school, please drop in to say "hello." I would like to meet as many parents as possible.

Sincerely,

FIGURE 2.4 Sample Student Teacher Letter

field trip, or as a guest speaker if they have some special knowledge related to the unit's content. A follow-up newsletter composed by students and teacher, which summarizes the unit's activities and learnings, could be one of the culminating activities of your unit.

As a student teacher you should make every effort to attend as many official parent-related meetings as possible (PTA, school site council, parent–teacher conferences, etc.). As you observe, you should take notes on what the teachers and administrators do to make a wide range of parents feel comfortable about participating in the school setting. In addition to attending these meetings, you should continue to expand your knowledge of parent-involvement strategies. One excellent resource for this purpose is *Communicating with Parents,* a resource manual for principals and teachers designed to assist them in communicating with and involving parents at home and at school.[38] Another excellent source of parent-involvement strategies are the teachers in your school and school district. By interviewing your master teacher and principal, you can identify and then interview teachers who have developed a reputation for excelling in the area of parent involvement and parent partnerships. Teachers stimulate high parent involvement in a variety of ways. Some make extensive use of the phone; others use newsletters to entice parents to visit the classroom and actually plan projects, exhibits, and evening workshops that parents will find intriguing; others are adept at meeting parents in homes, restaurants, and other neutral settings. Your interviews with such teachers will provide you with valuable information and will help you realize that student teaching is a wide-ranging field experience, one that focuses on a particular classroom but also extends into other classrooms, the school, and most significantly the community the school serves. Interviewing and observing are major strategies for developing the knowledge base that will allow you to see, plan, and teach with a multicultural perspective. Thus in the section below we will present some tools to facilitate your use of these strategies during student teaching.

Interviewing and Observing during Student Teaching

Prospective and new teachers should understand that educators do not learn how to teach solely by reading, observing, and engaging in practice teaching. Much that is important in good teaching arises from an awareness of curriculum, community, and culture that is difficult to discern from observation alone; some very pertinent knowledge is local in nature and can only be known and derived from the multiple experiences of local practitioners (teachers, instructional aides, principals, counselors, and others). For example, an essay, text, or special presenter in a methods course can inform you about the discontinuity between American nonverbal cues (smiling and nods) and the different meaning that smiles and nods may have when delivered by some newly arrived Vietnamese immigrants. This knowledge about a specific immigrant group will be helpful in general, but it will be the practitioners in your school district who will give you insight into how such knowledge is used by teachers as they try to distinguish between new immigrants and immigrants who are in the process of trying on "American" forms of nonverbal communication. Our recommendation is that prospective and new teachers should regularly question teachers, university supervisors, parents, students, instructional aides, principals, and community leaders. In short, student teachers should become patient, well-organized, energetic interviewers and should *always* remember the individuality of their students and families. The risk of oversimplification and stereotyping is constantly with us as we attempt to use wisely cultural information about various groups.

In the busy student teaching–learning environment it may prove difficult to have extensive interviews with various community and agency leaders and citizens, but at the school site there are many interviewees who can enhance your potential for teaching with a multicultural perspective. Your primary sources of local information about the cultures of your students will be your master teacher and her principal, the school psychologist, and the students themselves; other valuable sources could be a migrant coordinator, migrant aide, bilingual teacher, or parent volunteer. The next section discusses in detail your initial interviews with your master teacher and your principal.

Initial Interview with Teacher

If possible the first interview with the master teacher should occur several weeks prior to your student teaching. This timing will allow your master teacher to share books, articles, and other material to help you develop the specific and local knowledge base you need to achieve maximum success with her students. As you review the questions enumerated below and our occasional commentary (in parentheses), please note the following:

1. in some cases the questions will relate directly to one or more of the goals of multicultural education;
2. some questions will serve other purposes;
3. student teachers are not required to ask all the following questions.

The Questions

1. I would like to know a bit more about your teaching background. For example, how many years have you been a teacher, and at what grade levels and in which school districts?
2. In terms of general ideas about teaching, which beliefs strongly influence the way you organize and manage the learning in your classroom?
3. Do you utilize a set of specific rules or standards to help establish and maintain an effective learning environment? If yes, which rules or standards do you work with,, and how were they selected or developed?
4. Is the development of self-esteem or self-direction in learning an explicit part of the curriculum in your class, and if so, what strategies do you use to help students develop self-esteem or self-direction in learning?
5. What roles do parents play in helping you achieve your educational objectives? In what different ways do you communicate with parents?
6. Do you place your students in groups to facilitate instruction, and if yes, what kinds of groups are employed and what criteria do you employ to structure these groups?
7. Is multicultural education or educational equity an important curriculum emphasis in your school district, and if yes, what kinds of staff development support the growth of multicultural education? (Please note that your major goal with questions 7 and 8 is to learn how a school district and master teacher relate to and conceptualize multicultural education. You should be open-minded and nonjudgmental as your master teacher responds. As you continue your questioning, you may well discover that she employs teaching strategies associated with multicultural education but does not use the same terminology that your teacher education program does. In this area, the master teacher's response to question 11 should be revealing.)
8. Do you provide multicultural education in your classroom, and if yes, what specific strategies help you to do so?
9. What types of evaluation and grading procedures do you use in your classroom? In this district, what are teachers required to do in the area of evaluation and grading, and what is left up to the teacher's discretion?
10. How is homework handled in your classroom, and does the school district have a specific policy that requires teachers to give a certain amount of homework on a regular basis?
11. Are there individual students or groups of students in your class who receive special attention, special services, or modified instruction because of one or more of the factors listed below. If yes, I'd like to gather some specific information about each of these students today and then continue to discuss them in later sessions. So, are there students who receive special planning and treatment because of
    a. learning disabilities or capabilities?
    b. language background or capabilities (i.e., limited, near, or potential English proficient—LEP, NEP, PEP, or bilingual proficiency or bidialecticism)?
    c. recent immigration to, or migration within, the United States (and neighboring countries)?

    d. cultural, ethnic, or religious background?

    e. socioeconomic status or gender?

    f. other factors related to recent family events, such as separation from a parent, divorce, or death in the family?

    (Your teacher's responses to question 11 serve as a surrogate for interviews with parents when you have your own classroom. If you choose to work with this strategy during student teaching, or are required to, it might be wise to save question 11 for a separate session in which you and the master teacher can work together to complete a *classroom demographic profile.* The profile will be discussed in greater detail below.)

12. When did you first have access to the record card or portfolios of your students? What information is kept in these files, and how do you utilize this data base? At some point during the school term may I review these files?

13. What strategies do you use in this class to help students relate to each other in positive ways?

14. What do you consider to be your most important legal responsibilities? In this district, how do teachers become aware of their legal responsibilities?

15. In our teacher education program I will be expected to teach at least one unit of instruction during this assignment, and I will also be expected to spend approximately five weeks planning the unit and employ a multicultural perspective as I design and implement the unit. With this in mind, are there any specific units you would like me to plan or special areas of the curriculum you would like me to direct my unit assignment toward?

Initial Interview with Principal

If there are other student teachers at the school site, you should try to arrange a joint meeting with the principal and also with the school psychologist. The principal will likely want to greet you when you arrive at the campus but may be surprised when you request an interview. With the principal, we recommend that you keep your interview short. You should ask the principal if he would like to see your questions in advance. Possible topics and questions for the principal include the following:

1. School and Community Characteristics and Special Programs
   a. Compared to other schools in the district does your school have special demographic and economic characteristics?
   b. Does your school have special programs to meet the educational needs of special groups of learners? If yes, can you provide a few examples?
   c. How would you describe the overall mission of this school and your school district?
   d. In terms of mobility and cultural patterns, resources for children, health facilities, and other data, how would you describe the surrounding community?
   e. How would you describe the relationship between your school and the community, and would you please describe some programs and activities that help to create this relationship?

2. At-Risk Children

   If at-risk students were not mentioned above, the following questions may prove illuminating.

   a. I have seen the term *at risk* used in recent educational articles. Are there children in your school who are considered to be at risk?

   b. If yes, how are such students identified, and do they receive special attention from teachers and other specialists on your staff?

   c. If yes, can you give some specific examples of such special support?

   d. Do you think this label is a functional and productive label for educators to employ? Why? Why not?

3. Educational Equity and Multicultural Education

   a. Do teachers and administrators in this district and school talk about educational equity and multicultural education, and if yes, what do you think these terms mean to most of them?

   b. In this school district are there any districtwide policies pertaining to educational equity and multicultural education?

   c. In terms of ethnic and cultural background, has the student population in your school or school district been changing during the last five or ten years?

   d. If yes, have these demographic shifts led to changes in curriculum and instruction and specific patterns of communication at your school?

   e. Do you think it is important for future teachers to think, plan, and teach with a multicultural perspective, and can you provide some reasons for your response?

With your principal, as with your master teacher, you may find an educator carrying out practices associated with multicultural education but not using the same terms employed by the teacher educators at your university. With the school psychologist you can use the questions delineated earlier in the chapter, and you can also ask her or the principal to name some of the specific community agencies and organizations that serve the children in your school (libraries, parks and recreation, Boy Scouts and Girl Scouts, weekend cultural programs for specific immigrant groups, and others). If you have not already done so, now might be a good time to walk around and drive through the community your school serves. The more aware you are of community conditions and community resources, human and physical, the better able you will be to provide sensitive equity-oriented instruction and advice to your students.

The Classroom Demographic Profile

After you have had initial interviews with your master teacher, principal, and school psychologist and have spent time observing in your local community, and perhaps observing in special classrooms at your school site, you are ready to sit down with your master teacher to have a more detailed discussion about the individual students in his classroom. If possible this conversation should occur before your assignment begins so you can observe with a multicultural perspective from the very first day of your assignment.

You will recall that in chapter 1 we said that the educators who teach with a multicultural perspective will see their students as unique individuals and as members of family, ethnic, and cultural groups that influence their behavior. During student teaching, or in earlier field assignments, you can begin to collect data to inform this dual vision by filling out a classroom demographic profile with your master teacher.

The classroom demographic profile is a form (see figure 2.5) that allows your master teacher to accomplish the following:

1. introduce you to the ethnic, cultural, and instructional diversity that exists in his classroom;
2. provide you with instructionally relevant information about specific special learners who are included in the data base;
3. share with you new categories for students that the district currently finds useful for instructional or funding reasons. You may, for example, find some teachers who can readily identify their "at-risk" learners and the extra resources that are directed toward these learners to expand their potential for success.

FIGURE 2.5 The Classroom Demographic Profile

Student Teacher Name: _____ Cooperating Teacher Name: _____ Date: _____

Grade: _____ School: _____ District: _____

Types of Students [Students are or have a(n)]   Instructionally Relevant Information about Specific Students*

A. *Linguistically Different (LEP/NEP) first name only*
   1. _____
   2. _____
   3. _____

B. *Individual Education Plan (IEP/LEP)*
   1. _____
   2. _____

C. *Suspected Learning Disability but No IEP*
   1. _____

*This could include information about resource room instruction, modification of regular class instruction; special arrangements stemming from religious background; health and medication; IEPs, or Individual Language Plans (ILPs), Learning Style, and so on.

2. _____
   _____

D. *Of Ethnic Minority Background***
   (first name and ethnic identification)
   1. _____
   2. _____
   3. _____
   4. _____
   5. _____
   6. _____
   7. _____
   8. _____
   9. _____
   10. _____

E. *Migrant Students*
   1. _____
   2. _____
   3. _____
   4. _____

F. *Receiving Special Medication*
   1. _____
   2. _____
   _____

G. *Gifted and Talented*
   1. _____
   2. _____
   3. _____

H. *Other Categories Used by Classroom Teachers and/or School*
   _____
   _____
   _____
   _____
   _____

I. *Extra Spaces*
   _____
   _____
   _____
   _____
   _____

**Include here students of Hispanic-American, African-American, Native-American, Asian-American, Iranian-American, Punjabi-American background *only* if this classroom teacher believes the student's cultural background or ethnicity has, or might have, instructional implications.

FIGURE 2.5 *(continued)*

Please note that the demographic profile will provide you with some instructionally relevant information about a range of special learners in the classroom. This information should tie directly into your effort to provide equity-oriented instruction to help your students achieve their full academic potential. As valuable as this data base can be at the beginning of the student teaching experience, you should realize that the profile data base is only a point of departure for further observation and note taking for all the students in class, those mentioned in the profile and those not mentioned. For this purpose we encourage you to keep a loose-leaf binder at home in which two or three pages are set aside for each student, and the names are alphabetically arranged. Your profile data should be transferred to this notebook, which can also serve as a reflections journal and a catalyst for reflective planning and teaching. If you are like many other teachers, the act of writing about your students will stimulate new ideas for helping them maximize their learning.

The structure of the profile will encourage you to think about your students in terms of socially relevant groups (ethnic and cultural, for example), and the alphabetical structure of the loose-leaf notebook will encourage you to think about each student as an individual. Both documents serve the purpose of providing you with a knowledge base that will help you think and plan from a multicultural perspective. It is the synthesis of your *general* knowledge about the goals of multicultural education and related appropriate teaching strategies, your *general* knowledge about characteristics of selected ethnic and cultural groups, and your *specific* knowledge about each of your students that will allow you to teach insightfully from a multicultural perspective. Another instrument that helps prospective teachers comprehend the wide range of strategies associated with multicultural education is a tool we call the Typology of Multicultural Teaching. We will briefly discuss the typology below and its relationship to the demographic profile and planning lessons, lesson sequences, and units of instruction.

The Typology of Multicultural Teaching

The typology of multicultural teaching is a listing of tactics and strategies that help teachers achieve each of the various goals of multicultural education. Each goal has its own list, but certain strategies such as cooperative learning that help to achieve more than one goal will appear on more than one list. When prospective and veteran teachers ask us what strategies we employ when we teach with a multicultural perspective, we invariably mention a few and then refer them to the typology. Upon examination, most teachers will find some strategies that they use and a few that they could easily adopt or adapt. When you examine the full typology in appendix 1, you should have a similar realization—namely, that multicultural teaching is well within your reach.

Because this chapter focuses on educational equity we will enumerate below the teaching strategies listed under educational equity in the typology. Please note that the lists in the typology are meant to be suggestive rather than exhaustive.

The Typology
A. Examples of Type I Multicultural (MC) Planning and Teaching
   (Planning and teaching that is directly aimed at educational equity)

The teacher
1. makes sophisticated use of the elements of instruction (selecting an objective at the appropriate level of difficulty, teaching to an objective, monitoring and adjusting, using the principles of learning, etc.).
2. selects and utilizes a classroom management system that maximizes the amount of time he or she has available for individual tutoring.
3. modifies his or her oral pace and syntax to facilitate the learning of language and content material for limited English proficient students as well as other special learners.
4. allows one student to serve as a buddy tutor, interpreter, or assistant teacher to facilitate the learning of another student.
5. makes appropriate use of cooperative learning strategies.
6. uses a variety of techniques and content to demonstrate powerfully that in contemporary America men and women of all colors and ethnic groups are succeeding in a wide range of occupations. These can include:
   a. Friday afternoon "career awareness" interviews in which a wide range of successful Americans are interviewed by students
   b. classroom bulletin boards
   c. magazines such as *Ebony* and *Hispanic* (which regularly contain stories about successful African Americans and Hispanic Americans)
   d. book reports
   e. "Upward Bound" visitors (junior high school and high school students who attend special activities to prepare them for college).
7. uses teaching techniques and curriculum materials from specially designed projects such as Project Equals (Lawrence Hall of Science, U. C. Berkeley) and the Complex Instruction Project (Elizabeth Cohen/Stanford University).
8. promotes junior high school and high school graduation and college attendance by engaging in "follow through" and "future prediction" oral behavior, such as the following:
   a. "I want you (all) to let me know when you graduate from high school . . . or junior high school."
   b. "When you children are in high school (or college), you are going to remember this lesson."
   An example of follow through behavior is the work of one local first-grade teacher who sends out congratulation cards to her students 10 or 11 years later when they graduate from high school.
9. engages in student, peer, and self-evaluation to monitor, assess, and perhaps modify the distribution of attention, higher-level questions and wait-time, and leadership opportunities to various individuals and groups in the class.
10. employs a flexible mastery learning model of instruction (pretest/posttest, carefully constructed teaching units, carefully prepared backup teaching strategies).
11. includes self-confidence and self-esteem building as part of the affective/cognitive curriculum.

12. seeks out and makes professional use of parent volunteers and bilingual/trilingual aides if needed.
13. makes use of informal "interest" and "learning style" inventories so as to address the student's interests, learning preferences, and learning style or strengths.
14. develops a multi-ability curriculum that allows a variety of academic skills to receive classroom and teacher recognition as important.
15. creates a collaborative/supportive learning environment—"We're all in this together; we're here to learn and grow as individuals and partners; in this class we will be responsible for each other's success."
16. examines attendance records to get an early start on implementing plans designed to lower the absence rate of specific learners.
17. collects and analyzes data from a survey of television watching to increase the ability to modify patterns of excessive television viewing where appropriate.

SUMMARY

When you understand the goals of multicultural education, are aware of strategies associated with these goals, have completed a first round of interviews with educators at your school site, and have begun to extend the demographic profile database into a more expansive notebook, you are ready to apply your synthesis of this knowledge base to the lessons and units you will implement in your student teaching assignment. In the next chapter "before" and "after" examples of individual lessons and lesson sequences from various content areas and grade levels will be presented and discussed to show how lessons that reflect a monocultural, Eurocentric orientation can be modified to become more multicultural in nature. We call this process *multiculturalizing* the curriculum; we accomplish this expansion in many different ways as we draw on strategies associated with the various goals of multicultural education. However, before venturing on to chapter 3, we want to encourage you to spend some time with the discussion questions and recommended activities that follow. They were formulated to help you flesh out your own multicultural perspective and will encourage you to visit classrooms of teachers who are effective practitioners of cooperative learning and sheltered English instruction.

DISCUSSION QUESTIONS

1. Consider once again the words of the late Chief Justice Earl Warren and then select one or more of the following questions to respond to.

> In these days, it is doubtful that any child may reasonably be expected to succeed in life if he is denied the opportunity of an education. Such an opportunity, where the state has undertaken to provide it, is a right which must be made available to all on equal terms.

   a. Analyze the ideas of *equal terms* or *equal opportunity* from the perspective of a district superintendent, school principal, and classroom teacher. What are some important responsibilities each should assume or activities each can carry out to promote equality of educational opportunity for all their students?

   b. What are some practices in your university or former high school that you consider to be examples of strategies designed to promote equality of educational opportunity? From your perspective, how well did these strategies work? What are your personal feelings about equality of education opportunity and associated strategies?

   c. Have you or any of your friends directly or indirectly benefited from equity-oriented strategies? If so, please describe and discuss them. If there have been negative repercussions associated with these benefits, please identify and discuss these as well.

   d. When Justice Warren wrote his famous opinion, the issue at hand was segregated schools versus integrated schools. In the 1990s in schools where 90 to 100 percent of the students are White American, Black American, or Hispanic American, can you have equality of educational opportunity? If so, what conditions and programs in the ethnically homogeneous school would be associated with such equality? If you respond to this question, please consider both qualitative and quantitative conditions.

2. Earlier in this chapter we wrote: "Increasingly since the 1970s, educational equity and educational excellence have become intertwined concepts," and further, that "because of this integration of meaning we no longer look only at overall graduation rates, overall admittance to community colleges, overall anything . . . when we evaluate the quality of an educational organization." Excellence is "now strongly related to the organization's relative success with the varied ethnic and cultural groups that make up its total student body."

   a. Do you think this new group-oriented conception of organizational excellence is fair? Why or why not? In what sense might your opinion be only part of the truth?

   b. If the integrated multigroup conception of excellence is true and appropriate and you aspire to be an excellent teacher, what specific implications does the integrated concept have for you in terms of classroom teaching, evaluation of students, teacher self-evaluation, and your own professional development?

3. In the section on student records we wrote: "We consider the examination of [student] files [and portfolios] to be the professional responsibility of a multicultural educator and encourage you to pay attention to the information shared by your colleagues as well as your own professional instincts." After examining a duplicate set of real records (with all names removed and surrogates inserted) provided by your professor, discuss the strengths and weaknesses of our opinion about early, prior to school opening, examination of your students' files (and portfolios, if available). In your response specify (a) the type of information you discovered that would contribute to your ability to be effective as a multicultural educator and (b) the information you did not find but would like to see made a part of the official cumulative file.

4. In chapter 2 we suggest that teachers should strive to learn as much as possible about the traditional communication patterns, educational values, and general culture of new American immigrant and refugee groups they are interacting with, as well as the communication patterns of indigenous American minorities—African Americans and Native Americans.

   a. Does this seem reasonable to you, and if so, please explain why?

   b. Does this recommendation seem unreasonable to you? Do you feel that too much emphasis is being placed on Americans learning about immigrant cultures (from all over the world) when, in fact, these immigrants and refugees have come here to become Americans? If you lean toward this feeling, please indicate what you think teachers should try to learn about the various immigrant, refugee, and indigenous American groups they will be trying to teach.

    c. Do you think it is wise for schools to send home letters in the language that is spoken at home, as well as English? Why? Why not? Where possible, please share personal experiences as well as research pertinent to your opinion.

5. In a school or classroom where cooperative learning groups (with consistent heterogeneous grouping) are employed for approximately 40 percent of instruction and where cooperative learning and other strategies have produced, for three consecutive years, positive but modest overall test score gains on standardized tests, should the teacher or school faculty agree to accept a proposal that would dramatically reduce the amount of cooperative learning employed in the school or classroom? In developing your response indicate

    a. whether you are considering this issue from the classroom or school site perspective (in either case you take the role of teacher);

    b. what other kinds of data should be examined in considering this proposal and why they should be included; and

    c. some other recommendations that might be appropriate for a multicultural curriculum-oriented educator to make concerning this proposal.

Would your general position about cooperative learning (40 percent of time with emphasis on heterogeneous grouping) and your specific recommendations change if the test scores had shown a slight decline for the past two years? Where possible, please share personal experiences as well as research that supports your response.

6. In chapter 2 we suggest that classroom teachers should give serious and consistent attention to recruiting students of color (as well as White-American students) into the teaching profession. However, well-intentioned educators, like us, are constantly placing new demands on classroom teachers without significantly adding to their resources (fewer students, more school days or hours, more funds for instructional programs, etc.). Focus on the specific grades you teach or expect to teach (K–3; 4–8) and then answer one or both of the questions below.

    a. Do you believe that teachers (new and veteran) should be consistently concerned—month after month across the school year—with the short- and long-term recruitment of new teachers into the teaching profession? Explain your response.

    b. If you consider the recruitment recommendation to have merit, what are some specific tactics a teacher could employ as she developed an ongoing, subtle, and sometimes explicit, recruitment campaign? If you develop a response to (b), consider the possible use of the content of the curriculum you will be teaching.

7. In terms of socioeconomic levels, ethnic composition, and locale (urban, suburban, rural), describe the school that you would like to teach in for the first or next three years of your teaching career, and then answer the questions listed below:

    a. What prompted you to describe your ideal first school? Be as specific and candid as possible in delineating your reasons.

    b. Were you surprised by the characteristics of the school you described? Speculate about the reasons for your response.

    c. Does the school setting in which you would like to teach call for any special type of preparation, and if yes, what are you doing or planning to do to gain such experience and knowledge?

8. On occasion, the values embedded in the various goals of multicultural education (i.e., intergroup and interethnic harmony, cultural pluralism, educational equity) may conflict with one another if the teacher is simultaneously trying to achieve all goals with each student in her class. For example, it will be extremely difficult to promote gender, ethnic, and cultural equity and simultaneously provide respect and support for a family, ethnic, or cultural group that explicitly promotes racism or sexism. How would you, as a fifth- or eighth-grade teacher, handle the following situation?

> A husband and wife have asked you to stop reading and discussing a specific book in your class because they feel it promotes feminism. (You can slightly modify this question by substituting other terms such as *interracial dating, atheism, racism, satanism,* and *secular humanism.*) The couple has met with you to discuss the problem they have with the book you are reading to the class. You listened patiently and respectfully (you thought) and told them you thought they were overinterpreting both the theme of the story and your intent in selecting the story. Although you appreciated their concern, you fully intended to continue reading and discussing the story in question. Now, they and one other parent whom you have not met have complained to your principal, and they have enlarged their complaint to include what they call your "persistent use of cooperative learning groups to promote feminism and secular humanism." Your principal would like you to meet with all three parents one more time to hear their concerns.

Assuming that you agree to the meeting, how could you use the school district's support of multicultural education to address the concerns of these parents? Should you meet the parents alone or invite the principal to attend?

9. We recommend that elementary and middle-school teachers (in their effort to achieve educational equity) should consider speaking with parents whose children have had poor attendance at school. In this discussion the teacher would suggest that by collaboration, the teacher and the parents could improve the attendance rate and overall education of the student in question. We make this recommendation because of studies like the Aspira Five Cities High School Dropout Study, which suggests that absences, grades, and age are critical factors in predicting whether Latino students will finish high school or drop out.[39]

   a. Do you consider the monitoring of attendance to be a significant aspect of multicultural education? Why or why not?

   b. A student in fourth grade had been absent for 23 days in the first grade, 31 days in the second grade, 28 days in the third grade, and is one to two years below grade level in all tested academic areas. Would you share this information with the parents at an early meeting, and if yes, how would you go about it?

   c. If you would not share the information at the beginning of the year, what is your rationale for not doing so?

10. We believe that what the teacher selects to teach (concepts, books, films, etc.) and how the teacher chooses to present required content is strongly linked to educational equity. In other words, the selection and treatment of content will greatly influence the motivation and achievement levels in your class and will also influence students' perception of reality.

   a. Drawing on your own experience as a learner and your more general experience as a student who has interacted with other learners, discuss your reactions to these assertions.

   b. Assuming that the above assertion is true, do you think that the set of specific instructional decisions regarding content and treatment would be different for a teacher who was teaching a unit of the Civil War to a fifth- or eighth-grade class of students who were

(1) 90 percent African American with the remainder Hispanic American;

(2) 80 percent White American with some Asian, African, and Hispanic American students;

(3) 80 percent Hispanic American with some African-American and Asian-American students.

(a) If yes, please specify how your selection and treatment of content might vary and explain the rationale for the variation.

(b) If no, explain why the set of instructional resources and treatment of content would remain the same.

11. Earlier we wrote: "It is the synthesis of your *general* knowledge about the goals of multicultural education and related appropriate teaching strategies, your *general* knowledge about characteristics of selected ethnic and cultural groups, and your *specific* knowledge about each of your students that will allow you to teach insightfully from a multicultural perspective." In your own words explain what this statement is trying to communicate. In identifying the three categories of knowledge that will allow you to teach with a multicultural perspective, have we left out a fourth or fifth category of pertinent knowledge? If so, please identify and discuss its relationship to insightful multicultural teaching.

12. Programs that aim at equal educational opportunity and equal educational results can lead to some confusing situations. Some teachers think that to pursue these goals they must treat all their students equally . . . or the same, although the law and common sense suggest otherwise. For example, we believe it is practical and wise to distribute praise and classroom responsibilities in a fair and roughly equivalent manner but dysfunctional to try to give each child a quantitatively equal amount of attention or individual tutoring on a daily basis. Indeed, the at-risk concept would suggest that some students should receive more individual tutoring than others on a regular basis.

a. In what areas of schooling, if any, should teachers and administrators strive to achieve quantitative numerical equivalency?

b. In what areas of classroom and school activity should teachers ignore quantitative equality as they seek to establish a fair learning environment for all learners? Be as specific as possible in your responses and explain your choices.

13. Recently, a fifth-grade teacher, Mr. Roberti, in a graduate course that focuses on the interaction of culture, education, and learning, made the following statement:

> Now that I know that in Mexico many parents do not have a tradition of actively participating in their child's school life—they turn education over to the teacher—I will not criticize my Mexican-American parents or take it personally when they do not show up for events like Back-to-School Night.

a. What is your general reaction to this statement?

b. If this were a staff development meeting in which teachers were discussing how their new knowledge about Mexican culture and Mexican-American cultures had influenced their teaching, and you were the staff development specialist and moderator of the meeting, how would you respond if a teacher asked you . . . in the group setting . . . what you thought about Mr. Roberti's "application of new knowledge"?

c. What else do you want to know about Mr. Roberti's new attitude toward Mexican-American parents? What main message do you want him to take back to his classroom?

14. Create and answer your own questions about the educational equity component of multicultural education or any of the other components discussed in this chapter.

RECOMMENDED ACTIVITIES

1. On your own or with the help of your professor, arrange to observe in one or more classrooms where the instructor has a reputation for the creative and effective use of cooperative learning groups. If possible, observe on more than one occasion and try to observe closely the interaction within two different groups in the classroom. In addition, try to structure the observation so that you will (a) be able to interview a few students immediately after the lesson, (b) be able to interview the teacher after you have completed your observation in her class, and (c) be able to observe in the class with one or more classmates so you can observe different groups and share your perceptions. The Cooperative Learning Observation Guide in appendix 4 may help you focus your observation and provide a data base from which to generate questions for your follow-up interviews. Feel free to add, delete, and rephrase questions.

2. On your own or with the help of your instructor, arrange to observe in one or more classrooms where the teacher has a reputation for the effective use of 'sheltered English' teaching strategies. Sheltered English strategies are techniques that non-bilingual teachers use to increase the comprehensibility of instruction, particularly in content areas like science and math. In such classrooms the instruction by the teacher is typically in English, but students are sometimes encouraged to use their primary language to help themselves and other learners develop proficiency in the new language. Also, please note that bilingual teachers also make use of sheltered English instruction, but the technique is associated with teachers who are not fluent in their students' primary languages. To increase the value of your observation follow instructions (a), (b), and (c) above as you make use of the sheltered English observation form in appendix 3.

3. Working individually, or as part of a cooperative learning group,
    a. expand the list of strategies delineated in part A of The Typology of Multicultural Teaching; (see appendix 1)
    b. examine the entire typology (in appendix 1) and add one or two strategies to each category;
    c. in each category put an asterisk by the strategies you consider most appropriate for your classroom or your student teaching assignment?
    d. share your new items and selected strategies with a classmate or members of your cooperative learning group.

4. Arrange to have several local principals or superintendents address your class as a panel to discuss selected discussion questions from chapter 2. Structure the presentation so that it resembles "Meet the Press," the Sunday morning news show. If possible, arrange to have the panel discussion videotaped.

5. Listen to the Association for Supervision and Curriculum Development (ASCD) audiotape by James Banks entitled *The Battle over the Canon: Cultural Diversity and Curriculum Reform.* Summarize and react to the major points in this address. (This tape was a major address given at the 1990 ASCD Annual Conference. It can be ordered by phone (703) 549-9110 and in 1990 cost $9.00. The stock number if 612-900-55A12. The tape runs approximately 50 minutes.

6. Listen to and view the ASCD videotape entitled *Multicultural Education: Goals, Teaching*

Strategies, and Evaluation. Compare and contrast the goals presented in this videotape with the goals and strategies presented in chapters 1 and 2.

Journal Entry

As this chapter has attempted to put you in touch with a set of ideas related to the creation of equity conditions in your own classroom, or the classroom where you will teach during student teaching, your journal entry should concentrate on the most significant things you have learned about this important area of teaching. More specifically you could comment on the following:

1. what educational equity now means to you—when trying to create equity in your classroom, what will you be doing? (for the in-service teacher)
2. equity-oriented strategies that you think you will use during student teaching and then those you think you will use in your first year of teaching. (for the prospective teacher)
3. unresolved questions and feelings that you may have regarding educational equity and multicultural education.
4. the relationship between your older understanding and more recent understanding of educational equity.

NOTES

1. R. Freeman Butts, *Public Education in the United States: From Revolution to Reform* (New York: Holt, Rinehart and Winston, 1978), 262–267.
2. Influential lawsuits or pieces of legislation include *Brown v. Board of Education of Topeka,* 347 U.S. 483 (1954), the Bilingual Education Act, P. L. 90-247, *Lau v. Nichols,* 414 U.S. 563 (1973), Titles VI and VII of the Civil Rights Act of 1964 (P.L. 88-352), and the Education for All Handicapped Children Act of 1975 (P.L. 94-142).
3. *Cooper v. Aaron,* 358 U.S. 1 (1958).
4. *Alexander et al. v. Holmes County (Mississippi) School Board,* 396 U.S. 19 (1969).
5. *Cisneros v. Corpus Christi Independent School District,* Civ. No. 68-C-95 (D.C.S.D. Tex. Corpus Christi Div. 1970).
6. *John Serrano, Jr. et al. v. Ivy Baker Priest,* 96 Cal. Rptr., 601 (August 30, 1971).
7. *Brown v. Board of Education of Topeka,* 347 U.S. 483 (1954), p. 493 (cited in Butts, p. 328).
8. *John Serrano, Jr. et al. v. Ivy Baker Priest.*
9. *Lau v. Nichols,* 414 U.S. 563, 1973.
10. Education for All Handicapped Children Act of 1975, 20 USC 1401, 1975.
11. Elementary and Secondary Education Act of 1965.
12. The Indian Education Act of 1972, P.L. 92-318.
13. Title IX, Education Amendment Acts, 1973.
14. The Women's Educational Equity Act of 1974.
15. Isabel Bruder, "Restructuring through Technology," *Business Week,* December 10, 1990, 33–34, Special Education Section.
16. Robert Stephens, Supreme Court of Kentucky, 88-SC-804-TG, *Rose v. Council for Better Education,* Opinion of the Court by Chief Justice Stephens, p. 2.
17. For example, Jonathan Kozol, in a brief essay entitled "The New Untouchables," (*Newsweek,* Special Edition, *The 21st Century Family,* Winter/Spring, 1990) points out that the schools serving the relatively wealthy communities of Great Neck and White Plains, New

York, spend twice as much per pupil as the schools serving the children of the Bronx, New York. In a related article entitled "Children at Risk" (*Newsweek,* March 12, 1990), Kozol reports that "In 1980 the wealthiest school districts in New Jersey spent $800 more per child than the poorest districts. Today they spend $3,000 more." Similarly, the same gap in Texas was $600 in 1978, and today it is $5,000. Kozol summarizes and extends his remarks on inequality in American public schools in *Savage Inequalities* (Southbridge, Mass.: Crown Publishers, 1991). An interesting critique of one of Kozol's themes, equalization, appears in Peter Shrag's essay entitled "Savage Inequalities," *New Republic* 205, no. 25 (December 16, 1991): 18–20.

18. Aaron M. Pallas, et al., "The Changing Nature of the Disadvantaged Population: Current Dimensions and Future Trends," *Educational Researcher* 18, no. 5 (1989): 16–22.

19. In a series of decisions in 1972 (*Bradley v. State Board of Education*) and 1974 (*Millikan v. Bradley*) the U.S. Supreme Court made clear that it would not support "metropolitanization" plans that would achieve integration of Whites and Blacks by requiring the merger of city school districts with surrounding, largely White suburban districts. See Percy Bates, "Desegregation: Can We Get There from Here," *Phi Delta Kappan,* September 1990, 13, for a discussion of *Millikan v. Bradley.*

20. Butts, *Public Education in the United States,* 346.

21. Thomas Nagel, "Desegregation, Education or Both" (1988), unpublished manuscript. Nagel can be contacted through the School of Education at California State University, San Diego.

22. Ultimately, when considering educational equity, the investigator must compare school districts with other school districts and states of the union against each other.

23. Robert B. Reich, "Metamorphosis of the American Worker," *Business Week,* November 1990, 58.

24. William B. Johnston and Arnold H. Packer, *Workforce 2000: Work and Workers for the 21st Century* (Indianapolis, Ind.: Hudson Institute, 1987), 89.

25. John I. Goodlad, "The Occupation of Teaching in Schools," in *The Moral Dimensions of Teaching,* ed. John I. Goodlad, Roger Soder, and Kenneth A. Sirotnik (San Francisco: Jossey-Bass, 1991), 17.

26. Donald C. Lueder, "Tennessee Parents Were Invited to Participate and They Did," *Educational Leadership* 47, no. 2 (October 1989): 15–17; see also Jim Cummins's essay "Empowering Minority Students: A Framework for Intervention," *Harvard Educational Review* 56, no. 1 (February 1986): 18–36, in which he links student empowerment to improved communication between teachers and parents, student goal setting, and the use of minority students' language and culture in the school curriculum.

27. Madeline Hunter, "Join the 'Par-aide' in Education," *Educational Leadership* 47, no. 2 (October 1989): 36–41.

28. Robert E. Slavin, "Research on Cooperative Learning: Consensus and Controversy," *Educational Leadership* 47, no. 4 (December 1989/January 1990): 52–55.

29. Ibid., 53.

30. Ibid., 54.

31. John O'Neil, "On Tracking and Individual Differences: A Conversation with Jeannie Oakes," *Educational Leadership* 50, no. 2 (October 1992): 18–21; see also Jeannie Oakes, *Keeping Track: How Schools Structure Inequality* (New Haven, Conn.: Yale University Press, 1985) and Jeannie Oakes, *Multiplying Inequalities: The Effects of Race, Social Class, and Tracking on Opportunities to Learn Mathematics and Science* (Santa Monica, Calif.: RAND, 1991).

32. See chapter 9, "Counseling Vietnamese," by Imogene C. Brower in *Counseling American Minorities: A Cross-Cultural Perspective,* 3rd ed., ed. Donald R. Atkinson, George Morten,

and Derald Wing Sue (Dubuque, Iowa: William C. Brown, 1989). Margaret A. Gibson makes a similar point about Punjabi-Sikh immigrants to America in her chapter, "Punjabi Immigrants in an American High School," in *Interpretive Ethnography of Education: At Home and Abroad,* ed. George and Louise Spindler (Hillsdale, N.J.: Lawrence Erlbaum). Bruce Thowpaou Bliatout et al. make a similar comment about Hmong Americans in chapter 2 of their work, *Handbook for Teaching Hmong-Speaking Students,* Folsom Unified School District, California, 1988. This book can be ordered by calling (916) 635-6815.

33. Ibid. (both chapters).

34. Spencer Kagan, *Resources for Teachers* (San Juan Capistrano, Calif.: Resources for Teachers, 1989), chapter 2, 2.

35. Ibid., chapter 8, 4.

36. Ibid., chapter 7, 1.

37. Ibid., chapter 7, 3.

38. *Communicating with Parents,* by Marcia Boruta, Janet Chrispeels, and Mary Daugherty, is available from the San Diego County Office of Education, Graphic Communications, Room 212, 6401 Linda Vista Road, San Diego, CA 92111-7399 (619-569-5391). In 1990 the cost was $28.00 for one copy.

39. Ana Maria Schuhmann, "Learning to Teach Hispanic Students," in *Diversity in Teacher Education: New Expectations,* ed. Mary E. Dilworth (San Francisco: Jossey-Bass, 1992), 94.

CHAPTER 3

Teaching with a Multicultural Perspective in Activities, Lessons, and Lesson Sequences

CHAPTER OVERVIEW

We believe that in the 1990s classroom teachers at all levels of instruction will be strongly encouraged, and in some cases pressured, to modify the way they conceptualize and deliver instruction. Although teacher-directed instruction, in which teachers parcel out information to 25 to 35 students in the traditional competitive mode, will continue to be an influential model, in this decade we expect K–8 learners to experience more interactive and collaborative instruction, helping each other learn in various cooperative learning formats. The collaborative teacher will spend more time working with students in an indirect facilitative way, and students will have greater opportunity to engage in self-directed learning, determining the direction and magnitude of their own learning. In addition, students' interaction with technological facilitators of learning will increase dramatically as the decade unfolds. Despite these expected changes, for the purpose of further elucidating what teaching with a multicultural perspective means, we believe that the curriculum K–8 students will receive can be usefully categorized into four types of planned instructional events. These events are part of the traditional way of describing and discussing teacher-directed instruction but are easily adapted to interactive and self-directed modes of instruction. They are classroom activities, lessons, lesson sequences, and units of instruction.

The content of these instructional events will be based on preestablished schoolwide routines as well as curriculum objectives determined by districtwide committees. For various reasons related to the European-influenced history of the United States and other Western nations, these routines and curriculum objectives will sometimes reflect a monocultural perspective (a Eurocentric or Western orientation) as opposed to a multicultural perspective (a European, African, Asian, and American orientation encompassing Western and Eastern points of view). As a teacher, your responsibility will be to modify monocultural routines, objectives, and curricula so that they more fully incorporate and reflect a meaningful multicultural perspective. To illustrate more clearly what such modification might look like, in this chapter a series of curriculum case studies, before-and-after treatments of activities, lessons, and lesson sequences will be offered. In addition, a set of evaluative questions based on the goals of multicultural education will be delineated, and the role of these questions in "multiculturalizing" selected instructional events will be illustrated.

INTRODUCTION

The content in chapters 1 and 2 has suggested that there are numerous strategies that classroom teachers can employ to create multicultural curricula. For example, we have seen that teachers help to create such curricula when they

1. create more time for instruction by utilizing time-efficient classroom management strategies;
2. plan and implement successful parent communication and parent education strategies;
3. develop and participate in class- and schoolwide student recognition programs;
4. provide ongoing inspirational talks to students about completing junior high school, high school, and college;
5. introduce their students to former students and community role models who have successfully entered the world of work after earning a high school diploma, associate in arts degree (two-year degree), bachelor of arts or science degree, master of arts degree, or other degree;
6. utilize instructional strategies such as cooperative learning, which give more students greater opportunity to achieve cross-gender and cross-ethnic friendships and academic success;
7. develop and implement strategies that increase the academic confidence and self-esteem of their students.

With these examples and others, and our description of the work of James Comer, Uri Treisman, Jaime Escalante, Bruce Smith, and Susan Sherwood, we have shown that teaching that aims to create a multicultural curriculum extends far beyond the content of the traditional formal academic curriculum. However, by illuminating the diverse nature and wide-ranging parameters of a transformational multicultural curriculum, we did not mean to diminish the central importance of the content and delivery system of the formal academic curriculum; namely, the facts, concepts, generalizations, skills, and attitudes, learned in mathematics, social science, art, music, science, and language arts.

In chapters 3, 4, and 5 we will underscore the importance of this formal curriculum as we focus on content that is delivered in the following instructional formats: activities, lessons, lesson sequences, and units of instruction. We will show how teachers can shape these planned instructional events so that they become vehicles for achieving one or more of the goals of multicultural education. In this chapter we will focus on before-and-after treatments of activities, lessons, and lesson sequences, and then move to units of instruction in chapter 4.

A major objective of this chapter is to provide you with a clear and diverse set of examples that show how to enhance the multicultural nature of an instructional activity, lesson, or lesson sequence; in the sections that follow we will enumerate some fundamental multiculturalization questions, define some key terms, and present several curriculum case studies. First to be discussed are the multiculturalization questions.

MULTICULTURAL PLANNING QUESTIONS

The basic strategy in our multiculturalization process is to evaluate activities, lessons, and lesson sequences in terms of questions that relate directly to the goals of multicultural education. In this exercise, each "before" activity, lesson, and lesson sequence will be examined with one or more of the following questions in mind.

1. Do the lesson content and strategies promote educational equity? For example, does the lesson content help to create an inclusive curriculum, one that attempts to maximize student participation in the everyday and overall class curriculum?
2. Do the lesson content and strategies make use of, or help to develop, collaborative empowering relationships among parents, students, and teacher?
3. Do the lesson content and strategies promote cultural pluralism in society or intergroup harmony in the classroom?
4. Does the lesson content help to increase the students' knowledge of various cultural and ethnic groups, including their own?
5. Do the lesson content and strategies increase students' proclivity and ability to see and think with a multicultural perspective?
6. Does the lesson content (a) help to correct distortions in the historical, literary, or scientific record that may be linked to historical racism or other forces linked to the oppression and exploitation of specific ethnic and cultural groups, and (b) present material in a manner that suggests that racism-related distortions are or may be part of the historical and scientific record that the students are studying?

We hope that your examination of the modified lesson content and structures that result from this evaluative process will persuade you to apply these questions selectively to your own curriculum planning and evaluation efforts.

DEFINITION OF KEY TERMS

At this point a caveat about the treatments is in order as well as some remarks about what the terms *lesson, lesson sequence, activity,* and *unit of instruction* denote in this text. The suggested modifications that appear in the "after" treatment and analysis sections will obviously not exhaust all possibilities, and the activities, lessons, and lesson sequences employed to provide examples will represent only a portion of the curriculum areas taught by elementary and middle-school teachers. Our choices here are dictated by educational logic as well as space considerations. Logic suggests that we do not need to select lessons from every content area to illustrate how content and instructional strategies in all content areas can be modified to create lessons and lesson sequences that are congruent with one or more goals of multicultural education. In addition, as we developed our examples, our choices were influenced by three assumptions. First, in terms of breadth and depth of lesson examples we assumed that less could be constructive. Second, we assumed that in moving from activity to lesson to lesson sequence and unit of instruction in our examples we would parallel the manner in which many teacher education programs introduce candidates to curriculum planning. Finally, experience suggested that the activity, lesson, lesson sequence, and unit of instruction categorization would also be meaningful to in-service teachers.

Regarding the meaning of *lesson plan, lesson sequence, instructional activity,* and *unit of instruction,* the following definitions have proven to be practical for prospective teachers at our university. Although we think it is appropriate for teacher education programs to define such terms as building blocks for clear communication, we would remind you that all of these terms, like most words in our language, have several valuable meanings.

Lesson Plan

A *lesson plan* is a plan of instruction for a single lesson, and the block of time can be anywhere from 15 minutes to 2 hours depending on the way instructional time is allotted in a given school situation. The plan covers a predetermined and specified block of time. There are different kinds of lesson plans for different purposes. Typically, a lesson plan will consist of most of the following components:

1. the instructional objective
2. the instructional materials to be used in the lesson
3. the procedures to be used by the teacher in "teaching to the objective"
4. the method(s) to be used in evaluating the students' learning
5. self-evaluation (the specific methods student teachers will employ during or after the lesson to evaluate their own teaching)
6. time estimate (an estimate of the length of time the lesson will take to complete from beginning to end)
7. lesson origins (Is this a lesson the student teacher adapted from one found in a library resource? Is it totally or largely original? Is it one that the master teacher gave the student teacher?)

During student teaching some master teachers and supervisors will want different amounts of detail in the procedure part of the lesson, and some supervisors will ask for more detail—a script almost—at the beginning of student teaching and less (or more) as the assignment unfolds. Later, during your probationary years of teaching, your principal, who will also visit you to conduct a form of clinical supervision, will likely also ask for a lesson plan. The lesson plan desired by the principal will probably consist of four or five of the above elements, but the principal may ask for a new component. The point is, during your teacher education program you should perceive your lesson plan as an agenda that gives you purpose and direction but also as an act of communication between you and experienced educators. These educators are trying to help you to develop your fullest potential and simultaneously trying to assure that their students are receiving thoughtful, high-quality instruction.

Lesson Sequence

The *lesson sequence* derives from the lesson plan and is defined as a series of individual lessons, each containing a single specific instructional objective. The individual lessons are a sequence because one objective and lesson typically builds on the lesson that preceded it. In a lesson sequence each individual plan and objective leads the learner in small increments toward a predetermined major goal or objective at the end of the sequence. A typical sequence will have between three and eight lessons but could have more.

Instructional Activity

A third type of planned event, the *instructional activity,* is an important element in the classroom curriculum and as used in the educational literature has at least several meanings. In our work we distinguish between two types of instructional activities. First, there is the activity that is an integral part of a lesson, designed to achieve one or more specific instructional objectives. In a mathematics lesson students might manipulate Cuisenaire rods or pentaminoes for a period of time as part of a sequence of events leading to the instructional objective. In another type of instructional event, the activity is not part of a specific lesson plan. The activity in this instance is the entire instructional event; and although a great deal of divergent valuable learning accrues during this type of instructional event, teachers typically do not plan or think about these events in terms of specific instructional objectives, lesson plan formats, and assessments (tests). Examples of this type of activity include

1. field trips to museums, work settings, and so on;
2. chapter-by-chapter oral reading by the teacher of a specific piece of literature on a regular basis (elementary teachers often read on a regular basis to their students immediately after recess);
3. oral presentations by, and interviews of, guest speakers;
4. self-directed learning periods when students can engage in any type of learning activity they wish;
5. classroom meetings to discuss current events, classroom rules, schoolwide controversies, or the proposed content for an upcoming unit;
6. the development of a class play;
7. class and schoolwide recognition programs like the "word of the week" program (This particular program as well as current events sharing will be

discussed in greater detail later in this chapter when we explore ways to increase the multicultural content of instructional activities);

8. weekly visits to the library and the computer room (teachers should ask themselves how, and if, the curriculum in these very important centers of learning contribute to the goals of multicultural education).

The reader will note that instructional activities come in all sizes and shapes, often have an emergent quality, are structured so that different learners will learn different things, and sometimes occur on a weekly basis. Instructional activities (a) call for thoughtful planning and execution, as anyone who has planned and led a field trip can attest, (b) can reflect a monocultural or multicultural perspective, and (c) often receive thin coverage in most teacher education and staff development programs because of their informal nature.

Unit of Instruction

The *unit of instruction* is our final example of a planned instructional event. We define it as a comprehensive multidimensional plan of instruction for learning inside and outside the classroom. A unit of instruction may contain several lesson sequences and typically requires a greater amount of time for planning and implementation than a lesson sequence. In comparison to a lesson sequence a unit will contain a wider range of lessons and activities, will incorporate a more precise type of evaluation, and will extend over a greater period of time, ranging from 4 to 10 weeks. In our program, units typically contain many of the following elements:

1. a guiding set of questions or generalizations linked to a set of unit objectives
2. a list of major ideas around which the unit will revolve
3. a list of the concepts that will be taught or reviewed in the unit
4. collaborative planning with students pertaining to the content of the unit
5. an exciting introductory activity to set the stage for the unit
6. a pre- and postassessment, or some other form of pre-teaching diagnostic activity
7. development of one or more bulletin boards and/or learning centers related to the unit
8. utilization of carefully selected and prepared guest speakers
9. a field trip
10. use of filmstrips, films, and videotapes that have been previewed and carefully integrated into specific lessons
11. a schedule of lessons and special activities and a bibliography of reading and visual material related to the unit
12. independent research and cooperative group activities for students
13. a special type of culminating event (a play, a musical presentation, or luau) that summarizes the group's learning, put on for themselves and invited guests (parents, other classes, the principal, etc.)

14. a decorated construction paper folder in which the student will keep documents related to the unit

With these definitions set, we can now examine our before-and-after curriculum case studies; we will focus first on instructional activities (section one), then move to lesson plans (section two), and culminate with lesson sequences (section three).

SECTION ONE Instructional Activities

I. THE WORD OF THE WEEK PROGRAM

Before Multicultural Restructuring

- **Major Objective:** Citizenship Education
- **Content Area:** Interdisciplinary
- **Grade Levels:** K–6 and 6–8 (Elementary and Middle School)
- **Time Period:** Entire School Year on a Weekly Basis

Background and Implementation Information

The word of the week program became popular in the late 1970s as schools across the nation attempted to design more powerful ways to influence positively students' behavior and social development. As typically implemented, it is a schoolwide program, but in non-adopting schools, individual teachers have implemented a modified program in their own classroom.

In its simplest form the principal or a committee of teachers picks one word for each week of the school year; this word is prominently displayed in each classroom and the school auditorium, and is announced in school assembly and the weekly newsletter. For example, a word such as *helpful* may be selected. On Monday of each week, as part of their ongoing language arts program teachers will discuss the meaning of *helpful* to make certain that each child understands. Each child also understands that on a weekly basis all teachers in the school will select one or two children from their class to receive special recognition as the student(s) whose behavior best exemplified the word of the week. The recognition is usually given at a schoolwide event, such as an assembly, on Friday mornings. Although schools implement this program in various ways, most schools will

1. have the teachers send in the names, or filled-in recognition certificates, on Thursday afternoon;
2. have school aides or volunteers make calls to parents or caretakers on Thursday afternoons or Friday mornings to give parents the opportunity to be at the awards ceremony;
3. take group pictures of recognized students and display them prominently near the principal's office;
4. list recognized students in a weekly or bimonthly newsletter;
5. use words that are widely accepted as positive attributes (in American culture) in the set of 25 to 30 words. Examples include helpful, friendly, cheerful, responsible, reliable, polite, courteous, considerate, positive, generous, independent, scholarly, hardworking, disciplined, punctual, tenacious, competitive, and imaginative.

Analysis

The structure of the typical word of the week program has many commendable features, but it lacks parental involvement, rewards only one or two students per week from each class, and does little to promote cultural pluralism, intergroup harmony, or the ability to see and think with a multicultural perspective. These, and other, limitations will be addressed in the "after" treatment delineated below.

I. THE WORD OF THE WEEK PROGRAM

After Multicultural Restructuring

- **Curriculum Area:** Citizenship Education
- **Content Area:** Interdisciplinary
- **Grade Levels:** K–6 and 6–8 (Elementary and Middle School)
- **Time Period:** Entire School Year on a Weekly Basis

Suggested Modifications

1. Representatives of the parent committee can work together with teacher and student government representatives to help identify the 25 to 30 words that will provide the focus for the year's word of the week program. This strategy ties in with multicultural education goal 2 (see chapter 1): creating empowering relationships among teachers, parents, and students on a class and schoolwide basis.

2. The teacher can explain that the two students who receive recognition at the award assembly will likely be *representatives* of a larger group of students in the class whose behavior in and out of class will merit recognition in terms of the "word of the week." For these students, the teacher can provide oral recognition in class and provide written recognition (on a weekly or bimonthly basis) by class certificates, letters sent home to parents, or identification in a bimonthly newsletter. These strategies will tend to reduce competitiveness in this area and will thus increase the potential for intergroup harmony (multicultural goal 4).

3. To promote greater equity in this program, that is, to allow a larger number of deserving students to be recognized on a weekly or bimonthly basis (multicultural goal 1), the manner in which the program is carried out can be modified. During the first week of the month, the first two words for a particular month could be announced, and during weeks one and two each teacher could nominate up to three students for each word. Thus, from this recognition program alone up to six children per week could receive certificates if their behavior were exemplary. In week three, the next two words could be announced; during these weeks the teacher could award certificates for all four words and could distribute from 6 to 12 awards per week. In the school assembly, the teacher could read the names of students receiving certificates, and the students could stand up as their names were called to receive recognition from fellow students and the principal.

4. To promote cultural pluralism (multicultural goal 3), intergroup harmony (multicultural goal 4), greater knowledge regarding selected ethnic and cultural groups (multicultural goal 5), and the ability to think with a multicultural perspective (multicultural goal 6), the traditional list of "good" words used in the program should be expanded to include some that are more explicitly congruent with the values and goals of multicultural education. We have in mind words such as open-minded, tolerant, bilingual, assertive, curious, pluralistic, bicultural, humorous, athletic, musical, creative, cooperative, collaborative, well rounded, and problem solving. When teachers explain what *curious* means, they can highlight some of the many useful things students can be curious about: knowledge about history, values, and contribution of specific American (and international) ethnic and cultural groups would be appropriate. In addition, because the teacher in weeks three and four can give recognition for all of the month's words, having a word like *bilingual* in the collection allows teachers to recognize publicly students who are striving to become bilingual,

without penalizing those children who are aiming to move through life as creative monolinguals. Finally, some words like *pluralistic* and *tolerant* should be presented as optional words in week three of the month because some K–3 teachers might find them difficult to explain to their students. In other words, the school can have its set of schoolwide words for all classes as well as a few optional words that individual classes can adopt.

5. To help teachers explain and use each word to its fullest, the school district could provide a packet of curriculum materials to accompany each word of the week. These packets could include brief biographical descriptions of Americans from a variety of cultural and ethnic backgrounds. The lives of these outstanding Americans should exemplify several different words of the week and will tend, therefore, to reinforce efforts to promote educational equity and cultural pluralism. In addition, materials that help to illuminate where prejudice, bigotry, and racism have stained American culture would help teachers when they attempt to explain what it means to be tolerant.

6. To promote positive collaborative relationships among parents, teachers, and students (multicultural goal 2) a description of the goals and procedures of the word of the week program should be sent home by school newsletter in as many languages as necessary, and the program should be reviewed on Back-to-School night. This activity will help to align parents' reactions with the goals of the program and help to avoid situations like the following, which occurred in Mesa Elementary School, one of the "newcomer" schools in Lucia Mar Unified School District in Arroyo Grande, California. In 1991, two brothers who were immigrants from Cambodia were attending the same newcomer class, along with other immigrants from Mexico and the Philippines, to establish a certain level of English proficiency and social skill before being reassigned to a neighborhood school. One of the brothers received a special award at the monthly awards assembly and when he showed the award to his parents he received another reward from them. Unfortunately, the parents, who were unfamiliar with the awards ceremony and objectives, also punished the son who did not get an award. Parenthetically, teachers should not assume that sending notes home in the native tongue will automatically solve the communication problem. Some immigrant parents may not be print literate in their native tongue. Subtle questioning of older elementary students or bilingual or migrant aides when these are available should help to identify the population for whom bilingual written communications will not suffice. Schoolwide efforts to explain key school programs orally—perhaps by cassette tapes—will then be needed.

II. CURRENT EVENTS

Before Multicultural Restructuring

- **Major Objective:** Citizenship Education
- **Content Area:** Social Studies and Language Arts
- **Grade Levels:** 3–8
- **Time Period:** Entire School Year on a Weekly Basis (15 minutes per day)
- **Objectives:**
  1. Students will demonstrate the ability to locate and summarize orally the contents of newspaper articles on current events.
  2. Students will develop the propensity to stay abreast of current events.

Background Information

In most elementary schools sharing is a part of the everyday and weekly routine of the classroom. During this time, primary grade students will come to the front of the classroom to engage in a show-and-tell presentation about something they have brought to show or discuss with classmates. Some teachers make this a required activity and others leave it optional, but practically all teachers encourage parents and students to participate in this informal type of public speaking event. Typically, the activity is arranged on a schedule so that students and parents will know the day of the week each student is expected to be a presenter.

In the upper grades (4th–6th and in some middle school classrooms) the sharing of personal experiences, toys, and other objects from home gradually gives way to activities that are more closely related to the academic curriculum. In one common extension of primary grade sharing, upper-grade students present one current events article on a weekly or biweekly basis in front of the entire class.

General Procedures

1. Teachers will establish a rationale and routine for current events sharing and will present it to their students. They might explain to their students that staying aware of current events is a natural part of citizenship responsibilities and survival strategies for most adults in our society, and that most adults get their current events update from a variety of sources including radio and TV news, newspapers, and various types of weekly news magazines.

2. The teacher might then say, "To help develop this positive inclination or desire to stay in touch with important news events, all students in the class throughout the entire year will have the weekly or biweekly responsibility to give an oral report on a news article of their choice."

3. Beyond this, the teacher will set up ground rules such as the following:

   a. Each student will be given a specific day of the week on which to give the oral report.

   b. On occasion, the students can pass up the opportunity to be a presenter but must let the teacher know before sharing time.

   c. Students will neatly cut out the articles they are summarizing so these can be posted on the current events bulletin board.

   d. On their presenting day, all students will be responsible for providing a written and oral summary of their news articles. The summary will, minimally, answer these questions:

      (1) Who or what was the news story about?

      (2) What happened in the story?

      (3) Where did the story take place?

      (4) Why did you find this story interesting?

      (5) What questions, if any, do you have about this news story?

   e. After the oral summary, students in the class can ask questions that can be answered by the presenter or other students in the class. The teacher moderates this part of the presentation.

   f. After the oral presentation, the student's written remarks will be submitted to the teacher, and the student's newspaper article will be posted on the bulletin board with his or her name neatly written in. Articles will be posted and removed on a weekly or biweekly basis. When taken down, students can keep or discard the articles.

Analysis

This format has several positive features but also notable flaws. It follows the traditional individualistic pattern of teaching and learning—students work alone—for an entire year with no modification of structure. The sheer repetition of the activity would likely dull student motivation long before June. Thus, as structured, the activity does little to promote educational equity or intergroup harmony. Regarding educational equity, it is noteworthy that the teacher assumes all children in the class will have access to newspapers. With one out of four young children growing up in poverty in America, this is an inappropriate assumption. Also, for limited English proficient speakers and others, a format that allowed the presenter to address a smaller group, say 8 students rather than 32, would likely be more constructive for this type of public speaking event. In addition, teachers utilizing this traditional format do not exploit the potential for involving students in collaborative deliberation in this year-long project, and typically do little to promote parental support for the activity. Finally, the routine nature of the instructional activity—where week after week the students have the same responsibilities—severely limits its instructional value. For example, as structured, the activity does little to promote awareness of

1. the manner in which the news media select and "create" news;
2. the distinction between local, regional, state, national, and international news;
3. the distinction between profit and nonprofit-oriented news organizations;
4. the fact that selected cultural and ethnic groups in the United States create their own sources of daily, weekly, and monthly news;
5. the various ways in which telecommunications can expand students' and teachers' perceptions of current events by creating two-way electronic mail communication between classrooms in different school districts, states, and nations.[1]

Some of the deficiencies will be addressed in the revised activity structure that follows.

II. CURRENT EVENTS

After Multicultural Restructuring

- **Major Objective:** Citizenship Education
- **Content Area:** Social Studies and Language Arts
- **Grade Levels:** 3–8
- **Time Period:** Entire School Year for Varying Amounts of Time (The activity may be dropped in certain weeks and months.)
- **Objectives:**
  1. The learner will demonstrate increased knowledge of news production and dissemination in the United States.
  2. The learner will demonstrate the ability to locate, summarize, and evaluate the contents of various forms of current events reportage (print, radio, and television news).
  3. The learner will develop an interest in staying abreast of the news.

Suggested Modifications

1. By newsletter, the teacher informs parents that a year-long study of news gathering and reporting will soon commence, and that within two weeks students will be asking parents to donate newspapers, magazines, and other print sources for projects. Parents with experience in news gathering or reporting are encouraged to

share their experiences with the class. Teachers can also solicit newspapers from professionals and various business organizations.

2. The teacher introduces the activity in an open-ended way by asking students what they think *current news* is, and what they think *current events* means; then the teacher has all students describe, in writing, what they do to stay aware of current events.

3. The teacher asks students to brainstorm the following question: "In what different ways could the students in this class *working together* become more knowledgeable about news gathering and reporting in our community, state, and nation?" The teacher then analyzes and uses some of the student ideas to establish the initial structure for current events sharing.

4. The teacher arranges to have a class library where a range of recently published newspapers and magazines will be made available for students to read and cut articles from; there will also be a weekly classroom newspaper from a source such as *Scholastic, Inc.* or *Weekly Reader,* if the school budget permits.

5. The teacher tells the class that for the first few months the class will employ several strategies to increase their knowledge base. "After the new year we'll evaluate our progress, and perhaps adopt some new strategies. The strategies we will employ now include cooperative group sharing of newspaper and magazine articles, presentations by and interviews of local journalists and publishers, individual and buddy research papers on news-related topics, and weekly or biweekly discussion of articles from the class newspaper, *My Weekly Reader.*"

6. Every student in the class has one partner and is also a member of a four- or five-student team. The teams are established in late September and stay together for 6 or 12 weeks, approximately—if 12 weeks, the students can switch partners. For reporting on newspaper or magazine current events articles as delineated in the "before" activity, two teams of four students each can be combined. Half the group of eight students can report on Tuesdays while the other half reports on the following Tuesday, or the groups can rotate on a weekly basis. By utilizing small cooperative group formats for the reporting activity, as opposed to having each child speak in front of 32 students, the teacher (a) creates a more supportive climate, (b) creates more time for other types of sharing because the four-student group structure takes less reporting time than the whole group model, and (c) places students in a setting that provides more active language involvement for a wider range of students.

7. With this extra time, during certain weeks the teacher could report on a current events article he or she found interesting. In addition, in a modified "Meet the Press" format the students could, on a biannual or more frequent basis, arrange to interview a local print or television journalist or publisher from the English and non-English media. If the more frequent basis is chosen, interviewing other community personalities like the junior high school principal, town sheriff, or school custodian may also prove illuminating. Student research projects about famous journalists, specialized ethnic and cultural publications, and current issues about problems facing the journalists and the newspaper industry could also be reported on an occasional basis.

8. The questions students ask journalists and publishers during the *Meet the Press* interviews should be as probing as possible. For this reason the students will be encouraged to ask their parents and older siblings for ideas, and parents will be invited to the Thursday or Friday afternoon interview. These sessions can also be videotaped. The teacher can suggest questions that reveal the economic basis and political dimension of local newspapers. For example, why do some papers cost

money while others are given away? How are "given-away" papers similar to television stations? In terms of expressing political preferences and opinions, what are some differences between newspapers and television? What is the difference between "public" radio and television and commercial radio and television?

9. During the course of the year teachers will bring variety to the weekly activity by
   a. using articles from the class newspaper as the basis for thought-provoking discussions;
   b. encouraging students to vary the type of current event they report on in terms of the source of the news (local, regional, state, national, and international levels of news), and type of news: sports, politics, entertainment, scientific, education;
   c. encouraging students to seek out current events from a wide range of newspapers and magazines;
   d. having students carry out comparisons of local newspapers, local newspapers versus local television in their treatment of a specific story, and analyses of what is included and excluded from local newspapers as well as the class newspaper;
   e. linking current events to historical anniversaries like the Columbus Quincentennial (1992), the fiftieth anniversary of *Brown v. Board of Education* (1994), and the integration of major league baseball (1997) and the U.S. armed forces (1998);
   f. having each group of eight students keep a scrapbook of the articles they have reported, and by occasionally inviting several students from each group to present one of their articles in front of the whole class;
   g. having student volunteers go out to interview and videotape fellow students, teachers, parents, and administrators about a specific controversial current event. The class could then view, discuss, and critique the videotaped interview.

Final Comments

The "after" treatment of the current events activity took a routine activity, almost a time filler, and transformed it into a more ambitious collaborative undertaking. Because the current events activity lacks a unifying theme and has the potential, with ongoing modifications, to last an entire year, it does not fall within the lesson sequence or unit parameters, but in expanding the horizons of the activity, it does take on some unitlike characteristics. In addition, in any given month the teacher could decide to make current events part of a more elaborate unit of instruction. For example, the teacher could lead the class into a unit related to the development and production of a class newsletter or paper.

III. ORAL READING BY THE TEACHER

Before Multicultural Restructuring

- **Major Objective:** Motivation toward Reading
- **Content Area:** Language Arts and Interdisciplinary Studies
- **Grade Levels:** K–8
- **Time Period:** Entire School Year on a Weekly Basis
- **Objectives:**
  1. Students will develop an enlarged appreciation for various types of literature.
  2. Students will develop a heightened appreciation of the enjoyment of reading.

Background Information

In grades K–6 and some 7–8 grade situations, oral reading of literature by the teacher is a regular part of the school curriculum. In the primary grades it is almost a daily occurrence and primary teachers, because of the brevity of storybooks at this level, will sometimes read more than one book per day. On the other hand, in the upper grades where books are lengthier, a teacher might take a week or two to finish the dramatic reading of a specific book, sometimes reading daily but more often reading on a flexible schedule several times per week. Because the traditional academic goals of this activity are largely motivational in nature, teachers typically select books they enjoy reading and that experience suggests their students will enjoy. Occasionally, teachers will read books related to a theme or unit they are teaching; sometimes they will read selected chapters from a book the entire class is reading. Typically, the teachers' focus in reading these stories is on presenting the literature in an enjoyable way rather than using the content for skill-related objectives, such as stimulating higher-level thinking. Increasingly, we see teachers employing these stories as a prompt for journal writing and class discussion.

General Procedures

The procedures here are pretty straightforward.

1. Teachers semirandomly select the book(s) they will read from the collection of books in their class or their own collection. Typically, the class collection has been selected from the school library to augment the language arts program, and the teacher's dramatic reading of these books will motivate the students to read them and others during a variety of regularly scheduled reading activities.
2. The teacher reads the book in a dramatic fashion, utilizing different voices for various characters to make the oral interpretation more interesting.
3. When the story is complete, the teacher may simply invite the students to read the book on their own or may ask broad questions such as "Who can tell me something they liked or didn't like about this story?" Sometimes the teacher might invite students to ask questions about the story or discuss the story with a partner.

Analysis

Many students and teachers look forward to story time as a desirable break in a school day that is often excessively oriented to skill-based lessons. It is a time to enjoy literature in a holistic manner rather than break it into little pieces for the purpose of learning discrete skills related to the test-oriented language arts curriculum. Here is material the student and teacher can relate to in an unhurried, relatively unfocused manner, material that is not tied to a specific instructional objective or test item, material that both student and teacher can approach in a spontaneous and creative manner. This does not sound like a picture one wishes to tamper with, and yet when examined from a multicultural perspective, this routine activity, like other desirable components of the K–8 curriculum, can be strengthened without totally changing its character.

There are several general ways to improve this routine instructional activity:

1. broadening the major objective to link it more clearly to the goals of multicultural education;
2. making the selection of stories less random and more purposeful;
3. placing less emphasis on "enjoyable" reading so that literature that is challenging and informative can be included;

4. encouraging the teacher to become more knowledgeable about the main characters in selected biographies and autobiographies.

Developing links to multicultural education is critical; literature can play too important a role in helping to achieve the goals of multicultural education to be selected on a random or semirandom basis. It is not enough for the teacher to select library books on the basis of variety and interest. Literature does more than entertain; it teaches important lessons. Literature has the power to develop self-respect, pride, and curiosity, as well as a deeper understanding of self, others, and history. Therefore, at least some of the books that are selected for oral reading should provide content that helps to accomplish these and other purposes.

Although these objectives can and should be achieved with various forms of literature—poetry, short story, novel, journalism—we encourage you to develop a repertoire of biographies to share with students throughout the year, and not just during Black History month (February) or Women's History month (March). We believe that children of all ethnic and cultural backgrounds can draw inspiration from the story of individuals such as Rosa Parks and Caesar Chavez whose courage and faith helped them transcend obstacles that racism, sexism, or religious bigotry placed in front of them. In addition, specific children will gain emotional nourishment and perhaps ethnic pride from these stories.

Such literature, which is after all a part of an American and world history replete with cultural and ethnic antagonism, will sometimes describe conflicts between White Americans, African Americans, American Indians, Mexican Americans, and Asian Americans. The introduction and presentation of such stories in multiethnic and monoethnic classrooms calls for thoughtful preparation rather than spontaneous interpretation, and the preparation, where possible, should extend beyond the single biography the teacher will read to students. To illustrate the type of focused selection and special preparation we mean, in the restructured example below we will draw on Eloise Greenfield's 1973 biography of Rosa Parks, a captivating biography that is quite suitable for second to fourth graders, and one that could be adapted for use with older students. This book was originally published by Thomas Y. Crowell and is now distributed by HarperCollins.

III. ORAL READING BY THE TEACHER

After Multicultural Restructuring

- **Major Objective:** Motivation toward Reading, Self-Esteem Development, Cultural Pluralism, and Citizenship Education
- **Content Area:** Interdisciplinary
- **Grade Levels:** K–8
- **Time Period:** Entire School Year on a Weekly Basis
- **Objectives:**
  1. Students will develop a heightened appreciation of the enjoyment of reading and various types of literature.
  2. Students will gain a heightened understanding of the contributions specific individuals and groups have made to American and world history.
  3. Students may gain increased pride in themselves as members of specific ethnic and cultural groups (as African Americans, Hispanic Americans, or simply as Americans).

Suggested Modifications

1. Please note that the major and specific objectives of this weekly, year-long activity have been expanded so that the activity is better positioned to help achieve multicultural education goals.
2. As noted, instead of selecting books exclusively on the basis of variety and student interest, the teacher should choose books that will inform students about different ethnic and cultural groups, both in the United States and abroad.
3. Some should be biographical in nature and contain content that will be inspirational to students by providing role models who have helped Americans overcome complex political and socioeconomic problems.
4. Some of these biographies should portray scenes of cultural conflict; these valuable stories should be carefully studied by the teacher and thoughtfully presented to students. Instead of interpreting these stories spontaneously as they are read, teachers should read them several days in advance. The early reading gives them time to think about (a) an appropriate introduction, (b) questions students might ask about key characters and events, (c) questions they might want to ask students, and (d) points they might wish to make that extend beyond the specific content of the biography or story in question. The biography of Rosa Parks written by Eloise Greenfield, part of an excellent series of elementary level biographies developed by Crowell publications, provides a case in point. This is a story about America's past and present. Although it does not mention racism, it is about racism; it contains important lessons that illuminate our common heritage and provides examples of strategies future citizens might use as they grapple with the social problems of their day. The story of Rosa Parks is one link in the long chain of individual and collective heroic struggles that are part of the centuries-long battle African Americans have waged to achieve full equality in the United States of America. Because of its heroic dimensions and lessons in character and citizenship, Mrs. Parks's story is one that should be widely told. However, for some White, Hispanic, and African-American teachers, the challenge will be first, to tell the story, and then to tell it well. Because the story describes several White people in a negative light and because it is a part of our contemporary history, White teachers, in particular, may be hesitant to read this story to ethnically integrated or nonintegrated classes. The following suggestions should leave all teachers more inclined to share this story, and similar material, with elementary school students.
   a. The teacher should *not* lead into a reading of the Greenfield biography with a simple remark like, "This morning I'm going to read another story about a famous American." Students should be emotionally prepared to hear this type of story. They should be told that this story is about a heroic African American who overcame some terrible obstacles to make her community and all of America a better and freer place to live. An introduction for any third- or fourth-grade class could begin as follows:

> "Future historians, this morning I'm going to read and tell you a story about a courageous American, a very brave African American who nearly _____ years ago helped African Americans confront and triumph over the unfair, humiliating, and oppressive conditions they faced in different parts of America. Her work specifically helped African Americans, but it also made America a freer and fairer place for all Americans. Does anyone have

an idea of whom I'm talking about? Yes, that's right, and there are lessons we can all learn from a review of some of the key events in Mrs. Rosa Parks's life. To help us discover these lessons, right after I finish reading you Eloise Greenfield's biography entitled *Rosa Parks,* I'd like each of you to be prepared to share your thoughts and questions about the struggles Mrs. Parks faced as she grew up as an African American in America. We'll all do our best to answer your questions, and the ones we can't answer, we'll research."

This introduction sets an appropriate foundation for the children because they now know they will be hearing a story that deals with racial conflict and struggle. Thus, they will not be shocked at the explicit racial encounter with which the story opens:

> Rosa was not afraid although the white boy was near his mother. When he pushed her, Rosa pushed back. "Why did you put your hands on my child?" the mother asked. "Because he pushed me," Rosa said.

This type of introduction should also raise the teacher's comfort level with the story because any concerns that he had about the story's being divisive will be diminished by his own remarks, which emphasize that Mrs. Parks's freedom struggle was for *all* Americans. Although many White Americans struggled against Mrs. Parks and the African Americans who joined her in collective struggle, her victory was for Americans of all colors, including Whites.

b. As he has done in the last sentence of his opening remarks, the teacher should emphasize that he has come to this biography as a student himself, and that the class as a group will seek out the lessons in the story. This opportunity to think cooperatively is valuable for students and it should alleviate any concern teachers have about needing to be the expert for every biography they read to their class. On the other hand, as a result of the group inquiry process and the strategy of developing a repertoire of biographies, teachers, as they share this biography with different classes, will become increasingly knowledgeable regarding the lives of Rosa Parks, Thurgood Marshall, Charles Hamilton Houston, and others and may find themselves seeking out more detailed biographies of Rosa Parks. For such extended reading teachers can consult the nine-volume series entitled *The History of the Civil Rights Movement* published by Silver Burdette in 1990. This series of well-written biographies for young people includes the book *Rosa Parks: The Movement Organizes* by Kai Friese, as well as others about Fannie Lou Hamer, Jesse Jackson, Ella Baker, Thurgood Marshall, and A. Phillip Randolph. Teachers will also want to read Rosa Parks's autobiography (written with the help of Jim Haskins) entitled *Rosa Parks: Mother to a Movement* and published by Dial Books in 1992. After teachers finish the reading and discussion stimulated by Eloise Greenfield's 32-page biography of Rosa Parks, they can read a page or two from Friese's lengthier biography, or Rosa Parks's autobiography. Such exposure will increase the possibility that some students will delve more deeply into Rosa Parks and her contribution to the civil rights movement.

c. To the extent that time permits, prior to reading the Greenfield biography to the class, teachers should list three to five questions they think their students might ask, and consider how they would answer them. The teachers' responses should be accurate and at the appropriate level of complexity and should deal with issues like collective struggle and racism. For example, if asked why the White people were so mean to the Black people, after listening to student responses to the question, a teacher might say the following. (Please note that our response is one we feel is accurate and comprehensible for third and fourth graders. However, teachers should not perceive it as the only one and should experiment with their own versions of an accurate comprehensible response.)

> "Racism was at the root of racial problems in the United States at the time of this story. Many White people believed that they were superior to Blacks and that Blacks had to be kept in their place, and this meant below and away from Whites—in separate schools, pools, hospital rooms, and in separate parts of buses, and theaters. As the story tells us, to keep African Americans in their place and dominate them, some Whites, in organizations like the Ku Klux Klan, terrorized African Americans. Things have gotten a lot better, but today we still find unfortunate examples of racism in our nation and world."

Teachers should also realize that when they explain the motivation of Whites and explain why racism made sense to them but had to be fought by African Americans, they will be teaching with a multicultural perspective. Such teaching may help young students make sense of the racial conflicts they see portrayed on television or played out in their own neighborhoods; it is also quite likely that the teacher's reading of *Rosa Parks* and related stories will lead to questions and discussions about current ethnic and racial relations in America, Canada, Iraq, Japan, Israel, Nigeria, India, and other nations.

d. Teachers should perceive the story of Rosa Parks and similar stories as more than occasions for transfer and sharing of historical knowledge. As they accurately teach the facts of the story, they should be prepared to probe, dignify, and respond sensitively to the feelings such stories evoke. Students should have the opportunity to share these feelings privately in their journals (to be read just by the teacher) and publicly during the class discussion. During these discussions teachers should be prepared for a wide range of reactions. For example, in their preliminary work, teachers may prepare themselves to answer questions about the Ku Klux Klan, the National Association for the Advancement of Colored People (NAACP), and boycotts as a strategy for collective struggle against economic and political oppression. They may find that many of the student responses are personal and local, having more to do with playground and community conflicts than with the plight of Blacks in South Africa. Teachers, when dealing with the complex issue of race relations, should meet students conceptually where they are and then transport them to higher levels of understanding. For instance, after discussing with students the important issue of bullying or name calling on the playground, the teacher can remind children that young Rosa's confrontation of a bully was a part of her preparation for the battle she and her fellow African Americans would ultimately wage against the whole system of legalized segregation in the state of Alabama.

e. Teachers should consider having more than one level of the Rosa Parks biography in the classroom: the Greenfield biography (3rd–4th grade), the Friese biography (5th–8th grade), and a brief, two-page treatment of Rosa Parks by Kathie White in "Women as Members of Groups" (2nd–6th grade) from the *National Women's History Project*. This variety will allow upper-grade students to read material about Rosa Parks to younger students and will also provide more challenging material for advanced readers. The strategy may raise productive questions about the difficulty of writing biographies, of getting all the facts "just right," and may stimulate in students a desire for further reading and research. Regarding the facts, a comparison of Greenfield's biography with Friese's suggests a difference of opinion about how old Rosa Parks was when she was pushed by a "white boy who was standing near his mother." In Greenfield's book Rosa is depicted as a child when this happens, but Friese reports that Rosa was married and over 20 years old when the shoving incident occurs. Whose depiction is more accurate, or could there have been two similar pushing incidents? Some future historians might well enjoy the opportunity to search out the answer to this discrepancy. In terms of stimulating a desire for additional knowledge, students reading the Friese biography will be intrigued, and perhaps surprised, to learn that Sojourner Truth, another courageous African-American woman, successfully struggled to integrate the street cars of Washington, D.C., during the Civil War, and that Mary Ellen Pleasant waged a similar struggle in San Francisco in 1866. With some properly worded invitations for inquiry, several students will likely want to track down more information about these nineteenth-century civil rights workers. It is even possible that some very motivated upper graders can do original historical work by letter writing and other methods. For example, Friese reports that in 1900—55 years prior to the boycott stimulated by Rosa Parks's refusal—there was another boycott conducted by the Black citizens of Birmingham, Alabama. At that time the goal was to increase the number of segregated seats in the streetcars. Who were the African Americans who led this successful boycott, what pressures did they face, and how can fourth through eighth graders making use of local as well as distant resources pursue the answers to these questions? Other students might be interested in a research project pertaining to Irene Morgan who in 1944 was arrested and convicted of refusing to move to the "colored" section of a Greyhound bus. The outcome of her struggle for freedom is described in "Forty-Five Years in Law and Civil Rights" by A. Leon Higginbotham, Jr., in *Ebony*'s forty-fifth anniversary edition (November 1990, pp. 80–86). Finally, other students might be interested in reporting on the life and legal triumphs of Vilma Martinez, one of the major contemporary leaders of the Mexican-American Legal Defense Fund (see the 1993 National Women's History Project catalogue for curriculum resources pertaining to Vilma Martinez, for information regarding this catalogue call 707-838-6000).

f. Finally, to prepare themselves to make a positive contribution to the development of their students' ethnic, cultural, gender, and racial identity, teachers should consider reading books and articles that discuss the various stages through which students travel as they develop a healthy integrated personality. A good place to begin such reading would be with Beverly Tatum's article entitled "Talking about Race, Learning about Racism: The Application of Racial Identity Development Theory in the Classroom." The article appeared in the Spring 1992 issue of the *Harvard Educational Review* (vol. 62 no. 1, pp. 1–24).

SECTION TWO Lesson Plans

•••

I. TO TELL THE TRUTH

Before Multicultural Restructuring

- **Major Objective:** Scientific Literacy
- **Content Area:** Science and Language Arts (Interdisciplinary)
- **Grade Levels:** 3–8
- **Time Period:** 90–120 minutes (two to three sessions)
- **Objectives:**
  1. Students will be able to identify orally the major achievement of outstanding scientists.
  2. Students will demonstrate the ability to use various language arts skills (reading, writing, speaking, listening, selecting key facts) to play the game "To Tell the Truth."

Background and Implementation Information

In contemporary language arts, science, mathematics, and social studies education there is a great deal of emphasis on involving students in meaningful and enjoyable activities that allow them to do science and mathematics and language arts. The development of meaningful activities that allow students to use writing, reading, speaking, and analytical skills has assumed a new importance in K–12 settings and teacher education. In this context, enjoyable, multiskill activities like "To Tell the Truth," based on a past popular television game show, have gained a new legitimacy and popularity. They allow various language arts and thinking skills to be used by students and are not guided by one specific instructional objective.

The version of "To Tell the Truth" described below has been circulated in California by several county offices of education as one way to use writing to teach science. The instructions that accompany the suggested activity are these:

Instructions

1. Divide the class into groups—three people per group.
2. Each group is assigned a letter from the alphabet.
3. Each group looks in the index of their science textbook and selects a person whose last name begins with that letter.
4. Each student in the group reads the pages that deal with their scientist.
5. The group decides who will be the "real" person and who will be the impostors.
6. The students use 5-×-8-inch cards to write down the autobiographical information they want to provide the class.
7. The groups quietly rehearse how they will present their information.
8. The groups make their presentations in the order designated by the teacher.
9. The moderator asks contestants one, two, and three, "What is your name, please?" At this time each of the contestants presents the autobiographical information.
10. The moderator asks for questions from the audience. Members of the audience can question any one of the contestants; the class may want to put a limit on the number of questions.

11. The class votes on who they think is the real scientist.
12. The moderator says, "Will the real _____ please step forward?"

Analysis

In providing an interesting activity in which students can use reading, writing, oral, and interpretive skills while learning real facts about the accomplishments of outstanding scientists, this interactive, multidimensional language game is a good instructional choice for most students. However, when considered in the light of multicultural education, you can see that with some modification of objectives and procedures, the lesson would have much greater potential for achieving multicultural objectives.

In promoting educational equity, the process of selecting scientists is severely limited. The students can choose only the scientists that are mentioned in their text and are further limited to selecting from these a scientist whose name begins with the letter they have been assigned. Given these constraints, it is quite possible that the students would discuss a group consisting largely of white male scientists. This potential result, which for some students would reinforce the notion that outstanding scientists are White men, is exactly the type of knowledge that works against the academic interests of White students and students of color, and the long-term interests of all citizens. As we move toward the year 2000, America and the world will encounter increasing shortages of scientists, engineers, and mathematicians. For this reason, we need to replace language games that may send negative messages to students of color and false impressions to White students with games that are designed to carry positive messages. The revised game described below should be evaluated with this positive message objective in mind. Please note the change in objectives.

I. TO TELL THE TRUTH

After Multicultural Restructuring

- **Major Objective:** Recruitment toward Scientific Careers and Scientific Literacy
- **Content Area:** Science and Language Arts (Interdisciplinary)
- **Grade Levels:** 3–8
- **Time Period:** Two Hours (two to three sessions)
- **Objectives:**
    1. Students will be able to identify various contemporary and past scientists and inventors who have made and are making contributions to scientific knowledge. These scientists will represent various ethnic and cultural groups.
    2. Teacher will get students interested in a career in science and will demonstrate to students that scientists come from both genders and various ethnic groups.

Suggested Modifications

1. The teacher should show a videotaped segment of the game, if available, and should provide a script that can be enacted so that all students will see exactly how the game is played. This demonstration will make the rules of the game more comprehensible to limited English proficient students who might be in the class.
2. For purposes of educational equity and intergroup harmony, teachers should use four-member cooperative learning teams. Three members of the team could be the contestants while one could serve as moderator for that group. Team members, as usual, could help each other with the reading and writing tasks.

3. The teacher should pass out a sheet with information about a specific scientist or inventor and then illustrate how the four team members will proceed to develop three sets of autobiographical remarks on 5-×-8-inch cards. The teacher and students can write one or more sets of remarks on the overhead projector.
4. Instead of limiting the selection of scientists and inventors to those listed in the index of whatever science text the class is using, the teacher should assign specific resources to the teams. For example, assuming that the school library or teacher has copies of these texts), the teacher could give each team the following resources:
   a. Robert Hayden's *Seven Black American Scientists* (Reading, Mass. Addison-Wesley, 1970) or Hattie Carwell's *Blacks in Science: Astrophysicist to Zoologist* (Norris, Tenn.: Exposition Press, 1977)
   b. Robert Hayden's *Eight Black Inventors* (Reading, Mass.: Addison-Wesley, 1972), and the June 1991 *Ebony* article entitled "Superstars of Science," pp. 42–50
   c. Louis Haber's *Black Pioneers of Science and Invention* (New York: Harcourt, Brace and World, 1979), and *Black Contributors to Science and Energy Technology* available from the U.S. Department of Energy, Office of Public Affairs, Washington, DC, 20585, Publication No. DOE/OPA-0035 (79)
   d. Clark Newlon's *Famous Mexican-Americans* (New York: Dodd and Mead, 1972)
   e. Ivan Van Sertima's (editor) *Blacks in Science: Ancient and Modern* (New Brunswick, N.J.: Transaction Books, 1983) and "African American Inventors" in the February 1992 issue of *Cobblestone: The History Magazine for Young People* (vol. 13, no. 2, pp. 2–23)
   f. Ethlie Ann Vare and Greg Ptacek's *Mothers of Invention: From the Bra to the Bomb, Forgotten Women and Their Unforgettable Ideas* (National Women's History Project—see appendix 6, section III this text, for ordering information)
   g. Louise Grinstein and Paul Campbell's *Women of Mathematics: A Bibliographic Sourcebook* (Westport, Conn.: Greenwood Press, 1987)
   h. the index of the science text, which several groups could use to make their choices
   These resources may not be in all elementary and middle-school libraries, but they can be ordered. In the interim teachers can photocopy pages from these books, *Ebony* magazine, and other resources that highlight the contributions of inventors and scientists from various ethnic and cultural groups. Enterprising teachers may be interested in developing computer software that can be used in conjunction with this game. An effort should be made to identify scientists and inventors from various Asian-American and Hispanic groups. One helpful resource for Mexican Americans is entitled *Mexican-American Biographies: A Historical Dictionary* (1836–1987) by Matt S. Meier (New York: Greenwood Press, 1988). In it we learn of the accomplishments of Francisco Sanchez Alvarez (1928–1980), a research chemist and former principal scientist of Syntex Corporation who is listed as the inventor in over 80 patents.
5. To reinforce what each team and the class has learned about the various scientists and inventors, each team will have the responsibility of writing a short article about their scientist/inventor for the class's monthly newsletter. The teacher could also invite students to create a crossword puzzle using facts from the set of 5-×-8-inch cards. In these and other ways, the accomplishments and inspirational messages of these creative individuals should become a part of the class's ongoing conversation.

6. The current adaptation or future versions of this game can include doctors, lawyers, and artists as well as scientists and inventors.
7. The teacher should consider following up this activity with guest speakers and videotapes. One videotape series entitled *Women in Science* is suitable for use in grades 5 through 12. Each tape is 30 minutes long, and titles include "Biomedical Fields," "Chemistry," "Computer Science," "Dentistry," "Engineering," "Geosciences, Physics and Astronomy," and "Scientific Careers for Women: Doors to the Future." The video series and the guide are available from the Agency for Instructional Technology, Box A, Bloomington, IN 47402; (800) 457-4509. Previews are available free of charge except for return shipping.

II. THANKSGIVING

Before Multicultural Restructuring*

- **Major Objective:** To Learn about the Origins of an Important American Holiday
- **Content Area:** American History (Social Studies)
- **Grade Levels:** K–2
- **Time Period:** 30–40 Minutes
- **Objectives:**
  1. The learner will be able to identify several key facts about the first American Thanksgiving.
  2. Working in small groups, the learners will create a flannel board story about the first American Thanksgiving and will share that story with another group.

Suggested Procedures

1. Create an anticipatory set for the lesson. "Who can tell me what this picture (a turkey) has to do with a holiday we will celebrate this month?"
2. "Do you know who brought the turkeys to the first American Thanksgiving?"
3. "These are good guesses. Let's listen to a story about the first Thanksgiving to see whose guess came closest to the truth; be prepared to tell me something you learned about the first Thanksgiving that you didn't know."
4. Read the following story to your class.

THE STORY OF THE FIRST AMERICAN THANKSGIVING

In 1620 a small ship named the *Mayflower* came to the United States, which was then an English colony. The people on this ship were Englishmen known asPilgrims and were among the first Europeans to settle the eastern part of our country. They were Puritans who did not wish to break away from the Church of England.

Arriving on the bleak, rocky Massachusetts coast in December 1620 in a

---

*This "before" and "after" treatment is based on Activity #156, "The First Thanksgiving in This Country," which is part of a collection of lessons entitled *US: A Cultural Mosaic: A Multicultural Program for Primary Grades.* The handbook was prepared by San Diego Unified School District curriculum consultants and teachers between 1975 and 1977 and is currently disseminated by the Anti-Defamation League of B'nai B'rith (823 United Nations Plaza, New York, NY 10017). The material is used with the permission of the Anti-Defamation League of B'nai B'rith.

place called Plymouth, the sick and weak settlers had to spend the winter in extreme hunger. Having very little food left after a dangerous ocean voyage, about half of them died of hunger, disease, and bad weather. Luckily for them, the Englishmen found the natives of this land, Indians of the Wampanoag tribe, to be friendly. They provided advice, food, and other important help. The Indians, one of whom was Squanto, taught their new neighbors how to build houses, hunt for food, and survive in the wilderness. The Pilgrims learned much from their friends of the Wampanoag tribe, whose chief, Massasoit, was one of the most powerful native rulers of New England. The treaty Chief Massasoit signed with them at Plymouth in 1621 was faithfully observed until his death many years later.

In the spring the Englishmen planted the seeds they had brought with them, along with corn and other crops the Indians taught them to grow. When autumn arrived, the Pilgrims gathered their bountiful harvest of food and stored away some for the next winter.

Everyone was grateful for the harvest, and the Pilgrims said, "We must give thanks for all the good food, our homes, our clothes, our Indian friends and all our blessings. We shall have a big feast and invite our Indian friends. We will call it a feast of thanksgiving." Well might they offer thanks; the Indians had helped the Pilgrims survive the terrible conditions in their new land.

Therefore, Governor Bradford invited Chief Massasoit and his braves to the celebration. On that memorable day of the first Thanksgiving feast in December 1621 the Pilgrims covered their tables with food from their gardens. Massasoit's braves brought turkeys, deer, and other game they had shot with their bows and arrows. The corn, pumpkins, squash, beans, clams, oysters, and fish provided by the Indians were added to the Pilgrims' food so that this famous Thanksgiving feast lasted for three days.

Typical of most of the Indians of the United States, Wampanoags were good hunters; growing crops was not as important to them as killing game. Unlike the Plains Indians, but like most tribes of the Eastern Woodlands, Wampanoags did not move their homes; they stayed in one place.

Chief Massasoit and 90 of his braves came in their best dress to celebrate the feast day. Some of the Indians had wide bands of black paint on their faces. Some had feathers stuck in their long straight black hair, and some wore furry coats of wildcats hanging from their shoulders; others wore deerskins.

Before anyone ate, they bowed their heads, offering a prayer of thanksgiving. That was the first Thanksgiving—a day that is now a legal holiday and one of the most popular days in the United States, especially since we do not have to come to school on that day.

The Indians danced, acted out stories, and played games with the children. The colonists sang their songs. In addition, a target was set up, and the soldiers fired at it. Then the Indians, standing in closer, shot at it with their bows and arrows to see which side would win the contest. Most important, hearty fellowship and goodwill was felt between the colonists and Indians. Peace and friendship had been established on a firm foundation. Without such a peace, the Pilgrims would never have won a footing on that bleak, rugged coast. Without it, Plymouth could never have survived.

Thanksgiving was not a new observance for the American Indians. We know that several Indian tribes were accustomed to observing several days of thanksgiving throughout the year. The Iroquois and Choctaw, for example, had an autumn festival known as the Green Corn Dance, which lasted three days. We are also familiar with the story of how the Wampanoags came to the first Thanksgiving feast at the invitation of Governor Bradford and the Pilgrims. It seems likely that the three-day period of Thanksgiving to which Massasoit and his Indians went was already customary for them.

The first Thanksgiving observance was held in December 1621, but it was not an annual affair as it is today. On July 30, 1623, Governor Bradford proclaimed a second Thanksgiving when a ship was sighted, heading for port carrying much-awaited, much-needed supplies from England. This second Thanksgiving Day was in no way connected with the harvest, but later on a day was set in the month of November that became associated with the gathering of the crops. Today Thanksgiving is a legal holiday in all the United States.

5. After reading the story, ask your students:
    a. "Which of our guesses came the closest?"
    b. "What did you learn from the story that was new information for you?"
    c. "Did any of the material in the story surprise you?"
6. Next, structure small groups so that each group will create a flannel board story of the first Thanksgiving in this country. Be sure that the stories include the *Mayflower*, several Pilgrims, several Indians, some crude homes for the Pilgrims, corn and other crops, and the Thanksgiving table laden with food.
7. As possible follow-up or extension activities, consider having your class learn the song "Thanksgiving Story" and "Indian Hunting Song" and listen to "Dances of Indian America."

Analysis

The lesson plan outlined previously is to be presented as part of a sequence of activities in *US: A Cultural Mosaic;* the entire set of 238 activities is designed to

1. help children see that the similarities among people are those traits that make them members of the human family, and that differences among people are those characteristics that make people special and unique; and
2. help children develop an understanding and appreciation of themselves and other persons in the communities.

The Thanksgiving lesson has a number of positive attributes: it illustrates the importance of friendliness and support from Native Americans—in this case, members of the Wampanoag tribe—to the survival of the Pilgrim contingent. In addition, it shows some of the diversity that existed and still exists among Native Americans; it also presents some basic information about the Pilgrims and their first American Thanksgiving.

On the other hand, the lesson could be improved:

1. It could incorporate some invitations for inquiry (Who can find out when Thanksgiving became a national holiday? Has anyone ever written a biography about Chief Massasoit? In the years after they celebrated Thanksgiving together, did the Pilgrims and members of the Wampanoag tribe come in conflict with each other?)
2. The lesson could make use of student partners to increase active student participation during the lesson; students could share the new information they learned from the story with their partners before the teacher asks a few to share in front of the entire class.
3. The story might have been entitled "The Second American Thanksgiving" to emphasize that Native-American groups had had celebration feasts prior to 1621 at which they likely thanked the "Great Spirit" for their good fortune. This would not diminish the historical significance of the first Thanksgiving the Pilgrims had in America but would help to dispel the idea that "American" history begins with the European experience in what would be called the Americas. These observations, and others not mentioned, will be incorporated in the revised lesson sequence below.

4. The lesson should develop the understanding that even though Thanksgiving has been a national holiday since 1863 there are religious communities in the United States that do not celebrate it.

II. THANKSGIVING

After Multicultural Restructuring

- **Major Objective:** The Development of a Culturally Pluralistic Attitude
- **Content Area:** Interdisciplinary
- **Grade Levels:** K–2
- **Time Period:** 60–120 Minutes
- **Objective:**
  1. The learners will identify and develop an appreciation of the way several different groups celebrate their own version of Thanksgiving.

Suggested Modifications

1. Implement the "before" lesson with the modifications mentioned above, namely, to (a) call the story "The Second Thanksgiving in America," (b) make use of partners to increase active participation and cooperative learning groups to facilitate the flannel board activity, and (c) incorporate invitations for inquiry to encourage critical thinking and self-directed learning.
2. Follow-up the presentation of "The Second American Thanksgiving" with lessons in which students learn about the following:
   a. the Jewish festival of Succot. Explain why many people believe that the Pilgrims patterned their Thanksgiving festival after Succot, which is described in the Bible as a festival of thanksgiving and rejoicing, related to the harvest.
   b. the Moon Festival, which is celebrated by some Chinese people in the autumn.
   c. the Octoberfest, which is celebrated in Germany at the end of the harvest in late September and early October.
3. Specific suggestions regarding lesson content and materials for the Succot, Moon Festival, and Octoberfest are included in *US: A Cultural Mosaic* (pages 178–186), and in additional appendixes in the document.

Final Comments

Note that in the "after" treatment in this comparison, we not only changed the major objective but also transformed a single lesson into a more elaborate lesson sequence. However, we also changed the Thanksgiving lesson itself in ways that make it more congruent with the goals of multicultural education.

US: A Cultural Mosaic is filled with thoughtful sequences that promote cultural pluralism (multicultural goal 3), intergroup harmony (multicultural goal 4), an expanded multicultural/multiethnic knowledge base (multicultural goal 5), and the propensity and ability to think with a multicultural perspective (multicultural goal 6). Because it works consistently to enhance the students' sense of group and individual self-esteem, the entire collection contributes to educational equity. Other sequences in the volume that are related to the Thanksgiving story include

- A Crosscultural Look at Some New Year's Celebrations.
- A Crosscultural Look at Some Independence Days.
- A Crosscultural Look at Some Special Religious Days.
- A Crosscultural Look at Some Days of Appreciation.

US: A Cultural Mosaic is clearly a resource worthy of your attention.

III. INTERVIEWING ANCESTORS

Before Multicultural Restructuring

- **Major Objective:** To provide students with the opportunity to learn specific facts about their ancestors and to develop an interest in learning more about their ancestors.
- **Content Area:** Language Arts
- **Grade Level:** 2
- **Time Period:** 60–90 Minutes
- **Objectives:**
  1. Given instruction on how to conduct an interview, the learner will
     a. demonstrate the ability to interview an ancestor; and
     b. share the results of the interview in class.

Background Information

This lesson was recently taught by a student teacher as part of several integrated language arts activities carried out over a 10-week period to help students become more familiar and friendly with each other. The setting was a second-grade class with 30 students in a school where most of the students and families were monolingual and middle class. In this class, three of the students were labeled limited English proficient (LEP), with Spanish as their primary language and the language spoken at home. One of the students was more proficient in both English and Spanish than the other two; all three second language learners were Mexican American; the remainder of the class were White Americans of varying ethnic background. The student teacher in this class made use of a modified seven-step lesson plan to communicate his plan of action and also submitted a letter of context along with the lesson plan. The "letter of context" is a device used in the California Polytechnic student teaching program and other programs that have adapted it. It allows the student teacher to provide special information about (a) the lesson plan itself in relation to prior and future lessons, (b) changes in the demographic profile of the classroom, and (c) targeted learners in the classroom. The student teacher's lesson plan and letter of context follow, along with a letter that was sent home to selected parents.

THE LESSON PLAN

Anticipatory Set

"Class, who remembers what we were going to do with our ancestor information?" "Very good, now show me with a thumbs up when you remember one of the things you are supposed to tell the class when you share your interview data." At this point I will elicit, and then orally reinforce, that students are to

1. tell which ancestor they interviewed;
2. recite the question they asked and what the answer was;
3. state what they learned from the interview.

Statement of Purpose

"Who thinks he or she can tell me one reason we are sharing our interviews today? Yes, we do want to develop good speaking and listening skills, and there is one more reason. We want to learn more about each other, the way we are alike and the way we are different. The more we know the easier it will be to form a helping community in our classroom."

Procedure

1. Review the characteristics of good speaking in this class.
2. Review the characteristics of good listening.
3. Role-play an interview presentation—I will share an interview that was conducted.
4. Proceed with the presentation.

Closure

"What are some interesting things you have learned from your classmates' presentations? Tell your partner first and then be prepared to share with the whole class."

THE LETTER SENT TO PARENTS

Dear Parents:

Next week the students in Mrs. Nulman's class will be sharing the results of an interview with one of their ancestors. Mrs. Nulman and I would appreciate it if you would help your son or daughter complete the interview. Here are some of the basic facts about this assignment.

1. The interview
   a. can be done with a parent, aunt, uncle, or grandparent;
   b. can have more than four questions;
   c. is due by November 20.
2. The student is to write out the answer to the questions that are asked.
3. The questions to be asked are these:
   a. Where did you go to school?
   b. What was school like when you were my age?
   c. What were your hobbies?
   d. What important event in history happened during your childhood?

Your support of this project is appreciated.

Sincerely,

Michael Deukmajian

Denise Nulman

THE LETTER OF CONTEXT

November 21, 1991

Dear Dr. Davidman,

Today you will see a neat presentation by some of the students. Their assignment was to interview an ancestor. This assignment was given to them last week and was due yesterday. Today will be a presentation of those interviews. I am predicting that some students will not be prepared because of absences and lack of effort. I did not ask the three ESL students to participate in this. But they will be required to listen and I think they will learn from this listening. The students will be asked to tell who they interviewed, read the question asked and the answer given, and tell something they learned from doing this interview.

Analysis

On the positive side this teacher candidate designed an integrated language arts activity that would allow most of the students to share an interesting language arts experience with a relative; he structured the activity so that students would have the opportunity to learn more about each other. In addition, the candidate reviewed speaking and listening standards at the appropriate time—when the assignment was first given and then again just prior to the recitations. The candidate also employed selected lesson design components (anticipatory set, purpose statement, modeling, and closure) in a manner that promoted active and appropriate participation by a wide range of students. The candidate also encouraged parent involvement by sending home a fairly clear letter. On the other hand, from a multicultural point of view, there is much room for improvement in this lesson. Several of these improvements will be mentioned below and then incorporated in the restructured lesson plan that follows the analysis.

1. From the perspective of the multicultural model a major flaw in this lesson is the total exclusion of the limited English proficient (LEP), potentially bilingual students and their Spanish-speaking parents from active participation. It is not exactly clear why the student teacher, and the cooperating teacher who approved the lesson, opted for exclusion. It may be because they could not easily translate their letter into Spanish or because they thought the overall activity was too complex for the three second language learners. But even if this was the case, the lesson should have been modified so that the second language learners could still conduct an interview with a relative or significant other. The student teacher apparently thought that if a student was going to participate in the lesson, he or she would have to participate at the same level as everyone else. Nothing could be further from the spirit of multiculturalizing/individualizing assignments according to individual students' special strengths, learning disabilities, linguistic capabilities, and home environments. This lesson could have been adjusted in any number of ways to accommodate and include all the students in this second-grade class.

   a. If the teacher has parents who do not speak English, he should immediately seek out human resources to help open up oral and written communication with the parents. The excluded parents in this class should have received a letter about this interview assignment written in Spanish and English. The teacher should have sought help from the English as a Second Language (ESL) teacher at the school site, and could also have received help from a parent or upper-grade bilingual student. In addition, the teacher should lobby the principal to bring a bilingual resource person to the school site.

b. The three English/Spanish-speaking students should have been allowed to interview their parents in Spanish and share their findings in written or oral form with each other. The student who was more bilingually proficient might have been able to help the other two prepare an oral presentation and might have volunteered to serve as a translator for the other two with the added benefit of showing this second language learner and the entire class why bilingualism is so practical and valuable. However, as we learned from our dialogue with the two students, they did not need a translator. They would have been able to report in English to their classmates what they had heard in Spanish from their parents. And the teacher or student teacher could have facilitated this recital by giving the second language learners an opportunity for rehearsal prior to the presentation before the entire class. The teacher could also have invited one or more English-speaking second graders to help the second language learners prepare their oral remarks. There are usually students, often budding teachers, who would be delighted to help; indeed, by association, some of these monolingual learners might be attracted to bilingualism at a propitious age.

c. The teacher could have structured the lesson so as to combine small and large group sharing; the students in this class were seated in groups of five, which served as cooperative learning groups. Students could have had the opportunity to report their interview data in the small group or the large group. As it turned out, the oral reporting in this class took much longer than was anticipated, and half the class did not have a chance to present their information with the whole class. Also, some of the students who did speak could not be heard because their voices were too soft.

d. From a precise vocabulary point of view, the lesson should not have been titled "Interviewing Ancestors." Ancestors are relatives from whom descent is derived, but an ancestor is often considered to be a person further back in line than a grandmother or grandfather. Typically, your ancestors are not alive when you are and thus cannot be interviewed. A better title allowing more flexibility and thus increasing the success potential of the lesson would have been "Interviewing Relatives and Close Friends."

e. The list of possible questions should be expanded so as to (1) increase students' knowledge regarding selected cultural and ethnic groups; (2) provide flexibility for students and interviewee allowing them to decide which three or four questions they wish to ask or answer; and (3) avoid placing students in a position of sharing information they might find embarrassing. For example, it is conceivable that some parents might not have attended school when they were young.

Additional questions related to (1) above include (a) When you were my age, what was your favorite holiday or celebration? (b) When you were my age what was most different from today's world? and (c) When you were my age where did you live and how was that community different from San Luis Obispo? Note that the last question opens up a potential connection with geography, and the teacher can now choose to provide a map with push pins and string indicating the towns, cities, and countries in which the interviewees lived when they were young.

f. The letter to parents might have to be modified unless the teacher knows that all of her students are indeed living with one or more parents. If this is not the case the letter should be addressed to parents and caretakers, and should refer to son, daughter, foster child, and so on. In addition, the last line should read, "Your consideration of this request is appreciated," as opposed to "Your support of this project is appreciated." We believe there is a subtle difference here and that the former ending treats the parent more like a respected client; the latter ending is slightly pushy. We realize that the difference here is small and that some educators might be quite comfortable with the ending just as it is. What do you think?

g. On a slightly different note, we suggest that the teacher consider using a microphone to increase the ability of students to project their voices more easily without shouting. If all can be heard, the whole group sharing will be more enjoyable for a wider range of second graders, thus increasing the equity potential of this lesson. Once connected with a microphone, the teacher might also choose to tape-record the presentations and then place the tape at the class listening post for future listening. Such embellishments require a bit of extra preparation but pay off handsomely in added motivation and additional potential for sharing. For example, some students who were absent can still hear their classmates' presentations.

III. INTERVIEWING ANCESTORS (NOW CALLED INTERVIEWING RELATIVES OR CLOSE FRIENDS)

After Multicultural Restructuring

- **Major Objective:** To provide students with the opportunity to learn specific facts about their relatives or close friends as well as the families and friends of their classmates.
- **Content Area:** Language Arts, History, and Geography
- **Grade Level:** 2
- **Time Period:** 120 Minutes (3 sessions)
- **Objectives:** Given instruction in how to conduct an interview, the learner will
  1. demonstrate the ability to interview a relative or close friend of the family;
  2. share the results of the interview in class.

Suggested Modifications

1. As noted above, change the name of the lesson, the major objectives, and the length of the lesson (one session to explain the project, two for the sharing and possible playback of selected presentations).
2. Include the three second language learners and their parents in this integrated language arts activity as delineated in the analysis section above. Set up a support team of second graders to help the second language learners prepare their presentations; allow these students to engage in a bit of behavior rehearsal prior to their oral presentations.
3. Expand the list of questions and involve the students in making up the final list of six to eight questions. Let the students know that on the day of the sharing each child will decide whether to make the presentation to the small group or the entire class. Model for them on that initial day how the microphone and tape recorder will be used to facilitate the oral presentations.
4. Let the interviewers and the interviewees know that they can choose the three to five questions the interviewers will ultimately share.

5. Add a geography component to this activity by using a map, push pins, and yarn to mark where the interviewees lived when they were young children.
6. Modify the letter to parents as noted in the analysis section. In addition, encourage interviewees to share material about holidays and celebrations that students might not know about because the holiday is associated with a culture the students are unfamiliar with.
7. Allow students to give their presentation with a partner. The partner could read the question that was asked, and the interviewer could share what the interviewee said.
8. As an invitation for inquiry, invite a second grader whose grandmother or grandfather is alive to interview the grandparent about the grandparent's mother or father, the child's most immediate ancestors. Invite the student to share these findings in an oral or written report. This invitation for inquiry might lead the teacher to discover that some of the children have grandparents living in different states and nations, and the invitation could lead to some joint parent–child letter writing to carry out the inquiry. In addition, this invitation might allow the teacher to learn about the extended or dispersed family of several of her students and could result in rapport building with parents who value school projects that reinforce the young student's connection with and respect for the extended family.

SECTION THREE Lesson Sequences

I. SMOKING PREVENTION

Before Multicultural Restructuring

- **Major Objective:** To make students more knowledgeable about the dangers of smoking so they will be more likely to avoid smoking if they have not begun, and more inclined to stop if they have already started.
- **Content Area:** Health, Language Arts, Science
- **Grade Levels:** 5–8
- **Time Period:** 100–120 Minutes (two lessons)
- **Instructional Objectives** The learner will be able to
  1. recall verbally or in writing the harmful ingredients in cigarettes: nicotine, tar, and carbon monoxide (lesson 1)
  2. explain verbally or in writing why or how nicotine, tar, and carbon monoxide are harmful to the human body (lesson 1)
  3. explain verbally and in writing why people smoke (lesson 2)
  4. understand and explain verbally and in writing the psychology of cigarette advertisements and their inherent fallacies (lesson 2)
  5. explain and/or model techniques on how to say "no" (lesson 2)

Background Information

These lessons were prepared by a pre-service candidate as part of a senior project. The lessons were implemented in several upper-elementary classrooms (fifth and sixth grades), and the candidate made use of elements associated with a specific seven-step lesson plan to design and implement these lessons. The lesson plans and selected materials follow.

LESSON PLAN ONE

Anticipatory Set

"How many of you have been near a person who is smoking?"
"How did the person's smoke affect you?"
"There are poisonous ingredients in cigarettes that cause unpleasant reactions in our bodies."

Students' Objective

"Today we're going to learn about the harmful ingredients in cigarettes and what harm they cause to people who smoke."

Purpose Statement

"By learning about the harm caused by smoking cigarettes, each of us will be able to make a more knowledgeable decision about whether or not we will be a smoker."

Input

"Cigarettes are made with leaves that come from the tobacco plant.

"Cigarettes and cigarette smoke contain three main harmful ingredients—nicotine, tar, and carbon monoxide—three items that I will now begin to tell you more about.

"*Nicotine* is a poison found in tobacco. It causes our blood vessels to constrict, reducing the flow of blood and oxygen through the body. This reduction causes an increase in blood pressure and heart rate that is not healthy. Nicotine also paralyzes the cilia in the bronchial tubes. *Cilia* are tiny hairlike structures that clean the lungs. When the cilia are paralyzed, dirt and germs are not removed from the lungs and sickness can result. There are billions of tiny particles of *tar* in cigarette smoke. When tar cools inside the lungs it forms a brown sticky mass that contains chemicals that are believed to cause *cancer.*

"*Carbon monoxide* is found in cigarette smoke. It reduces the amount of oxygen carried in the blood. This means that the cells are demanding more oxygen than the blood is able to supply. Now we are going to learn about harm caused to the *lungs* and *heart* from smoking. First, let's think about what the lungs do. What is their function? Yes, the lungs allow us to breathe. When we breathe, oxygen comes into our lungs and goes to the *alveoli* where it enters our blood and can then travel through our bodies and feed our cells. On our outline next to function of the lungs let's write, 'the organ that allows us to breathe.'

"Next, let's think about what the *heart* does. The heart is the body organ that pumps blood through our body so that our cells can get oxygen from the blood. The heart is a muscle. On our outline next to function of the heart let's write, 'the organ that pumps blood through our body.'

"Smoking is very harmful to our lungs. Cigarette smoking is a major cause of emphysema, chronic bronchitis, and lung cancer.

"*Bronchitis* is an inflammation of the bronchial tubes. Smoking can cause bronchitis by irritating the cells in these tubes. Chronic bronchitis means that the bronchial tubes are always inflamed; this makes breathing very difficult since the passageway for air is smaller.

"*Emphysema* is a stretching of the structures in the lungs. This makes it more difficult for oxygen to enter the blood at the alveoli.

"*Lung cancer* is a disease caused by the uncontrolled growth of abnormal cells. These abnormal cells destroy the healthy lung cells. Cigarette smoke contains chemicals that can cause the normal healthy lung cells to become the unhealthy cancerous kind of cells.

"Smoking is also very harmful to our hearts. Cigarette smoking is a major cause of heart disease, heart attacks, and atherosclerosis. *Atherosclerosis* is caused when nicotine and carbon monoxide damage the inner walls of the arteries. This damage allows fat cells and other abnormal cells to build up on the walls of the arteries. The arteries carry blood away from the heart. This thickening of the artery walls by fat and abnormal cells that have built up, causes narrowing and hardening of the arteries. When the arteries are hard and have a narrow opening, it is difficult for blood to pass through. This means the heart has to work harder to pump the blood.

"*Heart disease* is caused when the heart does not have the proper conditions to function. It means the heart is not healthy. Heart disease can lead to *heart attacks.* Heart attacks are caused when the heart does not get enough blood. The blood brings oxygen to the heart, so when the heart does not get enough blood it lacks oxygen as well. The lack of blood and oxygen to the heart during a heart attack causes damage to the heart since the heart cells can be killed when they do not get oxygen."

Check for Understanding

1. "I want all of you to look at your outline (see figure 3.1) and go over all the major points I just had you write down. Then discuss with your neighbor the harmful ingredients in cigarettes and how your lungs and heart are harmed by smoking.
2. "Now listen to me carefully and show me with thumbs up or down whether the material I mention is one of the three main harmful ingredients of cigarettes.
3. "Now let's do the same as I mention possible harmful effects that smoking produces in the lungs."

Guided Practice

"Check your outline with your neighbor and then color in the illustrations of the heart and lungs."

Closure

"I'd like each of you now to think about what we learned today, and then turn to your neighbor and tell him or her, first, what our lesson was about today, and, second, what some harmful effects of smoking are."

FIGURE 3.1 Example Lesson Outline 1

Day One Outline

Key

nicotine   tar   carbon monoxide   cilia   emphysema   bronchitis
lung cancer   heart disease   heart attacks   atherosclerosis

---

Function of the lungs:
The organ that allows us to breathe.

Function of the heart:
The organ that pumps blood through our body.

   I. Harmful ingredients in cigarettes:
     1. nicotine
     2. tar
     3. carbon monoxide
  II. Harm caused to the LUNGS
     1. bronchitis
     2. cilia
     3. emphysema (alveoli)
     4. lung cancer
 III. Harm caused to the HEART
     1. heart disease
     2. heart attack
     3. atherosclerosis

Key

carbon monoxide   bronchitis   tar   emphysema
cilia   nicotine   atherosclerosis

Using the words listed above, write in the correct word to complete each sentence.

1. A poison in tobacco that constricts blood vessels and paralyzes cilia is <u>nicotine</u>.
2. A substance in cigarette smoke that forms a brown sticky mass in the lungs when it cools is <u>tar</u>.
3. An ingredient of cigarette smoke that decreases the oxygen in our blood is <u>carbon monoxide</u>.
4. A disease that makes gas exchange at the alveoli more difficult is <u>emphysema</u>.
5. A disease causing inflamed bronchial tubes is called <u>bronchitis</u>.
6. The disease that would cause narrowing of the passageway in an artery of the heart is called <u>atherosclerosis</u>.
7. The hairlike structures that keep the bronchial tubes clean are the <u>cilia</u>.

FIGURE 3.2 Example Lesson Worksheet

Independent Practice (Homework)

"Complete this worksheet (see figure 3.2) by filling in the correct term in each sentence."

LESSON PLAN TWO

Anticipatory Set

"I'd like everyone to think back to our previous lesson on smoking and tell yourself one thing you learned about cigarette smoking.

"Who can tell us three harmful ingredients of cigarettes and cigarette smoke?

"Who can tell us some ways in which cigarette smoke harms the heart and lungs?"

Students' Objective

"We know that cigarette smoking is harmful in many ways, so today we'll discuss and try to figure out why people might choose to smoke. We'll learn the major reasons people smoke, and we'll study the tactics advertisers use to promote an image that will make smoking acceptable and desirable to many consumers."

Purpose Statement

"The information we study today should help us avoid the pressure to smoke and help us to say *no* to anyone who asks us to smoke."

Input

1. "First, let's discuss *why people smoke*. On our outline (figure 3.3), we can fill in the three reasons that people are most likely to smoke, and

---

Day Two Outline

Key

parents, friends, or idols   easy to obtain   nicotine addiction   hidden
message   false message   ignore   say no   say no, give reasons

---

I. Why People Smoke
   1. Parents, friends, or idols smoke
   2. Cigarettes, ashtrays, and matches are easy to obtain
   3. Nicotine addiction
II. Advertisements
   1. Hidden message
   2. False message
III. How to say "No"
   1. Ignore
   2. Say no
   3. Say no, give reasons

FIGURE 3.3 Example Lesson Outline 2

why they continue. (1) Parents, friends, or idols smoke; (2) Cigarettes, matches, and ashtrays are easy to obtain; (3) Nicotine is a very addictive drug.

2. "*Advertisers* spend over a billion dollars a year to get people to spend their money on cigarettes. These advertisements try to make smoking seem desirable. They do this by making the consumer want to be like the people in their ads. Different companies create different images of the people who smoke their cigarettes. They try to make you believe that by buying their brand of cigarettes you will be like the people in their ads. There are two things we should know about cigarette ads. They contain hidden messages, and the hidden messages contain fallacies.

3. "As you get older and go on to junior high and high school your friends or acquaintances may offer you a cigarette and pressure you to smoke. We know the health reasons for why we should say no to smoking cigarettes. I am going to tell you of three ways to *say no* to someone who asks you to smoke. These same examples can be used to say no to drugs: First, you could simply ignore the question and walk away or change the subject; second, you could say, 'No, I'd rather not'; or third, you could say, 'No, I'm not going to smoke because it is bad for the heart and lungs, and I want to stay as healthy as I can.' This is an example of giving reasons why you don't want to smoke. By using the third example you may even persuade the other person not to smoke. You should use the method of saying 'no' that you feel most comfortable with.

4. "Now, I'd like you to look at your outline (figure 3.3) and discuss with your neighbors why people smoke, how advertisers create a false image of smoking, and ways to say no if someone asks or pressures you to smoke."

Check for Understanding

"I'm going to ask some questions. Listen carefully and show me with your thumbs if the answer is correct or not. Why do people smoke? How do advertisers try to get people to buy their brand of cigarettes? What are some ways we can say 'no' to someone who asks us to smoke?"

Closure

"With your neighbor, do a role-play in which a parent or relative is asking you what you learned in school today that was interesting. In your response, among other things, identify the ingredient in cigarettes that is addictive and the ways you can say 'no' to a person offering you a cigarette."

Independent Practice (Homework)

1. "For homework complete the sheet with true/false and fill-in sentences." (see figure 3.4)
2. "Examine the activities listed on the Follow-up Activities worksheet and identify one you'd like to participate in, or add your own project to the list." (see figure 3.5)

Lesson Analysis

These lessons can be critiqued and improved from a variety of perspectives. On the plus side, the teacher candidate has selected a very appropriate content area for her fifth and sixth graders. Despite the warnings from the U.S. Surgeon General's office, the labeling

FIGURE 3.4 Example Homework Sheet

True or False

T F 1. Smoking is harmful to the lungs.

T F 2. Cancer and heart attacks can be caused by smoking.

T F 3. There is poison in cigarette smoke.

T F 4. Smoking is an easy habit to break for people who have smoked for a long time.

T F 5. Bronchitis and emphysema are diseases caused by smoking.

T F 6. Smoking does not affect the heart.

T F 7. Smoking makes kids look and seem grown up.

T F 8. If a friend asks us to smoke it is okay to say "No."

Fill in the blank with one of the following words:

Key

oxygen   cilia   lungs   heart   advertisements

1. When we breathe in, <u>oxygen</u> goes into our blood and feeds the cells.
2. <u>Cilia</u> are hairlike structures that sweep out our air passages to keep them clean.
3. We breathe with our <u>lungs</u>.
4. The <u>heart</u> is the body organ that pumps blood through the body.
5. <u>Advertisements</u> try to show an image that people will want to copy.

Possible Follow-Up Activities

1. Public Service Announcements:

   Have a contest among the students to write and recite public service announcements about the hazards of smoking. Do the announcements in class or contact radio or television stations beforehand to find out about airing the announcements.

2. Awareness in the School:

   Have the students design antismoking posters. The students could start a campaign to inform the entire school about the hazards of smoking.

3. Math:

   Have students investigate how much a pack of cigarettes costs and determine how much a one-, two-, or three-pack-a-day smoker would spend on cigarettes in a year.

4. Interview:

   Have students interview smokers and nonsmokers as to why they do or do not smoke and their attitudes toward smoking.

5. Current Events:

   Have students look for information about cigarette smoking in newspapers.

FIGURE 3.5 Example Follow-Up Activities Worksheet

on cigarette packages regarding the harmful effects of smoking, and the increasing sophistication of television antismoking commercials, in the United States we still have large numbers of teenagers who begin smoking each year. Thomas Glynn found that each day more than 2,000 American adolescents smoke their first cigarette,[2] and the University of Michigan Institute for Social Research reported that 18.1 percent of American high school seniors smoked every day in 1988.[3] Given the linkages between cigarettes and lung cancer and emphysema, and the status of cigarettes as a gateway drug with the potential to lead to other serious forms of drug abuse, prevention education related to cigarettes is clearly warranted.

In addition to selecting an appropriate content area, the teacher candidate, utilizing resources from the American Lung Association, has also selected meaningful facts to call to the attention of the fifth and sixth graders who received these lessons. In particular, the candidate attempted to incorporate a no-use message into her lessons. Beyond these positives there is ample room for improvement, and we will use several of the evaluation questions for multiculturalization to structure our improvement remarks.

Do the lesson content and structure promote or impede educational equity? These lessons were initially prepared for fifth and sixth graders in general and not a specific classroom, so as we respond to this question and the ones below, we will keep in mind the wide range of learners teachers often encounter, even in classrooms that are relatively homogeneous in terms of ethnicity.

For this wide range of learners and their various learning style preferences, points of view, prior knowledge of, and perhaps experience with cigarettes, the candidate's decision to view her learners as empty vessels who would be filled up with important knowledge is a weakness. Before you can consider more subtle questions related to teaching effectively with a multicultural perspective, you must consider some very basic questions about making the most effective use of the model of instruction you are employing. For these lessons the candidate employed a teacher-directed approach that leaned heavily on a seven-step lesson design format familiar to many prospective and veteran teachers. It is a format many teachers use well as they employ it flexibly and integrate it with other approaches to teaching and learning. In this sequence, however, there is no creative or flexible use of this lesson format. The format is disconnected from the mastery learning model of which it is a part. Thus, the candidate is cut off from the diagnostic and task analysis process that would put her in touch with what students already know about the topic and what they would like to know, and help her sequence the material she would ultimately teach.

In addition to diagnostic work, teachers who draw on the seven-step format as they make instructional design decisions often make use of selected ideas about learning to promote efficient learning for all students; these ideas lead teachers to employ teaching tactics related to anticipatory set, active participation, reinforcement, retention, motivation, and closure. In these lessons the candidate's attempts at active participation—keeping the students' minds consistently engaged in the lesson—were limited to having them fill out a worksheet after listening to her present information orally. Occasionally, the students would be directed to share and discuss their worksheet with a neighbor. The candidate, perhaps because she was working in classrooms that were not her own, fell back on the oldest and least effective way of transmitting information—the lecture. These lecture remarks were not illuminated by slides or other visuals, or punctuated by thought-provoking questions. The candidate does not know what her students know because she has not done any diagnostic work prior to sharing information about nicotine, carbon monoxide, and cilia. In lesson one she should ask students what they know about these terms and then connect her remarks to their comments. In addition to an increase in questioning, the candidate could create more active participation by incorporating more variety in modes of information delivery. Directed reading, thinking, and discussion activities would serve this purpose as would the selective use of videotape or slide/cassette tape presentations, role-playing, or brain-storming.

Another area worthy of revision concerns the relationship between the major objective of the lesson and the purpose statement in lesson one. The major objective incorporates a strong and appropriate no-use message. The goal of this lesson is prevention, to keep young people away from cigarettes, or to persuade them to stop smoking if they have already begun smoking or experimenting. In the statement of purpose, however, the candidate's words suggest that the objective of the lesson is to provide information that will help the students make a more informed decision about whether to become a smoker. Ultimately, of course, that is what each student will do, but current research suggests that the teacher should be a partial, rather than an impartial, disseminator of information. The teacher should be willing to say something like this:

> The purpose of today's lesson and this entire sequence is to persuade and prepare each of you to avoid smoking and cigarette smoke, and to stop experimenting with cigarettes if you've already begun. If you wish, you can consider today's lesson one big antismoking commercial. I care about you and your health, and that's why I don't want you to smoke.

It is noteworthy that the purpose statement and the entire approach employed by the candidate appear to be closely aligned to the "information-only" program of alcohol and drug prevention that was the dominant mode of drug prevention in the 1970s and 1980s. Writing in 1987, John Van de Kamp, attorney general of California described this method in the following way:

> This approach relies heavily on scare tactics and provides some information on the effects of drug and alcohol in the human body. It assumes that the individual uses drugs because of the lack of information, and that by providing that the individual will choose not to use drugs. This method is outdated and some researchers even claim that it may contribute to increased drug and alcohol abuse.[4]

Furthermore, in discussing constructive alternatives to the information-only approach, Van de Kamp said that "the essential ingredient seems to be the comprehensive approach of a K–12 curriculum. Such a curriculum must emphasize development of a strong level of self-esteem . . . must emphasize effective decision-making skills . . . and must be age-appropriate. It must give special weight to teaching social skills and refusal skills in difficult situations. And it must be supported by parental and youth involvement at every level with peer support being especially important."[5]

One of the main ideas in the model of instruction employed by the candidate is that after selecting an appropriate instructional objective, the teacher should teach directly to that objective with relevant behaviors (which is another way of saying appropriate strategies). In addition, in our Typology of Multicultural Teaching (see appendix 1), we say that teachers should use the direct instruction model in a sophisticated manner. This means knowing when to use and not use it, when to integrate it with other models, and how to use it well when using it. In this instance, Van de Kamp's statements strongly suggest that the candidate was not using appropriate strategies. The candidate included the idea of refusal in her lesson but thought that all she had to do was provide information about refusal. However, research suggests that to increase the age at which individuals begin to experiment with tobacco, alcohol, or marijuana, or prevent it altogether, students need the opportunity to role-play refusal and to discuss the difficult choice situations many will encounter. The addition of role-playing and discussion related to the role-playing scenarios suggests that this two-lesson sequence will need to be lengthened. A review of curricula designed to prevent drug and alcohol abuse reveals that several popular research-based prevention curricula for grades five through eight contain 10 to 12 lessons in their sequence. Although some prevention curricula and programs focus on tobacco exclusively, more recently designed curricula integrate prevention education for tobacco with prevention education for alcohol and marijuana and also link this content to larger health considerations. Such curricula are described in *Schools and Drugs: A Guide to Drug and Alcohol Abuse Prevention Curricula and Programs*,[6] and K–8 educators interested in designing sophisticated and multiculturalized lesson sequences in this area would be well advised to review the 19 curricula described in this document. Particularly noteworthy are *Project SMART*—grades six through nine (developed by the Institute for Health Promotion and Disease Prevention Research at the University of Southern California); *Ombudsman: A Classroom Community*—grades five and six (developed by the Drug Education Center, Charlotte, North Carolina); and *Parent and Substance Use Prevention*/PASS-UP—grades six and seven (developed by the American Lung Association of Los Angeles County and the Institute for Health Promotions and Disease Prevention Research, University of Southern California). In the latter curriculum, both classroom and homework activities involve parents; follow-up research conducted 18 months after the 10-session curriculum was implemented revealed that a high level of parent involvement was a critical factor in maintaining a low usage rate of alcohol and marijuana.[7] This research result relates to the second question in our multiculturalization process:

Does the lesson content or structure make use of, or help to develop, collaborative empowering relationships among parents, students, and teachers?   In our model the goal of collaboration among parents, teachers, and students is eminently sensible for a variety of reasons. Logic suggests that classroom teachers and parents, functioning as guides and educators in different settings and sometimes differing cultural contexts, will be more effective in motivating and supporting students when they share information about students' proclivities and progress and work together as a team.

What we learn from drug prevention research is that in this area of the curriculum parent involvement is not only desirable but is critical. The introduction to a recent drug prevention guide put it this way:

> There is little evidence to challenge the basic premise that prevention is the most human and cost-effective response to drug and alcohol abuse and related problems among youth. But preventing drug use takes more than classroom instruction. Research shows that no curriculum has much impact on students' behavior concerning drugs, unless it is delivered in the context of a comprehensive prevention program encompassing school instruction, parent involvement, and community support.[8]

Like many lessons designed and implemented by student teachers who are in classrooms for relatively short periods of time, the lesson sequence outlined above did not have a parent involvement component. However, whether the instructor is a student or veteran teacher, there are several good reasons for involving parents in drug prevention instruction. In terms of long-term prevention or overall effectiveness, parent involvement is an influential factor in the prevention equation. Even if parent involvement did not make the curriculum more powerful, the teacher working with a multicultural perspective would want to communicate with parents prior to implementing this sequence because this teacher, more than others, wants to maintain rapport and open lines of communication between parents and teacher and parents and students.

The maintenance of such smooth, two-way communication is a major goal of the multicultural model. Thus, because the multicultural perspective encourages the teacher to think about the learner habitually in the broader context of family and community, it will be second nature for the teacher oriented to multicultural instruction to consider the effects of the lesson content on the students' extended families. This consideration will likely lead that teacher to see that this content is not neutral, innocent, information devoid of social or family implications. Because parents or relatives of the students may be smokers, we believe the teacher, in planning this sequence, is ethically bound to consider the social implications of the content. Minimally, we believe that parents should receive an overview of the objectives and content in this set of lessons in the monthly newsletter that precedes the sequence, and parents should be invited to attend any of the sessions. Parents who have quit smoking can make brief presentations as part of a panel; homework assignments can be designed with a component that involves parents and child, so that parents are also learning or being reminded about the prevention content. In addition, students should have the opportunity to discuss the way this content, and antismoking advertising in general, might make smokers in their extended families feel, and how and if they should use their new knowledge in the family context. In leading this discussion, the teacher should make clear that although politeness is an obvious consideration, there are no easy answers to this question. Various responses should be expected because of the different values and relationships that exist in different families. This content might produce sadness or fear in some students because of their relatives' smoking. Therefore, teachers should encourage students to write about these and other feelings in their classroom journal so the teacher can address their individual concerns.

Another observation is that the structure of the candidate's sequence did little to use or develop collaborative relationships between students. The student teacher's plan had neighbors checking and discussing each other's worksheets, but *neighbor* is a vague term; students can change neighbors from one part of the lesson to the next, and some students may not find a neighbor easily. This sequence, in a variety of ways, would improve if it were implemented in a "classroom community" in which partners and cooperative learning groups were integral elements. Smoking is not just an individual problem. It is also a social problem and the solutions for the individual and the society are intertwined. Therefore, cooperative problem solving and support groups provide the logical context in which to receive prevention knowledge. Commitments made to peers, who in a cooperative learning environment have a responsibility to help each other, should strengthen everyone's individual resolve to resist pro-use media messages and local peer pressure.

Collective and critical analysis of pro-use and antismoking advertising can help to strengthen students' resolve not to smoke. It can also show students how certain corporations in America and elsewhere attempt to use knowledge of cultural groups such as women and ethnic groups such as African Americans and Hispanic Americans to sell products like cigarettes and alcohol. We will discuss this further under our next evaluative question, the last one to be considered in this analysis.

Does the lesson content help to increase students' knowledge regarding various cultural and ethnic groups?   The candidate's sequence, which dealt with advertising in a very general way, did not add to her students' knowledge of cultural and ethnic groups. Significant improvement could be made here in the lesson plan because cigarette product development has been described as "the epitome of what advertisers call *niche* marketing, with more than 300 brands, targeted by gender, race, and socio-economic group."[9] With concrete examples, students should be made aware that specific groups such as the poor, women, Blacks, Hispanics, and the young in general are routinely targeted by cigarette corporations, and that the objective of the corporations is to lure members of these groups into smoking. Consider the story of Uptown. In 1988, R. J. Reynolds developed Uptown, a new cigarette aimed at the African-American market. The new cigarette "had less menthol flavoring, was packaged in black and gold . . . and was packed with the filters facing down after market research indicated that Black-American smokers tend to open cigarette packs from the bottom. Six months of test marketing was scheduled to begin in January 1990 in Philadelphia, which has a Black population of some forty percent, through heavy advertising in Black newspapers, on billboards and buses, and through point-of-purchase displays"[10] The Uptown story shows students how individuals and groups can fight back to protect their own communities and children. In late January 1990, Reynolds canceled its plans to pilot and market its new product, losing an estimated five to seven million dollars. The cancellation resulted from the combined protest efforts of antismoking groups, African-American community leaders, and Louis Sullivan, then U.S. Secretary of Health and Human Services.[11] The story also reveals the tenacity of the cigarette industry. R. J. Reynolds is currently testing two additions to its Salem line, Salem Gold and Salem Box. Each has the lower level of menthol that Black smokers prefer, according to R. J. Reynolds's market research.[12]

Other case studies can be used to show products and advertising that have been developed to target different groups: Rio and Dorado cigarettes for Hispanics,[13] Virginia Slims for women, and Dakota, a new cigarette aimed at young uneducated White women, aged 18 to 24, who are considered to be virile females.[14] This may not be the type of ethnic and cultural knowledge practitioners have in mind when they think about multiculturalizing the curriculum, but in learning how to grow in a positive and healthy way in our society, students need to learn that some corporations and advertising companies will exploit cultural and ethnic patterns to attract individuals to various addictive and dangerous products such as cigarettes.

I. SMOKING PREVENTION

After Multicultural Restructuring

- **Major Objective:** To provide students with a variety of reasons and skills to help them (a) avoid the smoking habit and (b) stop smoking if they have already begun.
- **Content Area:** Health, Language Arts, Science, Social Science

- **Grade Levels:** 5–8
- **Time Period:** 4 to 8 Weeks
- **Instructional Objectives** The learner will be able to
  1. assertively and constructively turn down offers of cigarettes in role-playing situations;
  2. give specific examples of the way cigarette advertising, packaging (shape and design of box and cigarette), and promotion of sports events is designed to attract young people to cigarette smoking;
  3. identify and describe specific examples of cigarette companies developing cigarette products and advertising campaigns targeted at specific cultural and ethnic groups;
  4. identify several reasons for saying no to cigarettes;
  5. identify specific locations where smoking is prohibited (e.g., airplanes, Carl's Jr. Restaurants);
  6. identify the harmful ingredients in cigarettes (nicotine, tar, and carbon monoxide) and explain how these elements harm an individual's health;
  7. explain why young people begin smoking and why some veteran smokers find it difficult to stop.

Suggested Modifications

1. To enhance effectiveness, during the planning stage analyze curriculum packages that incorporate the latest knowledge regarding tobacco prevention; review periodical articles and texts to make certain your content and strategies reflect current research.
2. Consider expanding the sequence to include lessons on alcohol and marijuana prevention.
3. Design the sequence and class newsletter so that parents and other caretakers have the maximum opportunity to participate in the sequence as learners, volunteer instructional assistants, guest lecturers, and homework assistants for their child when possible. Help with homework should be requested in a polite and sensitive manner.
4. In the class newsletter, several weeks prior to the unit, provide an overview of the sequence content and objectives and invite parents and caretakers to discuss the content with you at a special meeting prior to sequence implementation. Provide other means of communication for the adults who cannot attend the special meeting.
5. During the planning stage conduct diagnostic work to learn what your students already know about this topic and what they would like to learn. To the greatest possible extent, incorporate collaborative and self-directed approaches to learning in this sequence.
6. Consider, during the planning stage, having students design inquiries to learn
   a. how many, or if any, fifth or sixth graders have experimented with cigarette smoking;
   b. what kinds of cigarette advertising they see in their communities and homes.
7. Organize the students into learning teams and give each team the responsibility for designing and implementing a special citizenship project related to the sequence. Brainstorm possibilities within groups and then the whole class.
8. Diversify the methods used to disseminate sequence content and significantly reduce the amount of time lecturing; devote at least one period to role-playing, giving each student the opportunity to practice refusal communication.

9. Disseminate brief descriptions of tobacco products and advertising campaigns that have targeted specific ethnic and cultural groups in the United States. Consider showing a film such as *Seeing through Commercials,* which is described in *Schools and Drugs* as a 15-minute film appropriate for fourth through sixth graders.[15] The film shows how commercials are made and certain techniques are used to induce people to buy products.
10. Design invitations for inquiry that will
    a. allow your students to play a role in shaping the ongoing sequence. You might encourage some students to preview films and videos available in your district's instructional media center and select one or two the class would benefit from seeing;
    b. give them the opportunity to analyze new cigarette advertising to learn whether they can discern who is being targeted for "disease recruitment";
    c. give them the opportunity to learn whether other nations like Mexico, Canada, France, or Nigeria put warnings on cigarette products, and if not, why not. Can American companies sell cigarettes in other countries without the warning labels? If yes, is this fair?
    d. give them the opportunity to correspond with or interview citizens like Louis Sullivan, U.S. Secretary of Health and Human Services during the Bush administration, who have publicly taken strong antismoking positions;
    e. give them the opportunity to learn whether the U.S. Congress and Department of Agriculture still provide subsidies to American farmers who grow tobacco.

Final Comments

The restructuring of this sequence was similar to prior restructuring in that a variety of techniques were used to "multiculturalize" the content. However, the restructuring in the "Smoking Prevention" sequence provided an opportunity to introduce a different type of multicultural/multiethnic knowledge. Students became aware that some American corporations actually target specific ethnic and cultural groups for what might objectively be called "disease recruitment." The impulse to think, wonder, and see with a multicultural perspective, over time, is shaped by "social facts" such as these. Such facts clearly indicate that some very powerful organizations think deeply about culture and ethnicity when they make influential marketing decisions. Informed citizens need to be aware that corporations use gender, culture, and ethnicity to sell their products; such knowledge helps consumers evaluate the real intent of the marketing message. Teachers can help their students in becoming informed consumers by a thorough examination of marketing strategies such as those discussed here.

II. DISCOVERING NEW PILGRIMS IN AMERICA

Before Multicultural Restructuring

- **Major Objective:** To enhance teacher awareness of a wide range of traditional Thanksgiving literature and ways to utilize it.
- **Content Area:** Language Arts and Social Studies
- **Grade Levels:** 3–8
- **Time Period:** One Week

Background and Implementation Information

The "before" and "after" sequence of lessons described below was designed by us and used in our graduate and undergraduate methods courses to illustrate how the selection of curriculum materials can promote or impede the development of a multicultural curriculum. The direction of the sequence is from more traditional Thanksgiving stories and activities toward those with the potential to promote intergroup harmony; increase students' knowledge of selected cultural and ethnic groups; and increase students' willingness and ability to examine an issue, word, or political situation from a new and perhaps multicultural perspective. Note that at the end of the sequence we tell our teachers and future K–8 teachers that the implementation procedures for the sequence of stories they will use can roughly parallel our procedures, but should also diverge creatively.

Because (a) our initial objective is to make our students more aware of a wide range of traditional Thanksgiving materials and (b) our classes are divided into cooperative learning groups, we structure this sequence in the following way:

1. Working in their cooperative learning groups, students tell whether their families have a tradition of celebrating Thanksgiving; if so, how they celebrate it; and what their own personal feelings are about Thanksgiving. (Is this a holiday they look forward to? Why? Why not?)
2. After this, we distribute to each group a different set of traditional Thanksgiving materials (stories, songs, poems, craft activities, etc.) from the university library. Each group collectively examines the materials and develops a consensus about the three or four they would most likely use in their own classrooms. The material distributed includes the following:
   a. "Thanksgiving" in *Twenty-Five Plays for Holidays* (Boston: Plays Inc., 1952), 124–177.
   b. "November: A Play for Thanksgiving—The Case of the Gone Gobbler," in *Teacher's Activity Calendar* (New York: Instructor Publications, 1981), 56–57.
   c. "Thanksgiving," in *Holiday Plays for Little Players* (Boston: Plays Inc., 1957), 92–111.
   d. *The First Thanksgiving* (New York: Knopf, 1942).
   e. *Let's Find Out about Thanksgiving* (New York: Watts, 1964).
   f. *The Plymouth Thanksgiving* (New York: Doubleday, 1967).
   g. *A Charlie Brown Thanksgiving* (New York: Random House, 1974).
   h. *The Harvest Feast: Stories of Thanksgiving Yesterday and Today* (New York: Dutton, 1938).
   i. "Thanksgiving," in *Holiday Storybook* (New York: Crowell, 1952), 290–314.
3. Each group indicates its consensus choices with one or two other groups using the following routine: the spokesperson, using notes created by the scribe, shows and identifies all the materials examined and then introduces the team members who will present one of the consensus choices, one or more reasons for the choice, and the grade levels they consider most appropriate for their selected materials.
4. The next step is to ask each group to identify what their materials have in common with those presented by the other groups. The answers for each group are put on the board, and the groups will generally discover that their material included traditional elements and symbols of the historical American Thanksgiving story: Pilgrims, Indians, a turkey, family togetherness, giving thanks.
5. When this analysis is completed, the teachers and student teachers are asked whether they have found any stories, songs, poems, or craft activities that introduce new elements into the traditional Thanksgiving story or treat the old elements

in a new and thoughtful way. The discussion that follows leads into the next step in the sequence where the authors present two stories and one film; these together help to achieve objectives related to multiculturalization questions three, four, and five enumerated at the beginning of this chapter.

6. In our sequence, the main story we offer is *Molly's Pilgrim* by Barbara Cohen (Bantam Skylark by arrangement with New York: William Morrow, 1990). The book was originally published in 1983. We use it because it is a touching, well-written book but also because the story was made into a film that is easily available to teachers in our region; the film, produced by Jeff Brown, won an Academy Award for Best Short Film in 1986. We discuss the book by using a set of into, through, and beyond activities to illustrate how this approach to language development can relate to effective teaching and multicultural education. *Molly's Pilgrim* introduces elementary readers to an immigrant Russian Jewish family who has moved to America to find religious freedom. In the story we find Molly, the protagonist, in conflict with Elizabeth and several other classmates who ridicule her, do not generously accept her differences in speech and dress, and are particularly insensitive to the wrenching change Molly's family has recently experienced. The story line moves from rejection and bigotry to acceptance and tolerance as Molly's mother encourages her to share in class the insight that she, Molly, and Molly's dad are modern-day pilgrims. Molly, in response to her teacher's homework assignment, nervously shows a pilgrim doll that closely resembles her mother dressed in Russian garb instead of a Puritan or Indian doll as requested. The stage is then set for Miss Stickley, who in several ways resembles an old-fashioned teacher, to tell Molly's classmates that "I'm going to put this beautiful doll on my desk where everyone can see it all the time. It will remind us that pilgrims are still coming to America." Then she says that the Pilgrims got the idea for Thanksgiving from reading in the Bible "about the Jewish harvest festival of Tabernacles." This festival is called Sukkot by contemporary Jews.

7. In our university classroom, to set the stage for appreciating and understanding our initial reading of *Molly's Pilgrim,* we review a number of words from the story and read the story in a slow dramatic way. This illustrates how we would attempt to make our oral rendition more comprehensible for limited English proficient (LEP) listeners. We review these words with contextual clues—the word in a sentence—with pictures and maps, and also with concrete experiences where appropriate, such as a peppermint stick. Some of the words we preview from *Molly's Pilgrim* are Cossacks, Russians, pilgrim, peppermint, tenement, synagogue, Goraduk, embroidered, tabernacles, religious freedom, "Oi Malkelah," "shaynkeit," "paskudnyaks," "Nu Malkelah," and Yiddish. With our largely English-speaking, monolingual teachers and prospective teachers we spent a bit of extra time explaining the meaning of the Yiddish phrases above to emphasize the value that this type of "sheltered English" preparatory activity will have for all learners, especially the limited English proficient learners who will be encountering strange-sounding, strange-looking, English and Yiddish words for the first time. For those who want to use *Molly's Pilgrim* in class, the following translations are based on information in Leo Rosten's *The Joys of Yiddish* (New York: Simon and Schuster, Pocket Book edition, 1970).

   a. "Nu Malkelah" as used in this book (p. 22) means "So, little Malke." However, the reader should know that "nu" (pronounced nōō to rhyme with moon) is a versatile expression that can have many meanings, depending on how it is said and where it is placed in a sentence. Rosten shows us that it can mean "How are things with you?" "What's new?" "Well," "So," as well as at least 15 other things. In addition, Malke is a Yiddish name, and was Molly's name when she lived in Russia.

b. "Oi, Malkelah" as used in this story (p. 10) is meant to communicate dismay and regret, as if to say "I'm sorry, little Malke." Leo Rosten says "Oy" is not a word but rather a vocabulary. Like "nu" it is an expression that can take on many meanings.

c. "Shaynkeit" (pronounced shānkīte) means beautiful child or "my beautiful child." "Schön" (pronounced shän) in German means pretty, and "shayner" in Yiddish means beautiful or pretty. In Yiddish shayner denotes goodness more than physical beauty.

d. "Paskudnyaks" is a Yiddish word that derives from "paskudne," a Polish/ Ukrainian word for nasty, dirty, or sloppy. A "paskudnyak" is a person who is nasty, mean, insensitive, petty, or simply contemptible.

e. Yiddish, according to Leo Rosten, is a language that is about 1,000 years old. Rosen writes that "Yiddish is descended from a form of German heard by Jewish settlers from Northern France about a thousand years ago,"[16] but the letters used to write Yiddish words were from the Hebrew alphabet rather than the German. The use of Yiddish in modern times was severely diminished by the destruction of East European Jewry during World War II.

8. After the vocabulary study we deliver the first oral reading by ourselves without the help of students, but students are asked to listen carefully and to jot down any questions they may have about the story. After the story is read we ask a general question such as, "Well, what did you think about this story?" Then we listen to the students' reactions before answering their questions.

9. After the question and answer period we discuss and list the different ways elementary students might read this story after the teacher's oral presentation. Some of these ideas include assigning parts to various readers for a whole class rendition, allowing cooperative learning groups to read the story within groups in a round-robin fashion, and allowing partners to read the story to each other page by page. As a part of this exercise we distribute questions to our prospective teachers, instruct them to discuss one or more questions of their choice, and create and answer a question of their own after the reading is completed. With this component we remind future teachers about the importance of self-directed learning and self-initiated questioning, and the fact that structure (a set of questions) and self-directed learning can go hand in hand. By providing meaningful choices and appropriate amounts of time, the teacher in a clear and deliberate way begins to share classroom power with the learners. In this component the opportunity to choose is also diagnostic because several of the questions deal with the nastiness and prejudice displayed by Elizabeth, Molly's antagonist in this story. Questions such as "Why do you think Elizabeth was so mean and intolerant?" and "Where do you think her ideas about Russian immigrants came from?" provide teachers and their students the opportunity to discuss their feelings about intolerance. Parenthetically, whether or not students have chosen to respond to the questions that relate to intolerance, we encourage our teachers to spend time discussing these important multicultural questions with their students.

10. When these discussions are completed, our students are asked to go back to the story one more time to identify the characters who spoke (Molly, Elizabeth,

Mama, Miss Stickley, and Emma), the characters who were mentioned (Papa, Mr. Brodsky, Hilda, Kitty, Faye, Emma, Arthur, Michael), and important icons, artifacts, or symbols from the story (Molly's Pilgrim Doll). This analysis sets the stage for viewing the 23-minute film version of *Molly's Pilgrim* from Phoenix films. As an advance organizer, students are told that in addition to discussing their general likes and dislikes about the film version, the class will focus on the following questions:

a. In the film what was new in terms of characters, dialogue, and setting?
b. What appeared in the novel that did not appear in the film?
c. What was left in but modified?
d. Why do you think there was a difference between the book and the film?
e. Which of the changes did you like? Why? Which changes did you not like? Why?

After the students assimilate the idea that storytelling in different media requires some changes we ask them through a series of invitations for inquiry to engage in some creative writing, drawing, acting, and general research. What follows is a sampling of these inquiries:

a. Develop a reader's theater script for *Molly's Pilgrim* or modify one that exists and then select a cast, perform, and possibly videotape it.[17]
b. Develop a movie script for one or more scenes from *Molly's Pilgrim,* select your actors and actresses, practice parts, perform and possibly videotape it.
c. Write an entirely new play based around the character of Molly—possible titles include *Molly's Christmas Story, Molly's Return to Russia,* or *Molly Visits Relatives in Mexico.*
d. Make drawings of several of the characters and possibly a doll representing your favorite character in the book.
e. Write a report that discusses the history of Yiddish.

11. In our college course, after we have completed a series of into, through, and beyond activities based on *Molly's Pilgrim,* we read another story that introduces or reminds our student teachers about another type of modern-day pilgrim, in this case boat people leaving their country to seek political freedom in the United States. The story we read is a picture book for primary graders and older students entitled *How Many Days to America: A Thanksgiving Story,* written by Eve Bunting (New York: Ticknor and Fields, 1988).

12. After we have engaged our students in the activities enumerated above, we have them review multiculturalization questions one through six. Then, with a partner, students design a sequence of activities based on *Molly's Pilgrim,* and other Thanksgiving resources to meet the objectives of several of these questions.

Analysis

The sequence described above contains a number of positive elements. For one, it shows how to build a multicultural curriculum by combining older curriculum elements with new resources. This is positive because it provides a response to critics of multicultural education. Often they claim that such instruction is anti-White, anti-European, and anti-male; they maintain that it consistently devalues European contributions to American culture at the same time that it uncritically celebrates the accomplishments of indigenous Americans and Americans of all colors save White. From this sequence, and other commentary in this text, it should be clear that we, along with many other advocates of multicultural education, favor an approach that is well rounded, balanced, and accurate in terms of its distribution of praise and criticism.

Second, the sequence demonstrates that awareness of relatively new literary resources, published in the 1970s, 1980s, 1990s, greatly facilitates the multiculturalization of a holiday that is a deeply entrenched part of the American K–8 curriculum. By extension, future and veteran teachers should perceive that the curriculum experiences for other widely celebrated holidays in February (the month of Presidents, Valentine's Day, and Black History month) and March/April (Easter, Passover, and Women's History month) can be multiculturalized by combining older and newer curriculum resources. The sequence also makes use of cooperative learning groups and integrated whole language teaching strategies that lead to higher-level thinking activities (the invitations for inquiry); it brings to the readers' attention a print and film resource that is useful for multicultural education, teacher education, and general literary enjoyment.

On the other hand, there is clearly room for improvement in this sequence at the university level or in an adapted format at the elementary or middle-school level. For example, as presented in our course, not much is done with *How Many Days to America: A Thanksgiving Story,* beyond reading it in class and asking students how they might use it in an elementary setting. Because this brief picture book does not name the island or nation the newcomers are fleeing, the story should be reinforced by books and other media that make it clear that we are talking about real people here. The following print resources could be used in a university or elementary/middle-school classroom:

1. Carol Olsen Day and Edmund Day, *The New Immigrants* (New York: Franklin Watts, 1985).
2. Joan McCarthy First, *New Voices: Immigrant Students in U.S. Public Schools* (Boston, Mass.: National Coalition of Advocates for Students, 1988).
3. James Haskins, *The New Americans: Vietnamese Boat People* (Hillside, N.J.: Enslow Publishing, 1980).
4. James Haskins, *The New Americans: Cuban Boat People* (Hillside, N.J.: Enslow Publishing, 1982).
5. Brent Ashabranner, *Children of the Maya: A Guatemalan Indian Odyssey* (New York: Dodd, Mead, 1986).

There is nothing in this sequence to remind students that some parents and students may not celebrate Thanksgiving at all, although some students may share such information in their cooperative learning groups. Even though the thrust of this sequence is on discovering new pilgrims to America, future and veteran teachers should be reminded that Thanksgiving has been, but should no longer remain, a holiday during which false information about Native Americans has been disseminated. As an example, Michael Dorris wrote in an essay entitled "Why I'm Not Thankful for Thanksgiving":

> A year ago my older son brought home a program printed by his school; on the second page was an illustration of the "First Thanksgiving," with a caption which read in part: they served pumpkins and turkeys and corn and squash. The Indians had never seen such a feast!" On the contrary. The Pilgrims had literally never seen "such a feast" since all foods mentioned are exclusively indigenous to the Americans and had been provided, or so legend has it, by the local tribe.[18]

The moral here, and the message to be included in the sequence, is that as we make use of new themes such as those embodied in *Molly's Pilgrim,* we should also do a much better job of conveying accurate information about Native Americans and Pilgrims and new immigrants to America, during Thanksgiving and throughout the school year.

II. DISCOVERING NEW PILGRIMS IN AMERICA

After Multicultural Restructuring

- **Major Objective:** To enhance teacher awareness of a wide range of traditional Thanksgiving literature as well as more contemporary literature that develops the theme of new pilgrims to America.
- **Content Area:** Language Arts and Social Studies
- **Grade Levels:** 3–8
- **Time Period:** One to Two Weeks

Instructional Objectives

The learners will be able to
1. specify how *Molly's Pilgrim* and *How Many Days to America: A Thanksgiving Story* can be used to incorporate new themes into the traditional Thanksgiving curriculum;
2. explain how they would use *Molly's Pilgrim* as the basis for a class discussion related to tolerance and intolerance;
3. identify and describe traditional and contemporary material they would use to create a meaningful Thanksgiving instructional sequence for a specific grade level.

Suggested Modifications

1. Utilize the new major objective to introduce the topic to future or veteran teachers so that everyone is working toward the same objective from the very beginning and to avoid the suggestion at any point in the lesson that the instructors are trying to reveal to the teachers what they, the teachers, do not know and should be aware of.
2. When teams are evaluating and selecting traditional Thanksgiving material, encourage the team members to (a) identify and set aside materials that treat Native Americans stereotypically or inaccurately, and (b) identify and select materials that describe accurately the interaction between the Pilgrims and the local Indians.
3. Allow teams to discuss the materials that have been set aside because of stereotyping and inaccuracies.
4. Develop a packet of information about Barbara Cohen, the author of *Molly's Pilgrim* and some of her other novels.
5. When presenting *How Many Days to America: A Thanksgiving Story,* discuss other nonfictional materials that accurately describe the varied experiences and feelings of new immigrants to America; develop new invitations for inquiry based on these materials.

DISCUSSION QUESTIONS

1. We identify four types of planned instructional events: instructional activities, lessons, lesson sequences, and units of instruction. Does this seem like a practical division to you? How do these categories compare to (a) the language used in your teacher education program, (b) the language used by teachers in your region, and (c) the realities of your own day-to-day teaching?

2. We suggest that the multicultural nature and potential of a given lesson or instructional activity can be evaluated by asking six basic questions that encompass the six goals in our model:

   - Do the lesson content and strategies promote educational equity?
   - Do the lesson content and strategies make use of, or help to develop, collaborative empowering relationships among parents, students, and teachers?
   - Do the lesson content and strategies promote cultural pluralism in society or intergroup harmony in the classroom?
   - Does the lesson content help to increase the students' knowledge of various cultural and ethnic groups, including their own?
   - Do the lesson content and strategies increase students' proclivity and ability to see and think with a multicultural perspective?
   - Does the lesson content (1) help to ameliorate distortions in the historical, literary, or scientific record that may be linked to historical racism or other forces related to the oppression and exploitation of specific ethnic and cultural groups, and/or (2) present material in a manner that suggests that racism-related distortions are or may be part of the historical and scientific record?

     a. To help evaluate the multicultural nature and potential of a lesson or lesson sequence, does this set of questions seem adequate? What would you add or delete and why?

     b. Should the fourth question be modified so as to focus on specific ethnic and cultural groups such as African Americans, Hispanic Americans, and Native Americans, or is the question phrased appropriately in your opinion?

3. Another popular example of a weekly, ongoing, instructional activity is Celebrity (or VIP or Star) of the Week. This activity is oriented toward building self-esteem. It is used most often in K–3 classrooms, but is occasionally found in fourth- through sixth-grade classrooms as well. In this activity each child in the class, for an entire week, becomes the focus of attention; in some classes two children may share the spotlight. In various ways during the week, the entire class learns about the life and family of the student VIP through photographs, favorite toys and art work, an autobiographical statement and/or class interview, a "my favorites" web, and possibly an experience chart written by the class. These materials and others are displayed on a bulletin board or in a learning center. Thus, during a given week the "facts" of each child's life become a central part of the class curriculum.

   In a specific grade, how could a teacher sensitively structure this activity so that the VIP of the Week activity, in addition to contributing to individual self-esteem, also helps to accomplish selected goals of multicultural education, such as the development of a pluralistic attitude and increased knowledge of the various cultures and ethnic groups represented in the class?

RECOMMENDED ACTIVITIES

1. In a local elementary or middle-school setting identify an ongoing activity such as homework and review, uninterrupted silent sustained reading or writing, or a 15-minute daily recess period; (a) describe the current structure (content/process) of the activity, and (b) make a list of proposed changes to increase the multicultural nature and potential of the activity.

2. Develop a plan for increasing student involvement in the word of the week program at the classroom or school level of operation. Your plan, on a weekly or monthly basis, should give as many students as possible the opportunity to shape the school world they inhabit.

3. Pick a biography, like *Rosa Parks,* in which the biographer's subject experiences some explicit form of political or economic discrimination that he or she overcomes. Prepare responses for questions you think students might ask as well as questions you would like to ask students. Read the story to your own or another class, and then answer one or more of the following questions:
   a. Was this the first time you had discussed discrimination (racism) with elementary school students? If so, how do you think it went?
   b. Which questions from students surprised you? Which questions, if any, were difficult for you to answer?
   c. Did your advance preparation lead to a fruitful discussion? Were you able to use any of your prepared responses in the postreading discussion? If yes, please specify the response.
   d. Do you think that discussing such stories helps to create a more intimate bond between you and your students? If yes, please explain your response.
   e. Do you think that consistent reading of such stories may help to reduce prejudice in the student body?[19]
4. Locate some printed material in which an author has written about Rosa Parks or some other historical figure inaccurately. Develop and describe a plan for using such material in a critical thinking lesson. For example, in *It Was on Fire When I Lay Down on It,* Robert Fulghum describes Rosa Parks as "a quiet, conservative, church going woman with a nice family and a decent job as a seamstress" and points out that "she was not an activist or a radical."[20] However, Friese's biography, cited in section one of this chapter, makes clear that from 1943 to 1955 Mrs. Parks was much more than a quiet, conservative, church-going woman. During this period she served as secretary of the local NAACP, helped register voters, and challenged the "bus laws" to the point of being ordered off a bus.
5. Using the six planning questions, write an evaluation of a key text or course in your teacher education program or major. If appropriate, write a set of recommendations for enhancing the multicultural nature and potential of the curriculum material or course. Do the questions appear to be helpful for evaluating materials and courses in higher education?
6. Locate several individual lessons, a lesson sequence, or a unit of instruction in your university library or with your instructor's help. Evaluate the multicultural nature and potential of this lesson. Discuss (a) the major instructional steps or procedures in the lesson, (b) your list of suggested modifications, and (c) the rationale for your modifications.
7. Pick one of the curriculum case studies in this chapter; (a) critique the "after" treatment, and (b) extend or improve the "after" treatment.
8. If you are designing a lesson, lesson sequence, or unit for another course in your teacher education program, your student teaching assignment, or your own classroom, use the six-question planning format to enhance the multicultural nature and potential of your lesson. If the questions lead to specific content or structural inclusions or modifications, make a list of these.
9. Evaluate the following lesson sequence; then, working with a partner, decide whether multiculturalization of the sequence is desirable. If it is, specify how you would multiculturalize this sequence. As you evaluate it, first imagine yourself in a class that is predominantly African American or Native American (90 percent), one that is predominantly White American (90 percent), and one that is ethnically diverse (Black, White, Hispanic, and Asian American) with no dominant majority. If you choose to multiculturalize the sequence, please indicate whether the different groups in the class would lead you to modify the sequence in different ways.

- **Sequence Title:** A Rainbow of Poems by Great Poets
- **Major Objective:** Poetic Literacy and Enjoyment of Poetry
- **Content Area:** Language Arts
- **Grade Levels:** 4–6
- **Time Period:** 90–120 Minutes (three to four 35-minute sessions)
- **Objectives:**
  Students will
  1. give specific examples of pairs of poems that illustrate the various ways poems can differ from each other (rhyming and nonrhyming, funny and serious, compressed and expansive);
  2. provide some biographical information regarding the following well-known poets: John Masefield, John Ciardi, Carl Sandburg, Robert Frost, and Shel Silverstein;
  3. be more likely to enjoy listening to poetry produced by others and to writing their own poetry.

General Procedures

1. In session one the teacher read poems such as "Sea Fever" by the British poet John Masefield and "Lost" by the American poet Carl Sandburg to contrast rhyming versus nonrhyming poetic structures, discussed the meaning of each poem, compared and contrasted the two poems, and shared background information about the two poets. Students were then invited to write their own rhyming or nonrhyming poems or listen to the teacher and other pupils recite favorite poetry.
2. In session two, selected poems by the American poets John Ciardi, Robert Frost, and Shel Silverstein were used to contrast humorous and serious poetry. The activities in session two were identical to those of session one except that students who had completed poems during or after session one were invited to read their poetry.
3. In session three, poems from all five poets were used to contrast brief compressed poems with lengthier, more expansive poetry. Again, the structure of the lesson was identical to the format of session two.
4. Session four was devoted to silent reading or poetry writing. Poetry that was produced, in first-draft form, was shared orally, and when revised, was sent home in the next class newsletter.

Journal Entry

This chapter focused on strategies for modifying the academic curriculum to bring it more in line with the goals of multicultural education. It would, therefore, be appropriate in your journal entry to comment on the questions below as well as your own questions or feelings about his chapter.

1. Did you learn anything of value from the chapter's "before" and "after" treatments, discussion questions, and activities? If yes, please summarize what you have learned.
2. Has the experience of reading chapters 1, 2, and 3 influenced the development or refinement of your own multicultural perspective? If yes, please describe and discuss the changes that have occurred.
3. Which aspects of the multicultural review and restructuring process recommended in this chapter seem questionable or ambiguous to you?

NOTES

1. For more information regarding the way telecommunications can positively influence classroom learning see "Telecommunications and Language Learning" by Patricia Mulligan and Kay Gore, *Language Arts* 69, no. 5 (September 1992): 379–384.
2. Thomas J. Glynn, "The Essential Elements of School-Based Smoking Prevention Programs: Research Results," *Journal of School Health* 59, no. 5 (May 1989): 181–188.
3. Sara Glazer, "Who Smokes and Starts, and Why," *Editorial Research Reports* 1, no. 11 (March 24, 1989): 151.
4. John Van de Kamp, "A New Solution to an Old Problem," in *Schools and Drugs: A Guide to Drug and Alcohol Abuse Prevention Curricula and Programs* (Sacramento: Office of the California State Attorney General, 1987), i–iii.
5. Ibid., ii–iii.
6. Ibid., 33–66.
7. Ibid., 47.
8. *Drug Prevention Curricula: A Guide to Selection and Implementation* (Washington, D.C.: Office of Educational Research and Improvement, U.S. Department of Education, 1988), iii.
9. Carol Matlack, "Smoke-Free Advertising," *National Journal,* February 24, 1990, 452–455.
10. *Standard and Poor's Industry Surveys,* May 17, 1990, F-36.
11. Ibid.
12. Walecia Konrad with Mark Landler, "Reynolds Draws a Bead on the Marlboro Man," *Business Week,* December 24, 1990, 47–48.
13. Jeff Bingaman, "Tobacco Has Dead Aim on Latinos," *Los Angeles Times,* February 11, 1990, M5.
14. Shari Roan, "Under Fire: Women and Smoking," *Los Angeles Times,* April 17, 1990, E5.
15. *Schools and Drugs: A Guide to Drug and Alcohol Abuse Prevention Curricula and Programs* (Sacramento: Office of the California State Attorney General, 1987), 111.
16. Leo Rosten, *The Joys of Yiddish* (New York: Simon and Schuster, Pocket Books, 1970), 439.
17. A set of supplementary activities for teachers working with *Molly's Pilgrim* has been compiled by Beverly Bain. The 14-page document, which includes a reader's theater script with 8 parts, can be purchased for $2.57 from the Ventura County Superintendent of Schools Office, Educational Services Center, 570 Airport Way, Camarillo, CA 93010. The full catalogue of materials from this center can be requested by phone (805-388-4407).
18. Michael Dorris, "Why I'm Not Thankful for Thanksgiving," *Spectrum: The Newsletter of Multiracial Americans of Southern California* 5, no. 5 (November/December, 1991): 3.
19. See James A. Banks, "Multicultural Education: Its Effects on Students' Racial and Gender Role Attitudes," in *Handbook of Research on Social Studies Teaching and Learning,* ed. J. P. Shaver (New York: Macmillan, 1991), 459–469, for evidence that sharing stories about ethnic heroes is a helpful strategy for reducing prejudice.
20. Robert Fulghum, *It Was on Fire When I Lay Down on It* (New York: Villard/Random House, 1988), 112.

Creating a Multicultural Curriculum with Integrated Social Studies and Science-based Units of Instruction

CHAPTER OVERVIEW

In chapter 4 various types of units are described—the basic unit of instruction, the content-specific unit, the literature-based unit, the resource unit, the integrated unit, and the multiethnic unit. In addition, several integrated units are discussed to illustrate how a teacher's awareness of the goals of multicultural education can help him or her multiculturalize the content and process of selected units.

The thought processes and evaluative questions employed in this multiculturization process are almost identical to those used with activities, lessons, and lesson sequences. However, the multiculturalization process with social studies and science-based units of instruction is, typically, more challenging, because we deal with more complex categories of knowledge such as generalizations, main ideas, and interdisciplinary concepts. Also, because of space considerations, in chapter 4 we use selected unit components rather than entire units to make our points and have integrated our "before" and "after" analysis into one set of remarks rather than the separate treatments employed in chapter 3.

INTRODUCTION

To gain a greater appreciation of how units of instruction in general, and integrated, social studies-based units in particular, can help you achieve the goals of multicultural education, several items are worthy of mention. First, you should understand that there are different types of units; some have greater potential for multicultural education than others, but all have some possibilities. Second, to be well prepared to apply a multicultural perspective in curriculum development you should be knowledgeable of a specific set of interdisciplinary concepts that James

Banks calls "key concepts for a multicultural curriculum."[1] Third, you need to remember that a multicultural perspective is both an orientation and a skill; it is simultaneously a way of viewing and thinking about the world, and a capability that is shaped by one's belief system and multicultural/multiethnic knowledge base. You must be convinced that cultivating a multicultural perspective and knowledge base is desirable and the perspective and knowledge are worthy of development in students. You should be concerned about, but not overwhelmed with, this responsibility, and be encouraged by knowing that your efforts in working with a multicultural perspective will inevitably lead to an enhanced multicultural/multiethnic knowledge base for you and your students. Last, please recall the six evaluative questions that can help you make judgments about the multicultural quality of units or other materials under consideration.

Before examining the different types of units, we need to explore the interdisciplinary concepts that are the fundamental building blocks for *anyone's* multicultural perspective. These include culture, ethnic group, ethnic minority group, cultural assimilation, acculturation, cultural conflict, prejudice, discrimination, race, racism, ethnocentrism, values, self-concept, socialization, intercultural communication, historical bias, power, social protest, collective struggle, colonialism, migration, and immigration. Some teachers will be quite familiar with these ideas; others will benefit from a review. An excellent text for this purpose is James Banks's *Teaching Strategies for Ethnic Studies*, particularly chapters 1 through 4.[2] This text, better than any other, introduces the reader to multicultural/multiethnic units of instruction that involve key multicultural concepts as well as the comparative study of two or more ethnic groups.[3]

Veteran teachers realize that units of instruction come in all sizes and shapes and that "the way units are planned and taught varies greatly from one teacher to another."[4] Because of this diversity and the key role units can play in developing a multicultural curriculum, teachers should be conversant with several types of units and the distinctions between them. Below, we discuss selected characteristics of a general unit of instruction, a content-specific unit of instruction, a literature-based unit of instruction, an integrated unit of instruction (sometimes referred to as a comprehensive unit), a multiethnic unit, and a resource unit.

TYPES OF UNITS

A *unit of instruction* is a comprehensive, multidimensional plan of instruction for learning inside or outside the classroom. A unit may consist of several lesson sequences, and in comparison to a lesson sequence typically requires a greater amount of time for planning and implementation. Compared to the lesson sequence, the unit will typically have greater diversity in lessons and activities and will incorporate a more precise type of evaluation.

In chapter 3 we presented 14 elements that are commonly found in the units produced by student teachers in our program. It would be helpful to review these elements before reading further. Also, note that the unit described above is often referred to as a *teaching unit* to distinguish it from a *resource unit*. The teaching unit contains only those objectives, activities, materials, bibliographies, and so on that the teacher and students will use during the unit. In contrast, the resource unit is an extensive collection of objectives, activities, and materials the teacher can use as a resource to help develop her teaching unit. Typically, the resource unit contains many more suggestions for study than any single teacher could pursue.

A *content-specific unit* shares a good deal of commonality with a teaching unit and could conceivably contain all 14 elements listed in chapter 3; typically, however, it would not be guided by generalizations unless it was a social studies or science unit. The chief distinguishing characteristic of the content-specific unit is that its contents are totally linked to one area of the elementary curriculum and there is little or no intent to stretch the unit's content beyond that one area. For example, we could have a content-specific unit in language arts entitled "Japanese Forms of Poetry." The focus of this unit would be the structure of various forms of Japanese poetry. Student activities would consist mainly of (a) reading and reciting Japanese poems and creating images stimulated by the Japanese poetry, and (b) using Japanese forms such as haiku to write original poetry. Students would be invited to illustrate selected poems, but this would be the only non-language arts-related activity. Japanese poetry would not be related to Japanese history, other aspects of Japanese culture, or the literary traditions of other Asian nations such as China. It is noteworthy that this particular unit, "Japanese Forms of Poetry," in addition to being a content-specific unit, has the potential to be a literature-based unit.

The development of *literature-based units* is a relatively recent phenomenon and is related to the evolution of "whole language" approaches to the teaching of language arts, including reading. These approaches represent an increasingly popular approach to language arts education and include an emphasis on (a) helping students read, write, and speak in a natural, less formal, way, and (b) allowing more time in class for students to use language in activities that receive less quantitative teacher evaluation. In addition, students are not divided into ability groups (high, middle, and low) where reading and related language arts instruction are delivered separately to each group by different level basal readers. All of the children simultaneously read the same whole piece of well-written, enjoyable literature, and the teacher uses the document as the primary resource from which a series of language arts-related activities are developed. Units that revolve around a single piece of literature are typically not guided by a set of generalizations and related main ideas. However, the literature-based unit need not be restricted to language arts activities. For example, a book about the life of George Washington Carver could easily serve as a catalyst for lessons related to science, history, geography, music, and art. If it involves language arts activities exclusively or primarily, the literature-based unit is a special type of content-specific teaching unit. But, like many content-specific units, the literature-based unit can incorporate lessons that extend into several different content areas. When this occurs we have created a different type of unit—the integrated unit.

An *integrated teaching unit* cuts across the boundaries of subject areas and integrates the curriculum. Students learn how the content areas relate to one another and how specific skills apply to real-life situations. They experience the application of reading and other language arts, mathematics, science, art, music, and physical education (P.E.) through meaningful and relevant life-related activities. Further, because it encompasses activities from a diverse array of content areas, the integrated unit is sometimes referred to as a thematic or comprehensive unit. Comprehensive units are often associated with social studies education, perhaps because social studies, as a content area, is itself informed by content from a variety of disciplines such as geography, anthropology, history, sociology, economics, and political science.

The final type of unit, the *multicultural/multiethnic unit*, has qualities that allow it to fit into the content-specific and integrated categories. The multiethnic/ multicultural unit involves the comparative study of two or more ethnic groups, typically from the same culture. Because ethnic studies in the university setting is increasingly considered a discipline or content area, a multiethnic unit can be perceived as content specific. On the other hand, as described by James Banks, a multiethnic unit is guided by interdisciplinary concepts that stem from a variety of social science disciplines. Therefore, almost by definition, it is an integrated unit. In Banks's conception, multicultural/multiethnic units will be part of an ongoing curriculum in which concepts such as racism, discrimination, prejudice, social protest, and culture will play a central role. Because these units allow for the consistent study of American ethnic groups, they contribute directly to the student's multicultural/multiethnic knowledge and indirectly to the capacity to think from a multicultural perspective. These direct and indirect contributions allow such units to provide a significant form of multicultural education.

CURRICULUM CASE STUDIES

With these units defined, we are ready to examine more closely the thought processes that educators employ as they shape and create material for a multicultural curriculum. Toward this end, the units we will analyze are "first draft" integrated social studies-based units that have resulted from collaboration between local school districts and the teacher education program at California Polytechnic University (Cal Poly) San Luis Obispo, California. Starting in 1987, several upper-grade elementary school teachers who were adjunct professors at the university began to work with the program as we attempted to model more precisely the design and implementation of units with a multicultural perspective. As a part of the modeling, the adjunct professor produces the first draft of a planned unit. This serves as a catalyst for creating an open-ended dialogue about the different ways a specific unit could be multiculturalized. Remember that the "before" versions examined below are first draft units created for teaching purposes within the Cal Poly teacher education program; the units that were actually taught emerged from these first draft plans after considerable revision. In addition, in our second example, elements from several units were synthesized to create the "before" version.

As you consider these first draft units and our multiculturalization recommendations, please keep in mind that although there are various ways to multiculturalize a unit, there is only so much a teacher can do at a given time. It would be incorrect to assume that we think the adjunct teachers, in creating their revised versions, should incorporate all the suggestions we make. The recommendations we offer are for teaching purposes. Our main objective is to illustrate how selective use of our six planning questions can help you develop a set of multicultural options as you conceptualize, revise, and implement multiculturally oriented units of instruction.

UNITS OF INSTRUCTION

UNIT ONE: WINNING OF THE WEST (1775–1850)

The first unit to be reviewed, entitled *Winning of the West: 1775–1850*, was developed by an adjunct, Mrs. Anderson (the names employed in this section are pseudonyms), for a bilingual fifth- and sixth-grade class where 95 percent of the students was Mexican American. Before discussing this unit several components from Mrs. Anderson's first draft unit will be enumerated so that you can form your own preliminary opinions about the content:

1. Categorization of unit content and strategies by content area
2. Unit objectives
3. Generalizations, main ideas, and supporting information
4. Introductory, closing, and selected developmental activities
5. Statement regarding incorporation of a multicultural perspective
6. Bibliography
7. A week-by-week schedule of unit activities

WINNING OF THE WEST (1775–1850)—SELECTED FIRST DRAFT COMPONENTS

Categorization of Unit Content and Strategies

SOCIAL STUDIES

Mountain Men/Trappers
First Women to Travel
Trails/Routes/Roads
Land Ordinance
Northwest Ordinance
Territories
Modes of Transportation
Frontier Life
Treatment of the Indians
Gold Rush
History of State Annexations
 and Statehoods
Indian Leaders:
  Sacajawea
  Tecumseh, Sitting Bull
  Black Hawk, Stand Waite
Contemporary Indian Personalities:
  Will Rogers
  Orville Moody
  Buffy St. Marie
  Jim Thorpe
  Carlos Montezuma
American Leaders:
  Sam Houston
  Daniel Boone

Jim Bridger
Lewis and Clark
George Rogers Clark
Andrew Jackson
Zebulon Pike
Davy Crockett
Stephen Austin

LANGUAGE ARTS

Simulations
Writing Newspaper Articles
Poetry
Outlining, Charting
Research Writing
Cooperative Grouping
Reading for Information
Role-Playing
Diary Entries
Oral Discussions
Tableaux
Oral Presentations
Biography Writing
Persuasive Writings
Reader's Theater
Interviews, Similes

Students will read *Sign of the Beaver*
  by Elizabeth Speare

ART

Make Covered Wagons/Conestoga
  Wagons Dioramas/Murals
Portraits of Famous Leaders
  and/or Pioneers
Tableaux
Make Flatboats/Keelboats/Forts
Build Wilderness Shelters

INDIAN CULTURE

Weaving, Food
Clothing, Cooking
Dancing, Customs

VALUES

Appreciation of the courage and
  determination of the pioneers
Understanding point of view of Indians
  and Mexican settlers in regard to their
  treatment during this period

MATH/CRITICAL THINKING

Mapping
Graphing
Similarities and Differences
Decision Making

Time Lines
Charting
Comparisons
Kilometers
Word Problems
Computer Programs

SCIENCE

Survival Skills in the Wilderness
Endangered Animals
Preservation of the Environment/
  Ecology
Animal Tracks
Natural Resources

MUSIC

Clementine
Oh! Susanna
Battle of New Orleans
Old Dan Tucker
John Henry
Wait for the Wagon
Sweet Betsy from Pike
Indian Songs

PHYSICAL EDUCATION

Invent a game from natural materials
Play games as described in *Sign of
  the Beaver*

Unit Objectives

COGNITIVE

1. Students will know why different groups of pioneers traveled west.
2. Students will know when the various states and sections of the country became a part of the United States and the history behind these actions.
3. Students will know the early pioneers and leaders of the Westward Movement and their contribution to the history of this period.
4. Students will realize the hardships endured by the pioneers as they traveled and settled on new lands.
5. Students will know the reasons the American Indians were treated unfairly.
6. Students will know the hardships the American Indians experienced.
7. Students will know the history of the Mexican Americans in California and in the Southwest and the impact of their culture in America.
8. Students will know of various contemporary Indian and Mexican personalities.

SKILLS

1. Students will be able to map the removal of the Eastern Indians.
2. Students will be able to map the westward growth of the United States.
3. Students will be able to map the United States at different times in history.

4. Students will work cooperatively and harmoniously in their groups.
5. Students will use reference materials independently as they seek information.

AFFECTIVE

1. Students will appreciate the perseverance of the American pioneers and their determination to settle new lands.
2. Students will appreciate the hardships and perspective of the American Indians regarding their plight during the Westward Expansion.
3. Students will appreciate the attitude of the Mexican-American people when they became outnumbered in their own land.

Generalizations, Main Ideas, and Supporting Information

Generalization   People with pioneer spirit will always meet challenges and endure hardships to improve their lives.

Main Idea 1   Early pioneers traveled west in search of better and more farm lands and opportunities.

Information

1. Some of the first Americans to move to the Old Northwest were land speculators.
2. Most pioneers were poor farmers who wanted land on which to build a home and start a farm.
3. By 1820, two and a half million people lived between the Appalachian Mountains and the Mississippi River.
4. Deserts, mountains, and rivers were explored by hardy fur trappers and mountain men.
5. In 1849 more than 80,000 hopeful newcomers arrived in California in search of gold.
6. By 1835 there were 30,000 settlers in Texas.
7. Pioneers endured many hardships and dangers in their travels and in settling the frontier.

Main Idea 2   Mexican Americans migrated to the United States in search of jobs and opportunities.

Information

1. In 1910, because of political problems in Mexico, many Mexicans migrated to the United States.
2. Today the Mexican people make up the largest Hispanic group in the United States.

Generalization   Adversity Breeds Leadership

Main Idea 1   A number of aggressive leaders were prominent during the Westward Expansion.

Information

1. Daniel Boone was the first White person to lead a group of settlers through the Appalachian Mountains.
2. Thomas Jefferson was responsible for the Louisiana Purchase.

3. Lewis and Clark and Pike were the pioneer pathfinders into the West.
4. Sacajawea guided Lewis and Clark much of their way through the unexplored areas.
5. President Jackson ordered the removal of Indians in order to make their fertile grounds available to the White man.
6. Jim Beckwourth was a famous mountaineer and trapper who later became a chief of the Crow tribe.
7. Davy Crockett was a famous hunter, scout, soldier, and congressman.
8. Kit Carson was a scout who guided some of the most important U.S. Army expeditions across great areas through which he alone knew the way.
9. Jim Bridger, a mountain man, led expeditions through the mountains.
10. Stephen Austin brought 300 American families to settle in Texas.
11. Sam Houston led the army that won Texas its independence.

Generalization   When an advanced civilization meets a less-advanced civilization, the less-advanced civilization will be assimilated or lose its national identity.

Main Idea 1   American Indians were dominated and eventually conquered by the White man.

Information

1. Treaties were made and then broken between the American Indians and the American government in regard to land.
2. In 1930 Congress passed a law ordering all American Indians to move west of the Mississippi.
3. The Cherokees were forced to leave in the middle of winter. Their march west is known as the "Trail of Tears."
4. American Indians were defeated in various battles and consequently lost their lands.
5. President Jackson did not support the Cherokees in their dilemma even after they had fought with him to defeat the Creeks in 1814.
6. By 1827, most of the tribes in the Old Northwest had moved west of the Mississippi.

Main Idea 2   In the middle 1800s, it became harder for Mexican Americans in California and in the Southwest to protect their rights and property.

Information

1. Mexican Americans were soon outnumbered in their own land.
2. Mexican Americans were not treated as well as English-speaking Americans in many ways.

Generalization   It is human nature to want to rebel when personal interests are not being represented in government.

Main Idea 1   Americans who settled in Texas wanted their independence from Mexico.

Information

1. Many of the Texans from the United States did not get along with the Mexican government and would not assimilate into the Roman Catholic culture of Mexico.

2. Mexico sent troops to Texas. Two hundred fighters held off about 5,000 Mexican soldiers for 12 days at the Alamo, a mission in San Antonio.
3. In 1836, the Texans declared their independence from Mexico.
4. The victory of Sam Houston's army over Santa Ana of Mexico led to the creation of the Republic of Texas with Sam Houston as president.

Introductory, Selected Developmental, and Culminating Activities

Introductory Activity A time line will be charted. After it is presented and various study prints and pictures have been previewed, students will be encouraged to ask questions for study in the unit. Their questions will be charted.

TIME LINE

1775	Daniel Boone opened the Wilderness Road and made possible the first settlement of Kentucky.
1778–1779	George Rogers Clark's campaign won the Northwest Territory for the United States.
1785	The Land Ordinance provided an orderly system for surveying and selling government lands.
1794	Victory over the Indians and a treaty with Great Britain brought peace to the Northwest Territory.
1795	Pinckney's Treaty with Spain opened the mouth of the Mississippi River to American navigation.
1803	The Louisiana Purchase opened a vast area beyond the Mississippi River to American settlers.
1804–1806	Lewis and Clark explored the Louisiana Territory.
1825	The Erie Canal opened, providing improved transportation westward.
1838–1839	The Cherokee Indians were forced to migrate to Oklahoma from Georgia.
1845	The United States annexed Texas.
1846	A treaty with Great Britain added the Oregon country to the United States.
1846–1848	War with Mexico resulted in the acquisition of California and the Southwest.
1848	The discovery of gold in California inspired the gold rush.
1862	The Homestead Act promised free land to settlers in the West.

Developmental Activities (Lessons) Some of the activities are self-explanatory; following is a description of the others (the complete list is included in the week-by-week schedule; see figure 4.1).

Activity No. 2 As a result of hearing about and discussing the various personalities who traveled west, children will pretend they are one of these individuals and will write creatively about their reasons for coming west.

Activity No. 7 Students will write a newspaper article on the adventures of Lewis and Clark. The article will include a headline. The first sentence will contain information answering questions of who, what, when, where, and why. Remaining paragraphs will elaborate on the incident.

Activity No. 10   Using *Instructor* curriculum materials on North American Indian Personalities, children will work in their cooperative groups to prepare presentations on assigned Indian personalities. Each cooperative will be responsible for two to three personalities.

Activity No. 12   After a study of the Alamo, students will present a brief tableau.

Activity No. 14   Students will imagine that they are in New York City in 1848. They have heard of the discovery of gold at Sutter's Mill and have decided to join the rush to California. Students will be divided into three groups—each taking a different route.

Each group will be prepared to (1) draw the route on a map provided, (2) describe the

FIGURE 4.1 Week-By-Week Schedule

January

Monday	Tuesday	Wednesday	Thursday	Friday
15	16	17	18 Introductory activity (see description under Introductory activity). Lesson plan will be provided.	19 What types of people traveled across the frontier? Activity #1: Mapping the Old Northwest on individual maps.
22 Activity writing. Activity #2: (see description under Activities).	23 Westward Movement. Activity #3: Chart advantages and disadvantages of settling West. Chart similarities and differences.	24 Daniel Boone. Activity #4: Write poem on Daniel Boone.	25 Frontier Life. Activity #5: Chart similarities and differences between frontier life and life today. Lesson plan will be provided.	26 Outline Daniel Boone's life.
29 Across the Mississippi. Louisiana Purchase. Lewis and Clark. Activity #6: Map the Purchase.	30 More on Lewis and Clark. Activity #7: Newspaper writing (see description under Activities).	31 War of 1812. Review meaning of words of "Star Spangled Banner." Activity #8: Teach song—"Battle of New Orleans."		

(continued)

February

Monday	Tuesday	Wednesday	Thursday	Friday
			1 "Trail of Tears." Cooperative groups. Lesson plan will be provided. For homework have students inquire of any prejudiced behavior toward family in history.	**2** Jackson and the Indians. Activity #9: Map the removal of the Cherokee and other Indian groups.
5	**6**	**7** Indian personalities. Activity #10.	**8** Manifest Destiny/trappers, missionaries, pioneers, Conestogas. Lesson plan wil be provided.	**9** Activity #11: Make Conestoga wagons.
12	**13** War in Mexico.	**14** Writing activity #13: Newspaper writing (see description under Activity #7).	**15** Learning centers.	**16** Resource person in for presentation to answer interview questions. Students interview parents about ancestors moving west.
19	**20** California Gold Rush.	**21** Simulation. Lesson plan will be provided.	**22** Values. Lesson plan will be provided.	**23** Paint murals and portraits.

FIGURE 4.1 (*continued*)

February/March

Monday	Tuesday	Wednesday	Thursday	Friday
26	27 Mexican Americans in the West.	28 Hispanic Americans today.	1 Graphics. Lesson plan will be provided.	2
5	6 Practice for culminating activity.	7 Practice for culminating activity.	8 Culminating activity. Lesson plan will be provided.	9

FIGURE 4.1 (*continued*)

weather conditions the group members expect to face, (3) explain how they will deal with those weather conditions, and (4) tell what other dangers they expect and how they plan to deal with them.

Also used at another time during the day will be an Interact simulation curriculum resource entitled *Pioneers*. This resource consists of various simulation activities involving decision making on a wagon train.

As settlers heading west during the 1840s, the students face problems such as floods, droughts, blocked trails, snakes, Indians, and a lack of food. The would-be homesteaders must make numerous individual and small group decisions. While learning about wagon trains and pioneer life, students participate in individual and small group decision making. In addition, they learn how to take notes, how to outline material, and how to write a brief research paper.

Culminating Activity   Throughout the course of the unit, a time line will be maintained showing important events in the Westward Expansion. Charts will also be displayed illustrating the addition of land to the United States and other information learned in this unit. Various groups of children will be assigned to portray these important events in a creative manner; tableaux, creative drama, choral verse, story writing, poetry, and readers' theater will be employed.

Statement of Multicultural Perspective

How do I plan to create educational equity?   In order to assure achievement and success for all, student groups of two or three will be used to encourage cooperative learning. These techniques help to ensure peer support that stimulates learning. Sheltered English techniques, such as the use of pictures to help make history come alive, will be employed.

Material is also provided in Spanish. Because our Social Studies Spanish material is not as comprehensive as that provided in the English texts I translate much of the material to ensure educational equity. I also make use of tableaux, creative drama, and films to stimulate understanding and comprehension.

How do I plan to create intergroup harmony?   In forming the cooperative groups, careful attention will be made to ensure that there are both boys and girls in each group and a mixture of Hispanic children and the rest of our classroom population. Rewards are provided for harmonious, cooperative behavior. All groups work together toward a total classroom reward.

How do I plan to help children recognize, value, and respect the diversity among their classmates?   Encouraging students to respect the opinion of their peers and of others has been the main method used to teach and encourage respect of others. I act as a model by listening attentively to my students.

Compiling a chart of our similarities and differences as human beings has been an effective strategy in realizing how we are the same and different. Through a discussion of how boring the world would be if we ate the same foods, played the same physical education games, dressed the same, looked the same, and spoke the same, students will learn the value of diversity. Again, using the chart, students can appreciate the commonalities we all share.

In this unit in particular, students will have the opportunity to appreciate their differences and commonalities as they share the results of family interviews in which they will attempt to discover

1. the reasons their family has settled on the central coast of California; and
2. hardships that their families have incurred and may still be experiencing in the settlement process.

How do I plan to help the children feel what the Indians felt or the Mexican Americans felt when absorbed or banished from their land and culture?   I will have the children express their feelings when I move them away from a friend or when groups of children move them and their friends away from a play area in the playground. Also, the students should provide insights if asked how they would feel if their family, against their will, was forced to move by a group of individuals who wanted to live where the family does.

Another strategy would be to ask how they would feel if they had to stand in line for quite awhile and before reaching their goal, they were sent to the end of the line to start waiting again.

I plan to read accounts written by Cherokee Indians and Mexican Americans of their feelings during this period when the "Americans" won the West.

Bibliography

Buggey, Joanne L., Gerald A. Danzer, Charles L. Mitsakos, and C. Frederick Risinger. *America, America!* Glenview, Ill. Scott, Foresman, 1982.

Eibling, Harold. *Great Names in Our Country's Story.* Sacramento: California State Department of Education, 1962.

Hoover, Sharon. *North American Indian Personalities.* Troy, MO: Instructor Publications, 1980.

Life History of the United States. New York: Time Incorporated, 1963.

McCracken, Harold. *Winning the West.* Garden City, N.Y.: Doubleday, 1955.

Peck, Ira, and Steven Jantzen. *A Nation Conceived and Dedicated.* Albany, N.Y.: Scholastic Book Services, 1983.

Vuicich, George. *United States.* New York: McGraw-Hill, 1983.

World Book Encyclopedia. Chicago, Ill. Field Enterprises Educational Corporation, 1970.

Analysis of Unit

Do the lesson content and strategies promote or impede educational equity? Overall, in planning for this unit Mrs. Anderson has done a very good job of providing for educational equity. She plans to use sheltered English strategies, cooperative learning, the bilingual capability of several of her students, and her own fluency in Spanish and English to facilitate comprehension and learning for all her students. In addition, to increase motivation she has selected interesting and diverse activities that should appeal to a wide range of learners (music, arts and crafts, writing, creative dramatics, and interviewing). She has modified the unit to include content that will be personally meaningful to many students in the class. For example, in an attempt to relate the historical material more directly to her students' lives, interests, and ethnocultural background, Mrs. Anderson broke out of the time boundaries of her unit. In doing so she included twentieth-century content about the Mexican migration to the United States as well as the work and contributions of contemporary Mexican-American and Native-American leaders. This addition will allow her students to compare the nineteenth-century east-to-west migration/emigration of mainly White Americans to the primarily south to north migration/emigration of Mexican Americans. As described below, Mrs. Anderson also found a way to make each parent or caretaker a resource for this unit through her homework assignments.

Do the lesson content and strategies make use of, or help to develop, collaborative, empowering relationships among parents, students, and teachers? Mrs. Anderson's plans call for extensive use of cooperative learning with groups as heterogeneously structured as possible. In addition, in two specific homework assignments Mrs. Anderson placed parents or caretakers in a position to serve as important information resources for this unit. Students would interview family members to learn whether (a) the family had experienced any prejudicial behavior and (b) any of their ancestors had been a part of the westward movement. The latter assignment would be more multicultural or "multiperspective" in nature if the homework assignment included the northern movement (of Mexican Americans and others) and the west to east movement of various Asian Americans and Pacific Islanders to America.

Analysis of the first draft of the unit suggests that it could be improved by some simple steps designed to elicit greater parent participation. For example, a class newsletter to parents could inform them about the upcoming interviews, as well as the unit content; parents could be invited to (a) offer any special knowledge they possess and (b) visit the class for the unit's culminating activity, in which the students will present a variety of creative unit-related projects. Parent involvement in the unit, if only as an audience for student presentations, should heighten motivation and learning for some students. A different point of view could be introduced to the unit content if one or more of the parents volunteers to be a guest lecturer, poet, artist, or dramatic actor with material related to the unit.

Do the lesson content and strategies (structure) promote cultural pluralism in society or intergroup harmony in the classroom? In terms of promoting cultural pluralism— the ability and propensity to understand and value different cultures—a unit entitled "The Winning of the West: 1775–1850" holds great potential. But many teachers who grew up in schools that denigrated Native-American cultures may find it difficult to present a balanced portrayal of the interaction and clashes between the European, Mexican, and Native Americans. Even teachers like Mrs. Anderson, who clearly intends to present accurate information regarding the way successive American administrations unfairly treated Native Americans, may fall into the trap of comparing "White-American" culture and "Native-American" culture in ways that

1. work against attempts to appreciate and understand various American-Indian cultures on their own terms;
2. imply that American civilization in all dimensions was more advanced than the culture(s) of the American Indian; and
3. obscure the diversity that was characteristic of the various American-Indian tribes.

For example, in several places in the unit plan there is language suggesting that in telling about the winning of the American West, Mrs. Anderson will favor the American settlers and soldiers. As most American teachers and textbook writers consciously or unconsciously identify with the white settlers and the soldiers—the victors—one might wonder if this favoritism were both natural and inevitable. In fact, it is neither, and it is the teacher's responsibility to provide an accurate, balanced portrayal of both cultures, key events, and key actors—heroes and scoundrels—on both sides of the struggle. To help achieve accuracy and balance when teaching this and related units, the following ideas are worthy of consideration:

1. The title or theme of the unit should be examined to see whether it orients the unit toward one or another perspective. In this unit, to increase the orientation to multiperspectivism, we would change the title to "The Expansion of the American Nation: 1775–1850."
2. The categorization of unit content should be reviewed for evidence of possible bias. For example, under "Values" in the web, why will students have the opportunity to appreciate the courage and determination of the pioneers, but not the courage and determination of various American Indians who, against all odds, steadfastly attempted to hold onto their land and way of life?
3. In describing unit objectives, the teacher should be more specific in describing the "plight" of the American Indian. Through the media, particularly motion pictures made prior to 1980 and shared folklore, American students become aware of Indian massacres and atrocities; rarely, however, do they hear about atrocities and massacres carried out by U.S. soldiers, such as occurred at the Sand Creek Massacre. Thus, unit objective six might read:

Students will learn about the forced marches, massacres, broken treaties, burnt villages, destroyed crops, and inadequate reservations the American Indians experienced during their struggles with the "Americans."

And where possible, when students learn of this tragic history, they should hear about it from Native-American authors as well as authors who bring a traditional Eurocentric viewpoint to the creation of their historical tale.[5]

4. Some of the generalizations in this unit and the main ideas and facts they lead to are also worthy of revision. Generalization number three states: "When an advanced civilization meets a less-advanced civilization, the less-advanced civilization will be assimilated or lose its national identity." As structured, this generalization and its related main ideas suggest that one civilization or culture (that of the White European) was more advanced or superior, across the board, than the less-advanced civilization of the American Indian and Mexican American. A related generalization, designed to avoid the less advanced/more advanced comparison, would read:

When cultures with different values come into conflict over land (and over other economic and political rights, the group with the technological advantage in weaponry will usually prevail.

Please note that the word "usually" is included in the generalization to indicate that this behavioral science generalization, like most others, is tentative and nonconclusive. As Banks notes, such generalizations "will have some exceptions," and "they often contain qualifying words."[6]

Generalization number two, "Adversity Breeds Leadership," has this main idea: "A number of aggressive leaders were prominent during the Westward Expansion." It, too, is worthy of rethinking. On the one hand it is a bit narrow, almost a cliche like "necessity is the mother of invention"; on the other, it doesn't seem to be supported by the main idea or the accompanying information. For example, Sacajawea and Lewis and Clark were not "aggressive leaders" and their exploits were not directly related to adversity or hard times. In addition, except for Sacajawea, who was not an Indian leader, all the men who are presented as "aggressive leaders" were White except for Jim Beckwourth whose racial heritage was a blend of Black and White. In planning integrated units, the generalizations, concepts, main ideas, and facts need to be logically related and mutually supportive and the generalizations should be testable and verifiable.

A broader generalization that simultaneously meets these criteria and continues to aim toward the material Mrs. Anderson wants to present is this:

As cultures struggle to thrive and survive, various types of leaders will typically emerge.

Main ideas supporting the validity of this generalization could incorporate information about Mexican-American, American-Indian, and White-American leaders. This would help to increase the students' knowledge of pertinent cultural/ethnic groups and would reinforce their growing inclination and ability to analyze events with a multicultural perspective. The following main ideas would serve these purposes:

1. The groups who came into conflict during the country's Westward Expansion were served by various kinds of leaders.
2. Various types of leaders played key roles in creating opportunities for White Americans to settle in the ever-expanding "American West."
3. Various types of leaders played key roles in the American Indians' attempt to maintain their way of life.

These main ideas would allow Mrs. Anderson to include all of the White-American leaders she originally listed and to discuss their lives and contributions in a well-rounded manner. It would also allow students to learn about a more diverse set of "American" leaders, namely those who made contributions as representatives of the Mexicans and American Indians who struggled to maintain their way of life.

Does the lesson content help to increase students' knowledge regarding various cultural and ethnic groups?   The unit's objectives, generalizations, and main ideas indicate that in addition to the historical figures mentioned, who are mainly White, information about contemporary Native-American and Mexican-American personalities would be included. Several of the suggestions above show how the generalizations could be modified to increase the amount of knowledge students gain about specific nineteenth-century ethnic groups, namely Mexican Americans and Native Americans. But the refinement and multiculturalization of this unit could extend beyond the generalizations and content proposed by Mrs. Anderson, and in a manner that would expand students' knowledge of ethnic groups outside the United States.

The story of the country's westward growth is filled with significant and traumatic conflict between the cultures that confronted each other on this part of the continent. Because of this, the concept of cultural conflict should receive special emphasis in this unit. Generalizations, main ideas, and facts related to this concept would undoubtedly provide the students with a richer understanding of why the Whites and American Indians found it impossible to coexist peacefully. A study of cultural conflict might also help students understand the complexity of contemporary U.S. relationships with nations such as Iran, Iraq, and Cuba, as well as conflicts in Peru, Venezuela, Brazil, and Malaysia where the land and economic and political freedom of indigenous rain forest tribes are rapidly being destroyed by a combination of private and governmental forces.

Units that link the past to the present and provide students with conceptual tools to help them understand ethnic and nation-to-nation interaction throughout history are both motivating and educationally appropriate, particularly from the perspective of citizenship education. What follows now is a broad generalization, a related main idea and several facts which, together, illustrate the type of understanding that cultural conflict-related generalizations can produce.

The Generalization

When cultures with very different beliefs about religion, land ownership and usage, and government confront each other on the same land, clear communication and peaceful coexistence will often be difficult to achieve.

A Related Main Idea

Major differences between European-American cultures and American-Indian cultures made clear communication and peaceful coexistence between the two cultures difficult to achieve.

Some Related Facts (or Supporting Information)

1. In European culture, it was assumed that land was a commodity that could be broken into parts and owned by individuals; these individuals could prevent others from using the land.
2. The Indians believed that all people could use the land as long as they treated it with

respect; they thought the land was sacred and could not be sold any more than the air or the sea.

3. When, in exchange for gifts, American Indians gave Europeans permission to use their lands, many did not realize that from a European viewpoint they were also giving up their own rights to use the land forever.

4. Because of their feudalistic background, the Europeans looked for kings among the Indians and assumed that Indian chiefs had absolute authority over their tribes. However, the authority of most chiefs was limited by the tribal council. In a sense, the Indian tribes and councils had a ratification process that the Europeans did not take into account.[7]

Final Comments

In teaching this unit, Mrs. Anderson used an integrated approach to language arts, one that allowed her to select whole pieces of literature (books, poems, newspaper articles, etc.) that *all* her students would read simultaneously to advance their literacy skills. To add depth to this unit and to help bring the historical period to life, Mrs. Anderson chose to have her entire class read (in English and Spanish versions) the *Sign of the Beaver* by Elizabeth Speare; this was an excellent choice for her generalizations as well as the ones we have added, and the choice is worthy of emphasis as we study how to increase the multicultural dimension of units of instruction.

The selection of written and visual materials for units is a pivotal aspect of multi-cultural teaching, and the content of a novel can work for or against the goals of multicultural education. In this instance the teacher's selection supports several goals of multicultural education as well as her own specific unit objectives. *Sign of the Beaver* highlights a pre-Revolutionary War (1768) relationship between two teenage boys, Matthew Hallowell, the son of a White settler in Maine, and Attean, the grandson of Saknis, a Penobscot Indian chief. The development of their relationship allowed Mrs. Anderson's students to see two boys transcend the barriers established by their own cultural stereotypes to establish a relationship based on respect and mutual support. In addition, the interaction between Attean and Matthew provided an opportunity for students to gain appreciation for the substantial cultural differences that led to conflict between the Indians and Whites, such as different beliefs about owning and using land, and the complexity and rewards of cross-cultural relationships. Such opportunities contribute greatly to achieving the general goals of multicultural education as well as the specific objectives of this unit.

UNIT TWO: ANCIENT EGYPT

The second unit to be discussed in this chapter, *Ancient Egypt*, will integrate elements drawn from several units. A number of teachers contributed to its content, but Mrs. Jackson was the major contributor, so we refer to her as the designer of the unit. Mrs. Jackson prepared this integrated unit for her sixth-grade class, which was diverse in terms of ethnicity and socioeconomic status; half the class was White American and the remaining half was Hispanic, Asian, and African American. As we did with *Winning the West*, prior to discussing the multiculturalization of Mrs. Jackson's unit, we will enumerate its various components.

Overview Statement

The purpose of this unit is to help students develop an understanding of how and why ancient Egyptian culture developed, selected characteristics of the culture, and the influence of Egyptian culture on other cultures.

Categorization of Unit Content and Strategies

HISTORY/SOCIAL STUDIES

Geography of Ancient Egypt
- Trade Routes
- Resources
- Regions
- Climate
- Location—Size

Life of the People
- Family Life
- City Life
- Language
- The People

Work of the People
- Agriculture
- Manufacturing
- Trade—Transportation

Activities of the People
- Education
- Religion
- The Arts
- The Sciences

Invasions

Contributions to Civilization

SCIENCE

Mummification/Embalming

ART

Murals
Draw/Create Hieroglyphics
Illustrate Family Life, Homes, Fashion

Make Mummies
Make Temple
Make Pyramid
Make Masks
Duplicating 'kas'

MATH

Egyptian Numerals and Fractions
Dimensions in Pyramids
- Height—feet
- Weight—tons
- Area—acres

LANGUAGE ARTS

Dramatic Play
Role-Play
Writing Projects
Poetry
Report Writing
Spelling
Simulations
Cooperative Learning
Oral Reports
Tableaux
Interviews
Outlining
Monologues
The novel *His Majesty, Queen Hatshepsut* by Dorothy Carter will be read to the class.

GUEST SPEAKER

Mortician

Selected Unit Objectives

COGNITIVE

1. Students will demonstrate their knowledge of the geography of ancient Egypt—its location, size, natural resources, and climate.
2. Students will demonstrate their knowledge of ancient Egyptian family life, city life, and language.
3. Students will demonstrate their knowledge of the various types of work ancient. Egyptians engaged in, including agriculture, manufacturing, and mining.
4. Students will describe various facets of ancient Egyptian culture, including its education, religion, arts, and science.
5. Students will identify different invaders and conquerors of ancient Egypt and reasons the invaders were successful.

SELECTED SKILLS

1. Students will be able to locate Egypt, the Red Sea, the Mediterranean Sea, and the Nile River on maps and globes.
2. Students will be able to trace on maps and globes the trading routes of the ancient Egyptians with other countries.
3. Students will be able to trace on maps and globes the coastal, desert, and fertile regions, plus Upper and Lower Egypt.
4. Students will be able to research, successfully complete, and present written reports about ancient Egypt.
5. Students will work cooperatively in their groups completing various assignments.
6. Students will use higher-level thinking skills in class discussions.

AFFECTIVE (ATTITUDES)

1. Students will appreciate the beauty of the pyramids and the great amount of labor required to build them.
2. Students will appreciate the way of life of the ancient Egyptians and the way it is both similar to and different from our contemporary way of life.
3. Students will appreciate the dependence of the ancient Egyptians on the Nile River.
4. Students will appreciate the beauty and antiquity of the treasures of ancient Egypt that today can be seen in various museums.

Generalizations, Main Ideas, and Supporting Information

Generalization   In both ancient and contemporary cultures we find human beings developing various ideas about life after death.

Main Idea   Ancient Egyptians took great care in preparing for life after death.

Information

1. They denied that death ended the existence of a person who led a good life.
2. They believed that the next world would be like Egypt in its richest and most enjoyable form.
3. They built stone tombs and filled them with clothing, food, furnishings, and jewelry for use in the next world.
4. They embalmed their dead and wrapped their bodies in layers of cloth.

Generalization   People tend to congregate and form societies in areas that have natural resources.

Main Idea   The ancient Egyptians built most of their villages and towns along the banks of the Nile River.

Information

1. Floodwaters of the Nile deposited rich, black soil on the land year after year.
2. Egyptian farmers planted their crops on this fertile soil.
3. Near the First Cataract, Egyptians mined granite and sandstone.
4. In the desert and hills to the east lay deposits of copper, manganese, and turquoise.
5. Without the Nile River no one could live in Egypt.

Generalization   In many ancient and contemporary societies the people are divided into separate groups along social, religious, and economic lines.

Main Idea   The ancient Egyptians were divided into four social classes.

Information

1. The four social classes were (1) royalty and nobles; (2) artisans, craftsmen, and merchants; (3) workers; and (4) slaves.
2. The professional army gradually became almost a separate class.
3. Egypt had no fixed caste system.
4. A person of the poorest class could rise to the highest offices in the land.

Generalization   In ancient cultures, as in contemporary cultures, people developed religious beliefs to help them deal with aspects of life they did not fully understand.

Main Idea   The ancient Egyptians believed that gods and goddesses took part in human activity from birth to death.

Information

1. The Egyptians believed in many different gods.
2. At one time each city had a god of its own.
3. Later, all Egyptians worshipped Amon—one of the great gods.
4. However, the people still felt loyalty to the god who lived in the temple of their hometown.
5. Following are three gods who were known throughout the land.
   a. Amon of Thebes was worshipped as King of the gods.
   b. Ptah, the god of Memphis, was the patron god of craftsmen.
   c. Bes, a comic dwarf god, brought good luck and happiness in the home.

Generalization   In both the ancient and contemporary world certain societies stand out as leaders in political, economic, and technological development.

Main Idea   In its time ancient Egypt was an enlightened, advanced society.

Information

a. Pyramid design and construction showed architectural expertise.
b. The embalming/mummification process is still studied and admired by scientists today.
c. Egyptians made significant contributions in terms of recorded history and language development.

Introductory, Selected Developmental, and Culminating Activities

Introductory Activity   A series of overheads will be shown to introduce the students to ancient Egypt, accompanied by a brief overview of the country and its culture. Students will be encouraged to create questions for study in the forthcoming unit. Students will work in their cooperative groups.

Possible Introductory Questions

1. Why and how did the ancient Egyptians build the temples?
2. How did they embalm their dead?
3. Why did they bury their dead with valuable jewels and treasures?
4. Where are the treasures today?
5. What do the different hieroglyphics mean?
6. Why did the ancient Egyptians gather papyrus?
7. What are the names of some of their gods?
8. Who was Tutankhamen and what were some of the treasures found in his tomb?
9. Where is Egypt on the map?
10. How did the ancient Egyptians live? What was their work like, and their family life? What kind of games did they play, and what were their homes like? How did they dress?

Developmental Activities (Lessons)

Activity #1   On individual maps students will locate ancient Egypt, the Nile River, regions of Upper and Lower Egypt, trading routes, surrounding countries, and important cities. The lesson on geography will stress five themes: location, physical and cultural features that give an area an identity, interaction between humans and the environment, communication and transportation systems, and regional considerations.

Activity #2   Children will work in their cooperative groups supporting and helping each other as they learn new information. A leader will keep the group on task. Questions are written on the board for the groups to work on. Groups receive points according to good cooperative behavior exhibited. When students return to their regular seats, all write the answers and two papers are chosen from each group as representative answers for further points for their groups. A reward is given when all groups accumulate 10 points.

Activity #3   After a study of hieroglyphics and their meaning, students will create hieroglyphics for each letter of the alphabet. Each cooperative group will be responsible for five to six letters. Students then will write notes to each other using their hieroglyphics. Also, groups will be responsible for recreating original hieroglyphics for display.

Activity #4   As a result of studying the mummification process, students will work in their cooperative groups and pretend they are creating a mummy. In each group there will be the priest, the embalmer, the cutter, the remover, and the organ wrapper. Each group will receive one dough body shape made out of salt and flour, two plastic knives, one shoe box, five cotton balls, and a small container of spices. The dough shape that the group will receive will have the internal organs inside represented with rubber bands and candies. Students work according to what their role dictates.

Activity #5   Alone or with the help of a partner, students will trace on craft paper their shadow picture. Each student will cut out his ka. Students in turn guess who each ka is. This activity reinforces the Egyptian belief that each person had a ba, or soul, and a ka, an invisible twin. When the individual died, his ba and ka were released from his body and lived on in the tomb. The ba would still maintain contact with the person's family and friends while the ka traveled back and forth at night from the body to the new world. In order for the person to live forever, the ba and the ka had to be able to recognize the body or they could not return to it.

Activity #6   This activity will focus on temple building. The book entitled *Make This Egyptian Temple* by Ashman (Tulsa, Okla: EDC Publishing, 1990) lends itself well to this activity because it is a cut-out model of a temple. Different portions of the temple will be distributed to the groups to assemble. Finished group products will then be joined so the class can see its recreation of a complete Egyptian temple.

Activity #7   This activity will focus on mask making. Papier mâché is applied to a paper plate that has had eyeholes cut out. The dried papier mâché is painted white. The face is brilliantly painted with tempera paints. Some students will continue to work on the recreation of the Egyptian temple.

Activity #8   This activity centers on poetry writing and reading. Drawing on material learned in this unit, students will be encouraged to write one or more poems that use patterns introduced in class, such as the cinquain, limerick, question poem, or biopoem. Students will be invited to enhance their writing with a drawing.

Activity #9   Working in their cooperative learning groups, students will exchange the most interesting facts they learned in the process of completing their research report and will ask questions of each other. Selected students will present their reports to the entire class.

Culminating Activity   During the unit's culminating activity each child, or a small group of students, will present one or more of the following:

1. a special poem, story, song, drawing or painting, craft project, original reader's theater presentation, or other expressive project related to the unit;
2. the results of their special report on ancient Egypt;
3. the information in the unit that they found most interesting; or
4. the questions they are still pondering.

For this activity the class will be transformed into an ancient Egyptian temple and special guests (parents and other relatives, the principal, His Majesty Queen Hatshepsut, the Pharaoh Djoser, and his great architect and adviser Imhotep). The latter three will be special "spiritual" guests to whom all the students would direct their remarks.

Statement of Multicultural Perspective

How do I plan to promote educational equity?   I will use various strategies that have been shown to stimulate widespread academic achievement. Most notably, I will make use of several forms of cooperative group learning during the unit. All the students in my class are members of a dyad or triad as well as a larger cooperative group, and students are quite used to helping each other learn. In addition, part of the direction of the unit will be influenced by questions the students themselves generate. My students like to engage in collaborative planning and enjoy seeing their names next to the questions they have created, even when they themselves do not follow up on research to answer the question. In my class, creating questions is an activity worthy of recognition. During the unit I will include activities that I know my students find interesting. This class is an expressive group, they like to write, paint, construct, perform, and listen, particularly when I read to them. Therefore, this unit will have a variety of imaginative and expressive activities. To bring history alive during the course of the unit I will read and tell them the story of *His Majesty, Queen Hatshepsut,* and will have Hatshepsut and others make an appearance at our culminating event. Finally, with regard to equity, I have found that my students like to contribute to the specific content of the culminating unit quiz; they find this motivating and it favorably influences the achievement of many of the students. In other areas of the curriculum, I make use of mastery learning strategies, but I find this approach less applicable for my integrated units of instruction.

How do I promote positive intergroup harmony?   My main strategy here is cooperative learning. I am quite open with my students; we all know from current events reports and class discussions during January and February about Black history, that in terms of getting along with each other, most Americans have ample room for growth. I share the research about cooperative group learning with them, and then throughout the year place them in cooperative learning groups that are heterogeneous in nature. In addition, during my current events time I will occasionally tell stories that illustrate integrated groups of people successfully working together to solve problems. Parenthetically, this unit will provide an example of an ancient multiracial civilization in which people of various colors apparently worked together with the relative absence of color prejudice and racism that has been a major part of modern history. Finally, I try to build in all my students a positive, success-oriented identity; when they feel good about themselves I think they will be in a better position to have positive relationships with others.

How will I promote collaboration among myself, parents, and students?   My parents know that I welcome their support and presence. About every six weeks parents receive a class newsletter that updates them on the general curriculum objectives for the next two-month period and invites them to participate in various ways. For this unit, for example, parents with special interest or expertise about ancient Egypt will be invited to contact me, and all parents will be invited to witness or participate in our culminating event. Parents have also accepted the responsibility of monitoring their child's homework packet for neatness and completeness.

How will I promote cultural pluralism?   I believe that exposure to the contributions that different cultures have made as well as to the complexity of these cultures will produce in my students a more positive attitude toward cultures and civilizations different from their own. The content of this unit on ancient Egypt will serve this objective well.

How will I use this unit to promote in my students a multicultural perspective vis-à-vis current events and history?   I will address this mainly by introducing my students to the socioeconomic diversity that existed in ancient Egypt. They will contrast the lives and attitudes of slaves and the royalty and artisans of ancient Egypt. This will remind them that history can be viewed from more than one perspective and as they study about different civilizations, they should wonder about the story that would be told by people in different segments of a society.

Bibliography

Aliki. *Mummies Made in Egypt.* New York: Harper & Row, 1979.

Allan, Tony. *The Time Traveler Book of Pharaohs and Pyramids.* Tulsa, Okla.: EDC Publishing, 1977.

Carter, Dorothy Sharp. *His Majesty, Queen Hatshepsut.* New York: HarperCollins, 1987.

Casson, Lionel, and the editors of Time-Life Books. *Ancient Egypt.* New York: Time Incorporated, 1965.

Champollion, Jacques. *The World of the Egyptians.* Bergamo, Italy: Minerva, SA, 1989.

Glubok, Shirley. *The Art of Ancient Egypt.* New York: Atheneum, 1962.

Hart, George. *Exploring the Past, Ancient Egypt.* New York: Harcourt Brace World, 1989.

Ions, Veronica. *Egyptian Mythology.* New York: Bedrick, 1983.

Macaulay, David. *Pyramid.* New York: Houghton·Mifflin, 1975.

Nesbit, E. *The Story of the Amulet.* New York: Dell, 1987.

Sethus, Michel. *The Days of the Pharaohs.* Morristown, N.J.: Silver Burdett, 1986.

Stuart, Gene S. *Secrets from the Past.* Washington, D.C.: National Geographic Society, 1979.

Unstead, R. J. *An Egyptian Town.* Lanham, Md.: Barnes & Noble, 1986.

World Book Encyclopedia. Chicago: Field Enterprises, 1970.

Unit Analysis and Multiculturalization Remarks

Once again we will use several of the evaluative questions for multiculturalization to guide our analysis.

Do the lesson content and structure promote or impede educational equity? There are various ways to think about educational equity in this unit. In our earlier remarks in this text we focused on maximizing the achievement of each student in the classroom and encouraged teachers to give special consideration to students who were members of groups who have experienced oppression and unequal access to various political and economic resources. The objective is to make certain that such inequalities are not reproduced in our contemporary classrooms. It is clear from Mrs. Jackson's remarks that she is taking steps to ensure that *all* the students in her class have a successful learning experience. To motivate her students toward the unit content, Mrs. Jackson will employ a number of commendable strategies. These include collaborative planning of unit content; heterogeneous cooperative learning groups; imaginative arts activities that include Mrs. Jackson's own telling of the story of Queen Hatshepsut; and presentations by intriguing visitors, in this case a mortician. In this class one senses, first, that the needs and interests of special learners have received professional consideration, and second, that the unit activities have been designed to stimulate intellectual growth in all the students, as opposed to a top-level of rapid learners. In short, in this class there appears to be equal access to learning for all 32 students.

This judgment notwithstanding, in the lives and lessons of teachers there is usually room for improvement, or at least for considering ideas. This unit is no exception. For her 32 students Mrs. Jackson did much to promote equity in terms of access to learning and actual participation and achievement. But, under the equity question it is also appropriate to ask: In what sense was the content of this unit equitable compared to what good sixth-grade students are learning about ancient Egypt in other parts of the country? In other words, are my students being challenged at the same level as yours? Is the content of my unit sufficiently rigorous when compared with units that have been designed elsewhere?

With this comparative sense of equity in mind, we believe there is some room for conceptual improvement in Mrs. Jackson's unit. To illustrate this point we will draw on selected components of a sixth-grade ancient Egypt unit designed by Jon Wiles and Joseph Bondi.[8]

In their interdisciplinary resource unit Wiles and Bondi identify the following conceptual goals among others. They want their unit to

1. acquaint students with the sources of our knowledge of the past: material remains, artifacts, oral traditions, pictorial data, and written records;
2. train students in the use of source materials so they can draw valid conclusions or frame reasonable hypotheses on the basis of the evidence, and thus learn elements of the historical method;
3. help students understand the values and limitations of various source materials in reconstructing our account of the past;
4. lead students to see that all racial and ethnic groups have similar innate capacities and intelligence and that historical circumstances and environment, as well as heredity, determine a people's cultural achievement.[9]

From these goals we can infer that Wiles and Bondi are not interested in merely exposing students to textbook chapters written for sixth graders by reputable scholars and pictures gathered by archaeologists. They want students to have the opportunity to *think* and *hypothesize* like archaeologists, anthropologists, and historians. The attempt to create situations wherein students will engage in higher and more complex levels of thinking is illustrated in one of the unit's behavioral objectives. They state that the learner will be able to "write a description of Egyptian religion and hypothesize reasons for the form it took."[10] By including such goals and behavioral objectives in their unit, Wiles and Bondi place teachers in a good position to remind their students of the difficulties in creating an accurate or definitive history of ancient Egypt. This, in turn, will help students understand why the history of ancient Egypt, indeed history in general, is open to ongoing review and reinterpretation. It is healthy for future scholars to see that the experts of their day still have important disagreements about ancient Egyptian civilization and further, that such debate is part of the continuing scholarly conversation, a dialogue to which they someday may contribute. In addition, because the reinterpretation is influenced by relatively new scientific tools, such as radiocarbon dating to determine the age of fossils and the use of the magnetometer to locate ancient cities, students should be invited to make special reports on these and other new procedures.

Although Mrs. Jackson's objectives and activities would engage her students in creative activities, Wiles and Bondi's goals and objectives more clearly view the students as future scholars and scientists. The overriding goal of their unit is not just to uncover information about ancient Egypt but to begin the training and recruitment process that provokes sixth graders to see themselves and their fellow students as the scientists, historians, and artists of the future. Educational equity and teachers' expectations are interrelated, and both influence future careers as well as current academic achievement.

The fourth goal of Wiles and Bondi, which pertains to the similar capacities and intelligence of various racial and ethnic groups, indirectly relates to the recruitment process listed above as well as to the continuing debate among scholars about important aspects of ancient Egyptian civilization. With regard to recruitment, what is it that stimulates twelve-year-old children to dream that someday they may be creative scientists, authors, teachers, entertainers, architects, or doctors? Surely, part of the stimulus comes from the world around them. In the world they live in, do they see people who resemble themselves serving in such positions? The study of the past can be a part of this stimulus if such study reveals (a) that men and women of various colors made important contributions to the civilizations that have paved the way to our own, and (b) that in different times and places racism and sexism prevented men and women from making the contributions they were capable of. In the case of ancient Egyptian civilization, students should learn that over a 3,500-year period, the leaders and creators of this civilization were people of various colors—tan, brown, and black. Although this multicolored depiction of ancient Egyptians may seem obvious or perhaps trivial to some contemporary teachers, it is noteworthy that for African-American scholars of the stature of the late W. E. B. Du Bois[11] and the late St. Claire Drake[12] the color and racial types of the ancient Egyptians was an issue of great importance. As Drake explained:

> Crucial in the Afro-American coping process has been their identification, over a time span of more than two centuries, with ancient Egypt and Ethiopia as symbols of black initiative and success long before their enslavement on the plantations of the New World. Great myths are always part of the group-coping strategies.[13]

At the same time that African Americans were identifying with the creators of ancient Egyptian civilization, however, influential twentieth-century European historians like Arnold Toynbee were writing a history that strongly contradicted the African contribution to Egyptian civilization. In *A Study of History*, a work that was later serialized in the widely read *Reader's Digest*, Toynbee asserted that "the only one of the primary races . . . which has not made a creative contribution to any one of our twenty-one civilizations is the Black race."[14]

Although Toynbee's remarks were made several decades later, it was to counter such flagrant distortions that Du Bois and others created the American Negro Academy in 1897. Today, because of the work of Du Bois and Drake, among others, when teachers introduce sixth, seventh, and eighth graders to what may be their first systematic exposure to Egyptian history, they can choose to ignore the debate about Egyptian racial and ethnic characteristics, focus on it as a main element in the unit, or introduce it through a series of invitations for inquiry. We recommend choosing one of the latter two options and will discuss our rationale under the next evaluative question.

Do the lesson content and structure increase students' proclivity and ability to see and think with a multicultural perspective, or is the content monocultural and/or inaccurate? First, we consider the content of Mrs. Jackson's unit slightly monocultural and inaccurate because it does nothing to suggest that for significant periods in ancient Egyptian history, Egyptian pharaohs, soldiers, priests, artisans, and slaves were Black Africans. If this basic fact is ignored, the unit silently endorses the contention that ancient Egypt was in no way influenced by Black-African men and women from Egypt and other African nations such as Kush, which in fact conquered ancient Egypt somewhere around 750 B.C.[15] This is an extreme Eurocentric perspective, and it is within this perspective that ancient Egypt is described as a "near Eastern" civilization rather than an "advanced African civilization" as Du Bois and other vindicationist African-American scholars stressed.[16]

In addition to essentially ignoring Black-African participation and contributions to Egyptian civilization, Mrs. Jackson, by reading passages of Carter's *His Majesty, Queen Hatshepsut* to her class subtly reinforces the contention that Egyptian pharaohs were non-Negroid. Where it is not subtly reinforcing, it is sending a mixed message. Consider the following data from the novel:

1. In the picture on the book cover Hatshepsut has copper or light brown skin, large lips, a broad strong nose, and eyes that appear more or less Asian. The women attendants have their hair in thick black braids similar to the "cornrows" one sees contemporary African-American women wear occasionally.

2. In the black-and-white pencil drawings in the book, the skin coloring of the Egyptians suggests some degree of darkness, but the noses and lips of the Egyptians—royalty and servants—have shapes commonly considered "white" as opposed to "black."

3. Descriptions of Egyptian, Libyan, and Syrian characters subtly reinforce the non-Black image. On page 40 it is suggested that Libyans have crinkly hair, but this adjective is never used to describe Egyptian hair (and the pictures uniformly suggest straight hair for the Egyptians).

> His majesty's pet monkey . . . Ini . . . yanked the wig off the Vizier's wife . . . then dropped it neatly on the Libyan ambassador's head. The very ambassador who is so vain of his thatch of crinkly hair.

And, in describing the Syrian ambassador and her future lover and adviser, Senmut, Hatshepsut, who is the narrator throughout the novel, gives us a contrast in noses and a slight sense of the Egyptian concept of beauty filtered through Dorothy Carter's imagination.

> The Syrian envoy is as always obnoxious. With his greasy face and dirty beard and little piggy snout.[17]

> His face [Senmut's] is strong rather than handsome, the nose a prominent beak, lines about the mouth deep as though slit by a knife, a brow cut off by the kind of short curly wig that went out of fashion years ago.[18]

Finally, in describing her 15-year-old stepson, Thutmose III, on his return from a 3-year sojourn in the Egyptian desert, we hear more about royal Egyptian noses.

> He appears bursting with health, taller, tanner, more robust. And his nose—that too, has grown. A true Thutmosid beak, wide and hooked, it dominates his face.[19]

So, in this novel published in 1987 we see two wide, prominent, beaked noses on two leading eighteenth-dynasty leaders, and tan skin on Thutmose III, but no metaphor or language to suggest that either of these individuals was Negroid in appearance. Provocatively, Drake, whose book *Black Folk Here and There: An Essay in History and Anthropology* was also published in 1987, notes that the pharaohs of the eighteenth dynasty, during the time Hatshepsut reigned, were Negroid in appearance. In describing the Pharaoh Tutankhamen and his family, Drake wrote, "This family was negroid, as was the entire Eighteenth Dynasty. The most highly respected Egyptologists admit that."[20] And in various other places in his text Drake makes clear his conviction that Negro pharaohs were a factor in all the Egyptian dynasties. For example, he states:

> Sculpture in the round, bas-relief friezes, and colored paintings on walls and papyrus provide enough data for stating conclusively that some distinctly Negro pharaohs appeared in all the dynasties and were numerous in a few. Portraits of others give the impression of a Negro ancestral strain. In addition to the Kings, their wives, and members of the courts, religious functionaries and officials of the state show similar tendencies, as do other individuals in a wide variety of occupations.[21]

What should elementary teachers do with the claims of respected scholars like Drake, when other apparently informed authors such as Carter and the writers of the ancient Egypt chapter in the 1991 Houghton Mifflin series choose not to mention the Negroid presence that Drake and other scholars see so vividly in ancient Egyptian history?[22]

We believe that teachers should not ignore the strong assertions made by Drake and others such as Martin Bernal[23] and Du Bois; but they should not accept them uncritically either. What they should do is keep an open mind to the idea that in ancient Egyptian history we might have another example of "Black" history lost, stolen, or strayed. Indeed, racist attitudes that were so prevalent in eighteenth-, nineteenth-, and twentieth-century

Europe and America may well have prevented European scholars from seeing the physical pattern so clearly perceived by Drake and others. On the other hand, it is not clear that identifying ancient Egyptians as "Black" or "negroid" based on nostril size and high cheekbones represents good scholarship.[24] But, as noted, it is not the fact of Negro-looking pharaohs that we want young Black, White, Hispanic, and other students to read about. It is the theory, or possibility of such a fact, that we would call to their attention, and then by pictures, essays, interviews, and other evidence we would encourage them to draw their own tentative conclusions. In this case, discussing the Eurocentric "Near Eastern" White version of ancient Egypt alongside the Afrocentric version of a Black/Negro-dominated ancient Egypt would provide students an important opportunity. They could consider history writing and making from different perspectives, and see that the history they read is sometimes shaped by the political purposes and social needs of the author.

Finally, although we believe that the precise ethnic and racial background of many Egyptian pharaohs is open to question, we consider it fair to assume that a good number of Egyptian pharaohs and queens did not look like Yul Brynner and Anne Baxter in Hollywood's *Ten Commandments*. At the minimum, a unit on ancient Egypt should convey that many of its pharaohs and citizens were people of color (non-White), people who were apparently much less color- and race-oriented than contemporary Americans, Canadians, Australians, Japanese, and others. Perhaps ancient Egypt has more to offer us than pyramids and mummies.

UNIT THREE: SUPPORT AND MOVEMENT OF THE HUMAN BODY

The third unit to be reviewed, entitled *Support and Movement of the Human Body*, was developed by a student teacher, Stacy Williams (pseudonym), for a combination fourth-fifth-grade class in a small, semirural, coastal school district. Her class of 23 students was 98 percent White American coming for the most part from middle-class or lower middle-class families (22 out of 23 students). It was relatively free of special learners. One child had an individual education plan (IEP) and was also designated limited English proficient; one other student participated in the school's free breakfast and lunch program. The IEP/LEP learner received one-to-one instructional support from a learning disability (LD) teacher who pulled her out for 30- to 45-minute sessions 3 days per week. The content of these lessons was heavily influenced by classroom teacher input. Prior to discussing the unit taught in this class, several components from Ms. Williams's unit plan are displayed below so that you can form your own preliminary opinions about the content:

1. Introductory statement
2. Generalizations and main ideas
3. General objectives of unit
4. Key questions
5. Introductory, closing, and selected developmental activities
6. Statement regarding incorporation of a multicultural perspective
7. Evaluation procedures and unit evaluation
8. Bibliography

Introductory Statement

This science unit is designed for both the fourth and fifth graders in this combination class. The unit focuses mainly on the skeletal and muscular systems of the human body, which provide for support and movement. The human body is a very complex organism, and through studying these systems the students will begin to understand that many components must work together to create a properly functioning body.

The unit will last approximately three weeks, and although it is primarily a science unit, literature, physical education, art, and math will be integrated into it. The fourth graders will read Lynne Reid Banks's *The Indian in the Cupboard*, which tells of a plastic miniature Indian who comes to life; the fifth graders, who have already read this book, will read Scott O'Dell's *Island of the Blue Dolphins*. During the unit we will draw on *The Indian in the Cupboard* by discussing "what makes something real" and will connect this discussion to the systems of the body that sustain life.

Generalizations and Main Ideas

A. Smaller components work together to create larger systems.
  I. The healthy human body is a complex organism of interdependent systems successfully working together.
    a. Individual bones work together to create the skeletal system.
    b. Individual muscles work together to create the muscular system.
    c. The skeletal system, muscular system, and other systems work together to move and support the human body.
  II. When a system is not working properly, complications occur that can often be compensated for or corrected.

   a. Injured bones and muscles often heal to become healthy bones and muscles
      again.
   b. Some disabilities are permanent but can be compensated for with special
      equipment or training.

General Objectives

1. Students will describe the functions of the skeletal system.
2. Students will identify several major bones of the human body.
3. Students will identify the four types of joints and give examples of each type.
4. Students will compare the functions of ligaments, tendons, and cartilage.
5. Students will describe the functions of the muscular system.
6. Students will compare voluntary and involuntary muscles.
7. Students will describe the effects of exercise on muscles.
8. Students will identify injuries to bones and muscles.
9. Students will become familiar with adaptations made by persons with disabilities.
10. Students will learn the proper care of muscles and bones.

Key Questions

1. What are the functions of the skeletal system?
2. What are the functions of the muscular system?
3. (From picture) Identify four bones that are labeled (common names).
4. What are the four types of joints? What is an example of each?
5. How do muscles move the body?
6. (From picture) Which muscle is contracting? Which is relaxing?
7. What do voluntary muscles do? What do involuntary muscles do? Why do we need
   both?
8. How does exercise affect muscles?
9. What are some injuries to muscles and bones?
10. What are some ways people compensate for physical disabilities?

Introductory, Culminating, and Selected Developmental Activities

Introductory Activity   Tell the students that they will learn about the human body and
systems that have specific functions. Discuss the definition of system. Assign students to
different systems, give them positions, and as a group have them simulate the human body.
Have them walk from place to place in a group to see that all components must work
together for the larger system to function correctly. The students will simulate the human
body by taking the roles of different systems in the body. The students will understand that
systems in the body must work together to perform properly.

Culminating Activity   Have a "healthy body" party with healthy snacks, healthy
games, and so on to promote the proper care of bones and muscles.

Selected Developmental Activities

1. Read textbook pages 314–318: "Your Body's Framework." Discuss functions of
   bones; begin notes. Activity: In small groups, make life-size skeletons and label
   bones. (The students will identify the functions of the skeletal system. The students will locate individual bones in the context of the entire skeleton.)

2. Discuss cartilage, ligaments, and the four types of bones. Add to notes. Continue to work on skeletons. (The students will identify the four types of bones. The students will locate individual bones in the context of the entire skeleton.)

3. Using a cow bone, discuss the parts of a bone. Add to notes. Activity: Compare strength of round bones to other possible bone shapes. (The students will identify the parts of a bone. They will experiment with different bone structures to determine the strongest shape.)

4. Using other objects, discuss the four types of joints and examples in the body. Read textbook pages 319–320. Add to notes. (The student will identify the four types of joints and will give examples of each type.)

5. Read textbook pages 321–323: "Muscles Move Bones." Discuss the functions of muscles and how they work, using your own muscles as examples. Add to notes. Activity: In pairs, students perform simple exercises to see how muscles fatigue over time when we exercise. (The student will identify the functions of muscles. The students will affirm that muscles fatigue as they are used.)

6. Activity: In pairs, students investigate blinking, discover that it is both voluntary and involuntary. Read textbook pages 325–326. Discuss voluntary, involuntary muscles, three types. Add to notes. (The students will compare voluntary and involuntary muscles. The students will identify the three types of muscles.)

7. Students do exercises and flexibility tests and answer questions about which muscles are used and how flexible they are. (The students will identify which muscles are used for certain exercises and will identify the extent of their flexibility.)

8. Read textbook pages 327–328: Bone and muscle injuries. Discuss injuries. Students complete "Determine the Fracture" worksheet, draw x-rays with broken bones. (The students will identify injuries to bones and muscles.)

9. In pairs, students take a blind walk around campus. Students try out wheelchair and discuss possible problems, feelings, compensations, and so on. (The students will identify problems faced by people with disabilities and become familiar with adaptations made by them.)

10. Read textbook pages 329–331. Discuss what is necessary for healthy bones and muscles. Brainstorm healthy choices. Plan "healthy body" party. (The students will identify what is necessary for the proper care of bones and muscles.)

11. During free time students will be able to play a matching game at the "Bone Zone" interactive bulletin board. The bulletin board will consist of a large drawing of a human skeleton along with two envelopes, one labeled "scientific names" and the other "common names." The students will be able to label bones on the skeleton with either the common names or the scientific names of the bones; they will tack the names in the envelope to the bones of the skeleton on the board. There will be a labeled skeleton available to help the students with the scientific names; the object is to give the students practice with the names.

Statement of Multicultural Perspective

Intergroup Harmony in the Larger Culture This unit will encourage students to see life from other people's perspective—specifically, the perspective of a disabled person. Through activities such as a blind walk and spending time in a wheelchair, students will be encouraged to think about the special challenges and obstacles that face persons with physical disabilities. These activities should help them see that not all people are the same, and that understanding and accepting people who are different is important.

Educational Equity   Each lesson is planned with specific objectives to be reached, and appropriate strategies are used to reach these objectives. A variety of lessons and activities are planned so that students with different learning styles will succeed. Reading, writing, oral discussion, drawing, experimenting, and physical activities will all be used. Cooperative learning will be used, with students assigned specific roles within groups to complete tasks as a team. The cooperative groups are diverse in terms of ability level and sex, so students can draw from each other's strengths and learn to work together successfully. Regarding the five R's (routine, relevance, rigor, ritual, and mutual responsibility) that we discussed in class as one approach to creating educational equity, I make use of the routines of taking notes and reading in class, and my assignments have students thinking about their *own* bodies (relevance). In addition, in this class the students answer in unison when a question is asked and the answer is clear (ritual). I maintain high standards throughout the unit (rigor). For example, students must retake a quiz if they misspell the names of bones. Finally, through the practice of cooperative learning we establish mutual responsibility.

Cultural Pluralism   The literature book *The Indian in the Cupboard* is being taught with this unit, and connections will be made to the book concerning what makes the miniature Indian in the book *real*. While studying this book, there will be opportunities to discuss different cultures, specifically, the Iroquois Indians and cowboys in American history. These cultures will be discussed with the view that not all peoples do things the way we now do in America. Through these discussions, students will realize that different cultures and ways of doing things have value.

Evaluation Procedures

The students will be evaluated throughout the course of the unit on their participation in discussions and their cooperation with other group members during group activities. On some days the students will receive marks of a check, check plus, or check minus depending on their participation and teamwork. I will stress to the students the importance of working with other classmates and participating in group discussions and they will know they are receiving grades for these activities.

The students will also be evaluated on their mastery of the content areas taught in the unit. There will be a test at the end of the unit over the major concepts covered, and smaller quizzes and activities that will be graded during the unit. Students will understand what they are expected to know for each quiz and for the end-of-unit test.

Unit Evaluation

Overall, I think this has been a very successful unit. The students have enjoyed learning about the systems of the body, and they have been meeting the planned objectives. I have learned that activities generally take longer than I think they will, so I did not accomplish everything I had planned, but I am pleased with what we did.

In my initiating activity, the students acted out the different systems of the human body to see that they have to work together to function properly, and this activity was quite successful. It was fairly simple but it was different and interesting for the students and I think the point of it was clear. It was rewarding to start the unit in a simple but unusual way.

We did experiments and activities throughout the unit that were always good learning experiences, even though they did not always turn out as I had planned. In an especially good experiment the students stacked books on paper structures to determine why bones were circular in shape. The results led all students to the correct conclusions. In an especially difficult and confusing experiment the students did exercises and extended periods of writing to see how muscles behave when they are tired. Many of the students got results that I did not anticipate and came to conclusions different from those I had hoped for. It was still a good learning experience, however, because we discussed the results, what should have happened, and how I might change the experiment in the future to make it better. I would use this experiment again, but I would definitely change to have fewer variables. I really liked having the students discover things on their own. I have seen that children need to be encouraged to think for themselves and draw their own conclusions, so I will definitely continue to incorporate these types of activities into my teaching.

If I could change something about my unit, it would be to integrate it more into other parts of the curriculum. There was a tie into the literature book *The Indian in the Cupboard*, but it was a very limited connection and little time was spent on it. I am still not exactly sure how I would integrate the unit into other subject areas, but this is something I would like to work on. Writing could be done, such as traveling through the human body, and art projects could also be tied in. If I had control of the material being taught in all subject areas, I would work on ways to integrate more. I enjoyed planning this unit and presenting it, and I am happy with how it turned out. I am especially pleased that the students enjoyed learning the content.

Bibliography

Allison, Linda. *Blood and Guts*, pp. 21–58. Boston: Little, Brown, 1976.

Conway, Lorraine. *Superific Science Series: Body Systems*. Carthage, Ill.: Good Apple, 1984.

Mallison, George G. *Silver Burdett Science 5*, pp. 314–331. Morristown, N.J.: Silver Burdett, 1985.

Analysis of Unit

Do the lesson content and strategies promote or impede educational equity? Overall, Ms. Williams, in her second student teaching assignment (11 weeks/full time) with approximately five weeks available for planning prior to unit implementation, has done a fairly adequate job. On the positive side, she used a diversity of activities (oral discussion, reading, drawing, experimenting) to achieve her instructional objectives, and also used cooperative learning in a manner designed to enhance learning for the various individuals in her class. Ms. Williams also reports that she maintained high standards, helped her students see the relevance of unit content by relating material to their own bodies, and made good use of routines, rituals, and feelings of mutual responsibility. Ms. Williams also promoted maximum learning for individuals and groups in the class (boys and girls, for example) by including in the unit some very interesting experiments and activities (e.g., the blind walk around the campus, the time spent in a wheelchair, the interactive bulletin board), and attempted to add an interesting dimension by linking the unit content to a popular fictional story her fifth graders had already read and her fourth graders were reading as the unit unfolded. These virtues notwithstanding, for providing maximum opportunity and motivation for learning unit content, there is significant room for improvement in the design of this unit.

Use of the following strategies and content would likely have improved the motivation and learning of more students in this class:

1. The content in this unit appeared to be dominated by the textbook chapter and this is somewhat inevitable, where textbooks exist teachers will likely use them, partic-

ularly for content areas like science and math. Nevertheless, some individual and collaborative brainstorming at the beginning of the unit might have created a need to go beyond the textbook in the search for information. In her introduction to the unit Ms. Williams could have said something like, "Children, a lot of what you and I learn in this unit will be determined by what these textbook authors (names on board) thought we should learn, but they might not have anticipated all our needs or our collective curiosity. Based on my own reading of this chapter I believe it would be quite valuable for us to spend some time generating questions based on what *we* want to know about muscles and bones. After the brainstorming I could let you know which of your questions are answered by the text and which will require external research. I can tell you already that the text does not answer three questions I am interested in: (a) Do men and women in the United States, and all over the world, have the same skeletal bones and muscles? (b) Are there new ways and materials used to help broken bones heal? (c) What are steroids, how do they affect muscles, and why are they illegal in sports but used by doctors to treat certain diseases?" With these questions and the opportunity for self-initiated questioning, the teacher moves the class toward inquiry-oriented learning in the self-directed learning mode. Parenthetically, the first question above might, in a limited way, contribute to a sense of community and intergroup harmony within and outside the class. Students, by themselves and on the street and through the media, will learn about the physical differences between men and women, and the alleged differences between members of different ethnic groups and so-called races. This unit provides an excellent opportunity to teach about what men and women all over the world have in common. In addition, question number two would allow the teacher to connect this unit to the topic of drug abuse (past, present, and future) in the world of sports.

2. Following up on the list of "student and teacher" questions, the class could have generated a list of individuals whose occupations or special interests might connect to the content in the unit. For example, a local chiropractor, medical doctor, surgeon, athletic coach, or gym owner could add to the content in this unit. It would also be appropriate, particularly in the context of a three-week unit, for the teacher to recruit guest speakers well before the unit was introduced and to attempt to locate non-traditional practitioners, such as a woman chiropractor, physical therapist, or medical doctor. The recruitment of minority practitioners as guest speakers could, as part of a cumulative program, contribute to increase equity in terms of opportunity and outcomes as well as a reduction of stereotypes.

3. This unit also appears to be devoid of invitations for inquiry. Requiring students to spell correctly all the names of the skeletal bones is one approach to high standards and expectations, but another powerful strategy is to communicate to your learners that you believe they can and you expect them to define and carry out their own inquiries. Perceiving your students as active creators of knowledge as well as energetic analysts of knowledge already created and packaged is another significant way to contribute to equity in your classroom. For example, any child who recently suffered a broken bone would be a natural to seek out information regarding new techniques for healing bones. Anyone who doubts the efficacy or feasibility of this activist, learning by doing, approach to knowledge creation should spend some time studying the *Foxfire* experience created and sustained by Eliot Wigginton and his students across 25 years of community interviews.[25]

4. On a different tangent, Ms. Williams's multicultural perspective statement says nothing of special steps taken to enhance the potential learning of Carmen, the LEP

student whose learning disability made reading and learning new words more difficult for her than for the average learner; indeed, no special preparation was made for Carmen. In this class where a learning disabilities specialist was available and quite willing to link her tutorial session to whatever content the teacher desired, it was the student teacher's responsibility to provide the specialist with ideas and materials to facilitate Carmen's academic learning and positive participation in the unit. Although the debate about the relative virtue of pull-out programs continues, it is quite clear that the full advantages of this equity resource will not be realized unless there is a rich dialogue between the classroom teacher and the resource specialist, and this holds true for Ms. Williams as well, who accepted the responsibility for educating Carmen when she stepped into this assignment.

5. Finally, although there was a diverse set of activities incorporated into this unit, there was no mention of films, videos, filmstrips, or computer software. This unit appears to have relied too heavily on the textbook as a source of information.

Does the lesson content or structure promote cultural pluralism in society or intergroup harmony in the classroom?   The use of cooperative learning may well contribute to classroom intergroup harmony as well as acceptance of different groups in society. The content of *The Indian in the Cupboard* might also contribute positively in this regard, but this novel has the potential to reinforce negative stereotypes about American Indians (p. 174) at the same time that it presents some stereotype-reducing information regarding Iroquois Indians (p. 21) and calls into question the portrayal of Indians on American television (p. 29). For promoting cultural pluralism this novel is not a good choice. In addition, as Ms. Williams notes in her evaluation, the connection between the plot of this story and her unit was quite thin. A biography much better suited to the content of this unit, and coincidentally available from the National Women's History Project, is *Wilma Rudolph: Champion Athlete* by Tom Biracree (New York: Chelsea House Publishers, 1989). This 112-page book is an inspiring story about a child stricken with polio who was unable to walk until age 11; with the help of her family, however, she won several Olympic gold medals in track. Parts of the story could have been read orally to the students during the three-week unit. It is an example of a child the same age as the students who overcame a severe physical disability, content that relates directly to the objectives of this unit. Also, in this class and community where there are very few African Americans, the story of Wilma Rudolph will give students the opportunity to identify with a courageous role model who comes from an ethnic group, and perhaps gender group, different from their own. Such exposure and possible positive identification experienced cumulatively across the school year and K–8 curriculum should contribute to greater acceptance of and more positive relationships with individuals who are culturally and ethnically different from the learners.

Does the lesson content or structure make use of, or help to develop, collaborative relationships among parents, students, and teachers?   Efforts to involve parents in this unit were minimal. For example, no letter was sent home notifying parents about the upcoming unit or inviting them to attend the culminating activity (the "healthy body" party). Until she asks, a teacher will not know whether a parent or friend of a parent possesses special knowledge that might tie into the unit. A parent who is a soccer coach, former ballet student or dancer, jazzercise instructor, or other athletic type might well have knowledge that could enrich the unit.

Does the content of the unit help to lessen distortions in the historical, literary, or scientific record that may be linked to historical racism or other forces linked to the oppression of specific ethnic and cultural groups?   As designed and implemented, this unit made no contribution toward discovering racial or cultural distortions in history and the content of this unit does not lead itself to this objective in a clear way. Nevertheless, the inquiry question we raised earlier regarding whether men and women from different parts of the world have the same skeletal structure and muscle groups can serve to show that the differences between the so-called races are skin deep at best.

UNIT FOUR: FAMOUS FAIRY TALES

The fourth and final unit to be reviewed, entitled *Famous Fairy Tales*, was developed by a student teacher, Carol Sanchez (pseudonym), for a second-grade class in a small, rural, central coast California school district. Ms. Sanchez's class had 28 students, was 93 percent White American with students for the most part coming from families who were middle and lower-middle class, (*N* = 25 out of 28 students), and had few special learners. One child in the class was designated limited English proficient (LEP), and another student was non-English proficient (NEP); both were Mexican Americans. Three students in the class participated in the school's free or partially subsidized lunch program. The LEP and NEP learners were pulled out of class five days a week (30 minutes per session) to participate in a second-grade ESL (English as a Second Language) class where they were taught English by a Spanish/English teacher. The classroom teachers in the second grade had little input into the content of the ESL class, and there was little effort to create continuity between the curricula in the school's three second-grade classrooms and the curriculum of the ESL classroom. Although there was little curriculum dialogue and continuity, relationships among all teachers in the setting were quite good, and the potential for more curriculum dialogue and exchange was favorable.

Listed below are several key components of Ms. Sanchez's unit from which you can form your own preliminary opinions about the content.

1. Introductory statement
2. Categorization of activities by content area
3. Main ideas
4. General objectives
5. Key questions
6. Introductory, closing, and selected developmental activities
7. Statement of multicultural perspectives
8. Evaluation procedures
9. Unit evaluation
10. Bibliography

Introductory Statement

This is a literature-based unit featuring well-known fairy tales and folktales. Such stories as "Jack and the Beanstalk," "Strega Nona," "The Frog Prince," "Little Red Riding Hood," "The Three Little Pigs," "Goldilocks and the Three Bears," "Cinderella," and "The Gingerbread Man" will be read, compared, acted out, and written about. This unit is to be incorporated into a four-week period for a second-grade class. The students will be engaged in many exciting and interesting activities that will make these well-loved stories even more important to them.

Categorization of Activities by Content Area

LANGUAGE ARTS

Beginning, Middle, End	Similarities/Differences
Sequencing Events	Point of View
Changing Endings	Characters
Oral Language	Setting
Charades	Create Own Fairy Tale
Drama	Magic Bean Writing

SCIENCE
Senses
  Taste
  Smell
  Touch
Growth of Plants
Wolf Information
Bear Information
Life Cycle of Frogs

COOKING
Gingerbread Men/Women
Porridge Making
Cookie Making

MATH
Counting
Graphing
Estimating
Map Reading
Sequencing
Measuring

Pumpkin Activities
  Estimating/Graphing
Time Lines
  Cinderella's Day
Jellybean Activities
Pasta Activities
  Classification

SOCIAL STUDIES
Italy—Map Reading
Reading Maps
Native Americans
Appalachian Mountains Location
Folktale Homes
Creating Fairy-Tale Maps

ART
Fairy-Tale Quilt
Gingerbread Men/Women
Making Pigs
  Basket Making

Main Ideas

1. Fairy tales and folktales differ from culture to culture.
2. There are similarities and differences between popular childhood fairy tales and folktales.
3. Fairy tales and folktales may be communicated in many different forms.

General Objectives

1. Students will gain awareness of fairy tales and folktales from other parts of the world.
2. Students will become aware of the similarities and differences between some fairy tales and folktales.
3. Students will gain knowledge in sequencing events of a story using pictures and words.
4. Students will be able to compare and contrast two similar fairy tales or folktales.
5. Students will gain knowledge in estimating and graphing their results.
6. Students will understand the different components of a fairy tale and a folktale: plot, characters, and setting.
7. Students will be able to explore their sense of taste, smell, and touch.
8. Students will be able to determine the difference between fantasy and reality.

Key Questions

1. What differences lie between familiar fairy tales and those of different cultures?
2. What is point of view?
3. What does main characters mean?
4. What is setting?
5. What is the difference between fantasy and reality?

6. How does our sense of smell affect our sense of taste?
7. Where is Italy located?
8. How do we sequence a story?
9. Are there differences between the same fairy tale or folktale told by different authors?
10. Are wolves that we read about in fairy tales and folktales the same wolves that are in the forest?

Introductory, Closing, and Selected Developmental Activities

Introductory Activity   This unit focuses on many different stories, and the introductory activity I have selected has something to do with all of them. The students will be involved in a lesson that asks them to differentiate between statements of reality and fantasy. This activity in turn will lead into a discussion about fairy and folktales and whether they are reality or fantasy. I will then read one of my favorite fairy tales from my childhood, "The Princess and the Pea," and will ask the students to guess why this tale was one of my favorites.

Closing Activity   The students will present the work they have completed in this four-week unit to all their parents. They will also present several of the stories we read in a play version for their parents to enjoy. Refreshments will be served to the parents and students.

Selected Developmental Activities

1. Opening lesson—Students differentiate between fantasy and reality. I read "The Princess and the Pea." (The students will gain knowledge about the difference between fantasy and reality.)
2. Introduce vocabulary for "Jack and the Beanstalk." Show students vocabulary cards, which have words and pictures. I will read the story and students will use the vocabulary words in sentences. (The students will be able to use the new vocabulary words in sentences of their own.)
3. Students will sequence the story of "Jack and the Beanstalk" by coloring pictures about the story and placing them in correct order. They then have their own story. (After reading "Jack and the Beanstalk," the students will color six pictures about the story and be able to sequence them in the correct order.)
4. Students will plant beans in cups and measure their progress over the next few weeks. We will talk about the different parts of the plant. (The students will take part in planting their own "beanstalk" and then measure the progress of its growth. They will also be able to identify the different parts of a plant.)
5. I will read "Strega Nona." The students will complete a map activity of Italy. (After reading "Strega Nona," the students will be able to find Strega Nona's hometown on their map of Italy; then they will color Italy.)
6. I will read "The Magic Porridge Pot" and the students will compare and contrast the two stories. (After reading "Strega Nona" and "The Magic Porridge Pot," the students will be able to tell the differences and similarities between the two stories.)
7. I will read "The Frog Prince"—students will learn about the life cycle of the frog and sequence the different phases in illustrations.
8. I will read "Little Red Riding Hood" in several versions. (The students will develop their sense of hearing and comprehension.)
9. I will read "Lon Po Po," a Chinese version of "Little Red Riding Hood," and we will

discuss the differences and similarities between the stories. (The students will learn how storytellers in China tell the story we know in a different way.)

10. Students will create their favorite scene in an illustration and then cut the picture into three panels to create the panel art work found in "Lon Po Po." (The students will gain knowledge about the Chinese art form of panel pictures.)

11. In "Little Red Riding Hood" the eyes were talked about, so students will create a class graph based on eye color to discover which eye color is the most prevalent in our classroom. (The students will gain knowledge in predicting eye color, graphing their results, counting their results, interpreting data, and comparing their data.)

12. I will read "The Three Little Pigs" in several versions. (Students will sit and listen attentively to the story and will be able to answer questions when it is completed.)

13. The students will act out the story of "The Three Little Pigs" as I read it again. (The students will be able to show their comprehension of the story by acting it out. They will also understand what a "part" or character is.)

14. I will read "The True Story of the Three Little Pigs," which is told from the wolf's point of view. We will then discuss point of view. (The students will understand what point of view means after reading "The True Story of the Three Little Pigs.")

15. I will read "Goldilocks and the Three Bears"; the students will learn about their sense of taste and smell since Goldilocks used these senses when finding and tasting the bears' porridge. (The students will be able to label items given to them to taste as sweet, sour, bitter, or salty. They will complete the assigned activity in groups of four.)

16. I will read "Cinderella." (The students will be able to sit and listen attentively.)

17. The students will become more familiar with telling time and will be able to sequence Cinderella's day based on time; they will also sequence their daily events. (The students will be able to match times written out with the corresponding times on clocks.)

18. I will read "The Indian Cinderella" and the students will compare and contrast the events in the story. (The students will be able to compare and contrast different and similar elements in the two Cinderella stories.)

19. I will read "Yeh Shen," a Chinese version of "Cinderella," and will compare this story to the version we know best. (The students will be able to compare and contrast the similar and different elements in the two stories.)

20. As "wrap up activities" the students will take a survey of 10 classmates to learn which of the fairy tales we read during the unit was their favorite. We will collect the information and compose a class graph showing the results. (The students will be able to collect data, graph the findings, and make an inference.)

21. As a class, the students will create a "Fairy Tale Quilt." Each student will cut out of construction paper one item that relates to fairy tales (frog, glass slipper, etc.), and we will make a class quilt out of construction paper to hang on the wall. (The students will be able to create one object related to fairy or folktales, cut it out, and mount it on paper. They will be able to use their creativity for this lesson.)

22. Students will present what they have done in their fairy tale unit to their parents and will perform several plays based on the fairy tales and folktales we have read in class. (The students will be able to take all the knowledge they have acquired throughout the unit and perform works informed by that knowledge.)

Statement of Multicultural Perspective

Educational Equity I hope that each student achieves success in my classroom. To help to ensure this, during the presentation and implementation of my unit I will incorporate appropriate teaching strategies that enable each student to acquire the necessary information. I have also incorporated heterogeneous seating groups, set up to ensure that each student has an equal opportunity to learn in my classroom. These groups will also enhance peer involvement, support, and teamwork.

To present vocabulary for the fairy tales that I will read during this unit, I have made vocabulary cards that have the word and a picture to illustrate the word. The pictures will give all students, including my non-English proficient student, a visual reference to associate with vocabulary words.

Intergroup Harmony   In forming the groups in which students will sit and work cooperatively, I will group them by gender, ability, and capability to work effectively together. I will also talk with the students to make sure we know what it means to work as a team. My bilingual student will be placed next to my non-English proficient student so as to increase both students' self-confidence and opportunity for success. As students are placed in groups, some may not get along. Students will understand that in life they do not always have to like someone but may have to work side by side with this person, and teamwork should help them learn cooperation.

Valuing Diversity   I value and encourage all the opinions of the children in my classroom. Through modeling, the students will learn that even when they disagree with someone, that person's opinion is also important. Diversity should be encouraged. I will look at diversity among classmates when we discuss the versions of fairy tales we each know best. Also, diversity will be addressed when we examine the same fairy tale as told in different cultures. All people are important, and that is what will be stressed.

Knowledge of Other Cultures   A large portion of this unit focuses on the students' examining the similarities and differences between versions of fairy tales from our country and from other countries and cultures. We will then talk about those cultures and why their fairy tales are different from the versions we know. This exercise will help students see that our knowledge of other cultures helps us to understand why their fairy tales are different.

Evaluation Procedures

During this unit on fairy tales and folktales, I will evaluate students' progress in learning the material on an ongoing basis. The students will be evaluated on participation, both in the large group and in their teams of four. Also being evaluated will be their completed assignments. By the end of the unit each child should have completed four sequenced picture books based on what we read in class. The students' final presentation for parents, classmates, and staff members will be evaluated and will also allow the students to share the work they complete during this unit. I hope this unit will be a very positive experience for the students, and in turn, they will be excited about participating and completing assignments.

Unit Evaluation

For my initiating activity I tried to incorporate something that would be useful for all the fairy tales and folktales we would be reading. The students participated very well in our discussion of what was reality and what was fantasy. They showed great imagination!

Overall, I feel the entire unit went very well. With unexpected things that occur in school days, I found that I had planned too many activities for the amount of time allotted. Writing lessons, for example, tended to take a few days. We incorporated math concepts such as graphing, estimating, classifying, and counting. In language arts we spent a great deal of time sequencing and distinguishing characters, setting, and point of view of the story. The students grasped the concept of point of view much better than I had anticipated. Hearing "The True Story of the Three Little Pigs" really made the concept clear to them. The students were also introduced to different versions of fairy tales and folktales, which we compared and contrasted. They seemed to enjoy hearing versions from different countries.

If I were to do this unit again with second, and perhaps third graders, I would use some fairy tales and folktales that they did not know, especially those from other countries. I think I might also read fewer stories and go into greater depth with the stories we studied. With second graders I felt as if I needed to keep their interest high by using many stories, but I think that older students could do much more with the overall topic without as much stimulation.

Bibliography

Children's Stories Utilized in Unit

1. "Cinderella," Marcia Brown, ed. (New York: Scribner, 1954).
2. "Goldilocks and the Three Bears," Jan Brett (New York: Putnam, 1987).
3. "Jack and the Bean Tree," Gail Haley (New York: Crown, 1986).
4. "Johnny Cake" in *English Fairy Tales,* Joseph Jacobs (New York: Putnam, 1904).
5. "Little Red Riding Hood," Jacob Grimm and Wilhelm Grimm (New York: Scholastic, 1986).
6. "Lon Po Po," Ed Young, ed. (New York: Putnam, 1989).
7. "Red Riding Hood," James Marshall, ed. (New York: Dial, 1987).
8. "Strega Nona," Tomie de Paola (Englewood Cliffs, N.J.: Prentice-Hall, 1975).
9. "The Frog Prince," The Brothers Grimm (Mahway, N.J.: Troll, 1979).
10. "The Frog Prince Continued," Jon Scieszka (New York: Viking Child Books, 1991).
11. "The Magic Porridge Pot," Paul Galdone (New York: Houghton Mifflin, 1976).
12. "The Soup Stone," Iris VanRynbach (New York: Greenwillow, 1988).
13. "The Teeny Tiny Woman," Paul Galdone (New York: Ticknor and Fields, 1986).
14. "The Three Billy Goats Gruff," Janet Stevens (San Diego, Calif.: Harcourt, Brace, Jovanovich, 1987).
15. "The Three Little Pigs," Gavin Bishop (New York: Scholastic, 1990).
16. "The True Story of the Three Little Pigs!," Alexander Wolf and Jon Scieszka (New York: Viking Kestrel, 1989).

Teacher Resources

1. *Fairy Tale Sequencing*, Evan Moor
2. Project AIMS, Fall into Math and Science
   Spring into Math and Science
   Glide into Winter

Analysis of Unit

Do the lesson content or strategies promote or impede educational equity? Overall, Ms. Sanchez, who was in her second student teaching assignment (11 weeks/full time) with approximately five weeks available for unit planning prior to unit implementation, has designed and delivered a strong unit. Among the positive attributes, several are important for promoting educational equity for the 28 second graders in this class. First, Ms.

Sanchez employed a wide range of lessons, activities, and teaching strategies to achieve her instructional objectives; this diversity no doubt reinforced the learning styles and preferences of specific learners at the same time that the variety probably increased the overall level of motivation in the class. In addition to the variety of methods and lessons, the selection of content and activities was diverse. The specific stories selected and the wide range of intriguing hands-on activities (cooking, map making, basket making, quilt making, and picture making), along with the well-developed integration of the fairy tales with math and science activities (the eye color graph and life cycle of the frog) and the presence of parents at the culminating experience all served to promote a high degree of student interest and achievement in this unit.

Ms. Sanchez made good use of cooperative learning, created word/picture flash cards for the two Spanish-speaking learners, and arranged her seating so that the limited English proficient student could help the non-English proficient student in her first steps toward the English language. For a student teacher this was certainly a well-rounded effort to promote equity. Nevertheless, as in most lessons and units, the advantage of hindsight and reflection leads to new ideas regarding teaching strategies and content. One idea, although intended to increase motivation for the two Spanish-speaking students, might also serve, in a limited way, to promote binguality for the second graders in this rural, heavily monolingual (English) community.

The strategy is to make available some Spanish language translations of selected fairy tales (such as "Caperucita Rojo/Little Red Riding Hood") for optional reading by Juan and Rosita, assuming that one or both can read in Spanish. Ms. Sanchez might read aloud one of the fairy tales in Spanish. Within the unit, the second graders will hear several versions of the Cinderella story from several nations. Why not also hear a version translated into Spanish so the children can experience a dramatic reading in a language other than English? If the teacher cannot read in Spanish, perhaps an older elementary school student, parent, bilingual aide, or another teacher could help out.

An excellent resource for locating literature that is available in Spanish is entitled *Recommended Readings in Spanish Literature: Kindergarten through Grade Eight* (Sacramento: California Department of Education, 1991). The book can be ordered from the Bureau of Publications, Sales Unit, California Department of Education, P. O. Box 271, Sacramento, CA 95802-0271. In 1992, the book sold for $3.25. Call (916) 445-1260 for current prices. Also, Group Editorial Grijalbo, Barcelona, Spain, publishes a series of fairy tales that are available in the United States. Series One and Two in their collection titled *Ediciones Junior S.A.* includes "El Mago de Oz," "Peter Pan," "Los Viajes de Gulliver," "Las Aventuras de Pinocho," and "Hansel y Gretel."

Does the lesson content or structure promote cultural pluralism in society or intergroup harmony in the classroom?   With regard to classroom intergroup harmony, the use of heterogeneously structured cooperative learning groups, as noted in chapter 2 is a very strong choice. In a more limited way, the choice of fairy tales from different nations of the world suggests to the learners that their teacher values the nations and cultures from which these fairy and folktales have emerged. A teacher will rarely say this explicitly; instead, over time from one grade to another, students form the impression by the weight of their teachers' cumulative choices about which tales and nations to include. In this unit we had two lovely tales from China—"Yeh-Shen" (a Cinderella story) and "Lon Po Po" (a Red Riding Hood story)—as well as "Strega Nona" (Grandma Witch), a delightful story with an Italian cast of characters. Because of the presence of this story in the unit, the second graders learned where Italy is located and colored a map of Italy. All this represents *very* good planning.

To promote appreciation and acceptance of a wider range of cultures, it would have been appropriate for Ms. Sanchez to include one or more tales from Africa and/or Central and South America. Teachers have a Caldecott Honor Book available to serve this purpose: *Mufaro's Beautiful Daughters, an African Tale* by John Steptoe (New York: Lothrop, Lee and Shepard Books, 1987). This story incorporates several Cinderella-like elements. Beyond the beauty of its illustrations and its well-crafted prose, this story has other virtues, ones not usually associated with fairy tales. For example, on the introductory page to *Mufaro's Beautiful Daughters* we learn that (a) the illustrations in the book were inspired by the ruins of an ancient city in Zimbabwe as well as the flora and fauna in that region, (b) the names of the characters in the story are from the Shona language, and (c) the author dedicated this book to the children of South Africa. We now have two more nations, Zimbabwe and South Africa, for students to locate on the map, and with the addition of this tale, the unit now transports the second graders to Asia, Europe, and Africa. In addition, we have an interesting question to share with the students: Why do you think Mr. Steptoe dedicated this book to the children of South Africa? After discussing the children's opinions, the teacher could use this question to stimulate interest in writing a class letter to Mr. Steptoe.

Does the unit allow students to expand their knowledge of other cultures and ethnic groups? In this unit students did not really study different cultures as much as they experienced literature from several different cultures. From these experiences they learn that cultures that existed long ago and very far apart from each other developed folktales and fairy tales that were quite similar. Thus, these stories allow the second graders to catch a glimpse of a common humanity unfolding, through literature, in several different cultures. In addition, the reading of *Mufaro's Beautiful Daughters*, which introduces the second graders to the idea of a beautiful and ancient African kingdom, could be augmented by several nonfiction articles about ancient African kingdoms. Taken together, the tale and extra readings could serve to diminish contemporary distortions regarding the content of African history. It is also possible that including content that pertains to Africa, along with efforts to provide accurate information about African Americans in American history, could help to develop better relationships between Blacks and Whites and people of color in general. At the minimum, children of all colors and cultural backgrounds deserve the opportunity to see themselves and their ancestors sensitively portrayed in the school's literary selections; it is the responsibility of contemporary teachers to know where to locate such materials. An excellent resource is the videos produced for the Reading Rainbow series, seen on Public Broadcasting Stations (PBS) around the nation. The series, hosted by Levar Burton, has one video that celebrates the music, dance, and literature of Africa. On the 28-minute video, entitled *Mufaro's Beautiful Daughters*, actress Felicia Rashad reads the story, which is accompanied by close-ups of the art work from the book. The reading is followed by a brief, informative discussion about drum making and other ancient African instruments made from indigenous materials, such as gourds, bamboo, and conch shells. In the final part of the video, several elementary school students provide book talks about other books with African themes. This video helps teachers integrate literature with music, art, craft, dance, and history. Teachers will likely find that local education agencies around the country have copies of the Reading Rainbow series.

Finally, if we were teaching the unit we would add at least one more variation on the Cinderella theme: a captivating little tale named "Atalanta" written by Betty Miles. This tale, which does not exactly fit into the traditional Cinderella mode, adds a modern twist that second graders would notice and enjoy. This tale introduces primary graders to a bright and clever princess who speaks her own mind and is determined to select her own husband. It will demonstrate to students that in the creation of their own folktales and fairy tales it is quite appropriate to develop and incorporate new themes and relationships. The story of "Atalanta" appears in *Free to Be You and Me* (New York: McGraw-Hill, 1974), a project conceived by Marlo Thomas, and developed and edited by her, Carole Hart, Letty Cottin Pogrebin, and Mary Rodgers.

DISCUSSION QUESTIONS

1. In discussing the unit entitled "The Winning of the West," we suggested that the title "The Expansion of the American Nation: 1775–1850" might lend itself better to a unit oriented toward multiculturalism.
   a. How do you think we would defend this title change?
   b. Can you suggest a different and possibly better title? If so, please explain.
   c. Is "The Westward Movement: 1775–1850" better than both of the above titles? Why? Why not?
2. We believe that elementary and middle-school teachers, using divergent inquiry-oriented questions and activities, should call attention to the various skin colors of the ancient Egyptians as well as the African context of the ancient Egyptian civilization.
   a. What strikes you as logical about this belief? Explain your reasoning.
   b. If you see little merit in this suggestion, spell out your reasons.
3. A frustrated teacher in one of our graduate courses recently lamented that multicultural education constantly seemed to highlight the achievements of people of color (non-Whites) and diminish or comment negatively on the behavior of Whites.
   a. Does this complaint seem accurate to you?
   b. How would you respond to this teacher?
4. In an essay entitled "The Danger in Multiple Perspectives," Albert Shanker, President of the American Federation of Teachers, presents a point of view regarding multiperspective teaching that we consider erroneous and misleading. In discussing the danger he perceives in teaching with multiple perspectives Mr. Shanker writes:

> Now "multiple perspectives" is an excellent phrase. It sounds open-minded, which is what the pursuit of knowledge should be. But when you put the concept into the classroom, what does it mean? For a teacher presenting a historical event to elementary school children, using multiple perspectives probably means that the teacher turns to each child and asks the child's point of view about the event. To an African-American child this would mean, "What is the African-American point of view?" To a Jewish child, "What is the Jewish point of view?" And to an Irish child, "What is the Irish point of view?" This is racist because it assumes that a child's point of view is determined by the group he comes from. But is there a single African-American or Jewish or Irish point of view? A child may have a point of view based on the fact that he is rich or poor or that he has read extensively or that he comes from a family of conservative Republicans or Marxists. In a society like ours, we are often, and delightfully, surprised that people do not carry with them the views that stereotypes call for. Is it a teacher's job to tell children that they are entitled to only one point of view because of the racial, religious or

ethnic group they come from? Should schools be in the business of promoting racial stereotypes and fostering differences where they may not exist?

Answer any or all of the following questions:

a. What do you consider to be insightful in Shanker's remarks? Explain your reasoning.

b. What do you consider to be questionable in Shanker's remarks? Explain your reasoning.

c. Why do you think we consider Shanker's remarks erroneous and misleading? Be as specific as possible in your comments and try to support your reasons with remarks made elsewhere in this text.

Please note that Shanker's article is part of the series of brief position papers that appear as paid advertisements under the auspices of the American Federation of Teachers. The essay mentioned above appeared in the December 2, 1991, issue of *The New Republic* and is reprinted in appendix 5 with permission of Shanker and the American Federation of Teachers. It is noteworthy that Shanker's concerns about "multiple perspectives" were provoked by a curriculum proposal entitled "One Nation, Many Peoples: A Declaration of Cultural Interdependence," which was recently accepted by the New York State Board of Regents. There are some serious problems with the idea of "multicultural perspectives" as it is discussed in this curriculum proposal, and Shanker insightfully discusses one of these problems in another portion of his essay.

5. In a revealing essay entitled "Sacrificing Accuracy for Diversity," Albert Shanker continued to discuss problems with the type of multicultural curriculum apparently supported by the New York State Board of Regents as a result of its recent approval of a social studies curriculum document entitled "One Nation, Many Peoples: A Declaration of Cultural Interdependence." In this essay Shanker develops his argument by presenting a critique of selected components—the science essay in particular—of the African-American Baseline Essays, a key element in the evolving Afrocentric curriculum movement. In the portion of the essay leading up to the critique Shanker says the following about ancient Egyptian civilization:

> The Portland essays present ancient Egypt as an African culture that strongly influenced the development of European civilization, and this is fair enough. It is a view most reputable scholars have agreed with for 40 years, and it corrects distortions of previous historians who were inclined to ignore Egypt's contributions or to disregard the fact that Egypt was an African civilization. But the baseline essays go far beyond discussing Egypt as an African society, and they assert a number of ideas that are inconsistent with the best scholarship. For instance, they maintain that the inhabitants of ancient Egypt were black Africans.
>
> Scholars of Egyptian history and archeology say that the evidence suggests an entirely different story. Far from being all black (or all white), ancient Egypt, they say, was a multiracial society with a variety of racial types much like that of modern Egypt. In any case, our concept of race—a relatively modern invention—would not have made much sense to the ancient Egyptians, who did not look at people in terms of skin color or hair texture. So the baseline essays not only misrepresent the evidence by insisting that Egypt was a black African society; they distort the example that Egypt has to offer our own multiracial society to make a political point.

Answer any of the questions below.

a. Do Shanker's remarks support our critique of Dorothy S. Carter's novel *His Majesty, Queen Hatshepsut*, or does it perhaps reveal grounds for a new line of criticism? Explain your reasoning.

b. Shanker and the historians and archaeologists he refers to suggest that ancient Egyptians did not look at people in terms of skin color or hair texture. But their artists did draw, paint, and sculpt Egyptians who looked different, suggesting that they were aware of physical differences. However, it seems likely that having noticed and depicted these differences, the ancient Egyptians did not categorize their people by race nor assume that people with different physical characteristics had different moral and intellectual capacity.

(1) In teaching a unit on ancient Egypt to sixth, seventh, or eighth graders, would you discuss the likely absence of racial categories in ancient Egypt, and if so, how could you make use of contemporary Egyptian society to characterize the diverse, multi-colored nature of ancient Egyptian society?

(2) Regarding the reduced emphasis on color consciousness in ancient Egypt, what questions might you ask your students, and toward what end?

c. In your junior high school, high school, college, and postgraduate education, were you taught that reputable scholars have believed since 1950 that (1) ancient Egypt was a multiracial African culture and (2) Egyptian culture strongly influenced the development of European civilization? If yes, in what circumstances did you learn this information? If not, why do you think this point of view was excluded from your education?

Please note that the article referred to above, another of Shanker's position papers, appeared in the December 9, 1991, issue of *The New Republic*. With the permission of Shanker and the American Federation of Teachers, the entire essay is reprinted in appendix 5.

RECOMMENDED ACTIVITIES

1. View the film *Black History: Lost, Stolen, or Strayed*, part of the "Of Black America" series, narrated by Bill Cosby, and identify specific ways the video could be used to enhance one or both of the units discussed in this chapter. The film was produced in 1968 and is distributed by BFA Educational Media, 470 Park Avenue South, Santa Monica, California. In a brief description, James Banks wrote that "the film is now an important historical document."

2. View the film *How the West Was Won . . . and Honor Lost* and do the same as the above for the unit on "Winning the West." The producer/distributor is CRM Films, 2233 Farday, Carlsbad, California 92008. If you would choose not to use this film, please explain why; identify other audiovisual or computer-based education products that would enhance this unit.

3. Identify specific resources from your school district, university, public library, museum, or other source that would allow you to create an inquiry-oriented activity on ancient Egypt—specifically, one that would allow students to speculate about the colors and racial background of ancient Egyptians. Develop a lesson to indicate how you would use such resources.

4. Examine chapter 7 ("Ancient Egypt") in Houghton Mifflin's (1991) sixth-grade text, *A Message of Ancient Days*. See specifically pp. 204–205—the exercise on "Interpreting Egyptian Art"; see also the activity on p. 100 of the Teacher's and Students' editions, which depicts Cro-Magnon people as very European looking.

a. With the goals of multicultural education in mind, which components of this chapter, if any, would you modify? Describe and explain the changes.

b. The Houghton Mifflin writers state: "Scientists say that in modern-day clothing Cro-Magnon people would look very much like Europeans." Why do you think these writers find it appropriate to comment on the physical and racial appearance of Cro-Magnons but choose not to comment on the physical/racial appearance of the ancient Egyptians?

   c. Identify those things you like about the Houghton Mifflin chapter.

5. Examine the way ancient Egypt is treated in a textbook series other than the one by Houghton Mifflin; describe and discuss the strengths and shortcomings of these chapters. Do the same for the chapters that deal with the westward expansion of the United States.

6. Working alone or with fellow teachers select a unit you have taught in the past or plan to teach in the future. Using our six evaluative questions as a point of departure, specify what you could do to increase the multicultural nature of this unit.

7. Plan a three-hour workshop for your fellow teachers or prospective teachers on multi-culturalizing units of instruction. Specify what information you would share. Do not hesitate to go beyond the content and prescriptions discussed in this text.

Journal Entry

This chapter has provided you with another opportunity for adapting content and strategies to increase the multicultural elements of the curriculum. The next chapter will link multi-cultural education to other curriculum areas such as citizenship education, global education, and environmental education. Before we move forward it would be helpful for you to write a summary of your current thoughts about multicultural education; before doing so, you should review your prior journal entries.

NOTES

1. James A. Banks, *Teaching Strategies for Ethnic Studies*, 5th ed. (Boston: Allyn & Bacon, 1991), 57.
2. Ibid., 487–509.
3. Ibid.
4. John Jarolimek, *Social Studies in Elementary Education*, 8th ed. (New York: Macmillan, 1990), 275.
5. See Dee Brown, *Bury My Heart at Wounded Knee* (New York: Bantam Books, 1971), 85–91, for an example of American history written from a Native-American viewpoint.
6. Banks, *Teaching Strategies for Ethnic Studies*, 47.
7. The related facts are based on information in James Banks's chapter, "American Indians: Concepts, Strategies, and Materials," in *Teaching Strategies for Ethnic Studies*, 131–166.
8. John D. McNeil and Jon Wiles, *The Essentials of Teaching: Decisions, Plans, Methods* (New York: Macmillan, 1990), 382–392.
9. Ibid., 382–383.
10. Ibid., 383.
11. W. E. B. Du Bois, *Black Folk Then and Now: An Essay in the History and Sociology of the Negro Race* (New York: Octagon Books, 1939).
12. St. Claire Drake, *Black Folk Here and There: An Essay in History and Antropology* (Los Angeles: University of California, Center for Afro-American Studies, 1987).
13. Ibid., xv.
14. Ibid., 158.
15. This date appears on p. 212 in chapter 7, "Egypt and Kush," in *A Message of Ancient Days*, the sixth-grade text in the Houghton Mifflin Social Studies Series. The copyright date is 1991.

16. Drake, *Black Folk Here and There*, xviii.
17. Dorothy S. Carter, *His Majesty, Queen Hatshepsut* (New York: HarperCollins, 1987), 38.
18. Ibid., 59.
19. Ibid., 131.
20. Drake, *Black Folk Here and There*, 218.
21. Ibid., 173.
22. Beverly J. Armento, Gary B. Nash, Christopher L. Salter, and Karen K. Wixon, *The Message of Ancient Days* (Boston: Houghton Mifflin, 1991), 186–217.
23. Martin Bernal, *Black Athena: The Afroasiatic Roots of Classical Civilization* (New Brunswick, N.J.: Rutgers University Press, 1987).
24. Robin Sewell, a Black-American graduate student working in Egyptian archaeology, expressed this viewpoint in a letter to *The New Republic*, December 31, 1990, 6. See also Mary Lefkowitz's article, "Not Out of Africa: The Origins of Greece and the Illusions of Afrocentrists," *The New Republic* 206, no. 6 (February 10, 1992): 29–36, for a thought-provoking article on this topic. Commentary regarding the article appeared on pages 4–5 of the March 9, 1992 issue of *The New Republic*.
25. Ann Meek, "On 25 Years of Foxfire: A Conversation with Eliot Wigginton," *Educational Leadership* 47, no. 6 (March, 1990): 30–35; see also Eliot Wigginton, *Sometimes a Shining Moment: The Foxfire Experience* (New York: Doubleday, 1985).

CHAPTER 5

Creating a Multicultural Curriculum with Content That Links Environmental, Global, Citizenship, and Multicultural Education

CHAPTER OVERVIEW

This chapter provides working definitions of global, environmental, and citizenship education and a rationale for creating units that link these curriculum areas to multicultural education. To illustrate the distinctive characteristics and special value of this unique type of multicultural unit, a profile of an integrated rain forest unit is given along with discussion questions and recommended activities.

INTRODUCTION

In chapter 4, two of the units we discussed had social studies themes: "The Westward Expansion" and "Ancient Egypt." These units were considered integrated because the teachers who planned them attempted to connect their social studies content to art, music, science, math, and language arts activities. Thus, the units integrated into one entity the traditional content areas of the K–8 curriculum. Now we present a different type of integrated unit, one wherein the teacher starts with themes that are *global* and *environmental* in nature, like rain forest depletion and then broadens these themes to include content related to *citizenship* and *multicultural education.* We refer to this special type of integrated unit as an environmental multicultural unit (EMC) and will show that the synthesis of these four interdisciplinary curriculum areas (global, environmental, citizenship, and multicultural education) can lead to units that are timely for students and society. As background we will discuss the synthesis approach to extending multicultural education, and then provide brief definitions for three of the four curriculum areas.

In chapter 1 we discussed conceptions of multicultural education that integrated it with other curriculum concepts such as multiethnic education (James Banks) and social reconstructionism (Carl Grant). In addition, various authors, particularly Christine Bennett,[1] have linked multicultural education to global education. In discussing our integrated multicultural model of curriculum and instruction, we noted that there were other important models of instruction worthy of teachers' attention. One such model would link effective instruction to a vigorous, open-minded form of citizenship education. Within this citizenship model "effective instruction" could be defined as instruction that successfully prepares students to be active, productive, citizens of their national and world societies. Carl Grant and Christine Sleeter, in their "Education That Is Multicultural and Social Reconstructionist" model have included a focused version of citizenship education in their conception of multicultural education by linking it to the philosophy of social reconstructionism. As noted in chapter 1 of this text, Sleeter and Grant distinguish their model from multicultural education as follows:

> Education that is Multicultural and Social Reconstructionist deals more directly than the other approaches have with oppression and social structural inequality based on race, social class, gender, and disability . . . it prepares future citizens to reconstruct society so that it better serves the interests of all groups of people and especially those who are of color, poor, female, and/or disabled.[2]

Clearly, this is a heightened, focused, and politically directed form of citizenship education that would presumably go far beyond preparing students to create a more efficient and dynamic version of our current capitalist democracy. For our target population, elementary and middle-school students, and our sense of what is appropriate in citizenship education, the reconstructionist emphasis is too focused, even though the oppressed groups they highlight are worthy of attention by younger and older citizens.

In contrast, our conception of multicultural education includes goals such as cultural pluralism, intergroup harmony, an expanded multicultural/multiethnic knowledge base, and empowerment of students and parents and, by implication, teachers; all of these develop skills and knowledge associated with citizenship education. But we chose not to include a specific goal for citizenship education in this model. We consider citizenship, environmental, and global education to be critical components of the overall K–8 curriculum, but we view multicultural education and citizenship education as distinct interacting elements within that curriculum. This view allows citizenship education, like any other content area, to be analyzed in terms of being more or less multicultural. Also, our approach to citizenship education is not as sharply defined or politically directed as Sleeter and Grant's. The citizenship content we propose does not explicitly aim at preparing K–8 students to reconstruct society in the interests of all people, or more specifically, those who are of color, poor, female, and/or disabled. Rather, the citizenship curriculum we espouse would develop in students a positive attitude toward being an active citizen in their class and school as well as the local, state, national, and world society. It would show K–8 students that by individual and collective political and economic action they can make a difference at one or more of these political levels. Because we are focusing on students 5 to 13 years old, most of the citizenship projects should be at the local school, community, and county level with active involvement in state, national, and world issues as appropriate. This, of course, does not preclude specific discussions about oppression, social structural inequality, or racism and sexism in the United States of America and other nations.

In our view, the formation of a positive attitude toward citizenship is the quintessential function of schools, and the major strategy for developing this attitude goes far beyond preaching to students and having discussions about citizenship responsibilities. On a recurring basis students should have the opportunity to read about, discuss, and *do* citizenship. However, for this to happen, teachers must vividly see their own classrooms, schools, and local communities as politically formed communities where power and conflict of interests exist; in these settings students can learn through citizenship projects that their own decision making and action can improve their classrooms, school, and local communities. In short, local politics is highly significant politics, particularly for developing a healthy attitude and inclination toward active, responsible citizenship.

A related nationwide research project was done in 1989 among American youth aged 15 to 24 by People for the American Way. The researchers concluded that the youth interviewed

1. considered personal success, family life, and personal happiness far more important than community involvement and public life,
2. equated being a good citizen with being a good person as opposed to being politically engaged, and
3. displayed no compelling drive to participate in the political system because their focus tended to be directed inward.[3]

With these results in mind, and because the citizenship projects discussed below are closely linked to global citizenship, three ideas are worthy of emphasis. First, it is critical that young students utilize democratic skills (voting, debating, writing letters, challenging authority figures, shaping class and school rules) *on a regular basis* in their own classroom, school, and local community. Second, teachers and students can engage in an important and productive form of citizenship education without committing themselves and their students to the more radical form of "reconstructionist" citizenship education. There is much good work to be done in directing students toward social responsibility in their own communities and away from an exclusive concern with personal success; K–8 teachers from all over the political landscape (Republicans, Democrats, Independents, Christian Democrats, members of Labour or Green parties, etc.) should see in multicultural education an approach to citizenship education that they can strongly identify with. Finally, as Jack M. Hamilton illustrates in his book *Main Street America and the Third World,*[4] students and teachers can discover in their local community many connections to the world community and therefore many opportunities for global education.[5]

DEFINITIONS OF CITIZENSHIP EDUCATION, GLOBAL EDUCATION, AND ENVIRONMENTAL EDUCATION

Set against these two approaches to citizenship education, the following definitions of citizenship education, global education, and environmental education should help teachers to make choices about creating or adapting the type of thematic unit described in this chapter. For the purposes of our discussion, *citizenship education* will consist of all the school lessons and experiences that help students develop the ability and desire to be an active responsible citizen at various levels in our emergent democracy. One major responsibility involves being a reflective and informed voter; this requires a growing knowledge about pertinent local, state, and national issues. Given the obvious importance of this knowledge, it is easy to view *global education* as a key component of citizenship education; a recent definition by Kenneth A. Tye and Williard M. Kniep affirms this viewpoint. They wrote, "Global education involves learning about those problems and issues that cut across national boundaries, and about the interconnectedness of systems—ecological, cultural, economic, political, and technological," and added that global education also "involves learning to understand and appreciate our neighbors with different cultural backgrounds from ours; to see the world through the eyes and minds of others; and to realize that all peoples of the world need and want much the same things."[6] Global education so conceived clearly enhances the citizenship curriculum because it places current and future citizens in a more informed position to attempt to influence the domestic and foreign policy of their nation and other nations by voting, writing letters, and creating special advocacy groups. Given the problems that cut across national boundaries, such as deforestation and nuclear proliferation, one could argue that global education should be a major component of a well-rounded citizenship curriculum rather than an add-on. For K–8 students, global education can complement an emphasis on learning to be politically effective in one's own local community. As teachers and students strive to accomplish this effectiveness, it is appropriate for them to discover that problems they experience locally, such as pollution, poverty, and homelessness, are global in nature, and that the political and economic behavior of Americans, Japanese, Mexicans, Canadians, and others can contribute in a positive or negative way to the local problems experienced in different areas of the globe.

Learning that human consumption affects local as well as distant communities brings us close to the central concerns of environmental educators. Although *environmental education* has been defined in various ways, most environmental educators would agree that an environmental curriculum attempts to teach people to live more harmoniously with the earth and each other. Some link it strongly to citizenship education. For example, Michael Weilbacher, in describing the central mission of environmental education, wrote, "It's to assist learners in developing awareness, knowledge, skills, and commitment that result in informed decisions, responsible behavior, and constructive action concerning wildlife and the environment upon which we all depend."[7]

These definitions suggest that environmental education, global education, and citizenship education are overlapping curriculum areas, and that each can mesh neatly with the major goals of multicultural education. Citizenship education will show K–8 students that by individual and collective political action they can influence the course of local political events. Environmental education will help them learn how to take constructive action concerning wildlife and the environment, and global education will teach them about problems and issues that cut across national boundaries. If we as classroom teachers define curriculum units that accomplish these objectives, and simultaneously achieve selected goals of multicultural education, we will productively link four critically important curriculum areas that too often receive brief, unsystematic treatment in the busy and overcrowded K–8 curriculum.

DEVELOPING ENVIRONMENTAL
MULTICULTURAL UNITS

Classroom teachers working in the 1990s and beyond will not have to start from scratch as they develop these multiemphasis, environmental multicultural units. An excellent resource for developing such units is the 18-volume, K–8 NATURESCOPE series developed and distributed by the National Wildlife Federation.[8] Each volume provides background information for the teacher, activities to help students understand key concepts, a set of copycat pages (ready-to-copy games, puzzles, coloring pages, and worksheets), and lessons aimed at specific age groups: the primary grades (K–2), the intermediate grades (3–5), and the advanced grades (6–8). Titles in the series include *Incredible Insects, Astronomy Adventures, Diving into Oceans,* and *Discovering Deserts.* A 24-minute video entitled *Special Report: You Can Make a Difference* shows how students around the country are taking action to protect the environment. It was developed to accompany the NATURESCOPE series. This video is an excellent vehicle for showing how environmental awareness and knowledge can lead to productive, age-appropriate citizenship activities.

All the volumes in this series are excellent resources for environmental education, but several are particularly well suited for the development of environmental multicultural units. This subset includes the volumes entitled *Pollution: Problems and Solutions, Endangered Species: Wild and Rare, Trees Are Terrific,* and *Rain Forests: Tropical Treasures.* For illustration, we will work with the tropical rain forest volume to show how a unit based on a specific volume of the NATURESCOPE series will successfully integrate all four curriculum areas. We will begin by analyzing content from the volume and will then show how this content can be selectively multiculturalized.

THE TROPICAL RAIN FOREST
AS AN ENVIRONMENTAL MULTICULTURAL UNIT

Analysis of the content in the tropical rain forest volume quickly reveals why this theme lends itself to a multiemphasis unit. The global and environmental education dimensions of tropical rain forests, both as an amazing physical reality and a human problem that cuts across national boundaries, are illuminated through various rain forest topics. Students study the forests in terms of their location, unique qualities, flora and fauna, indigenous human groups, and the various problems associated with the quickening pace of rain forest depletion throughout the world. Instructional objectives related to the lessons and activities in this volume could be stated in the following way. Students will demonstrate the ability to

1. describe the four levels of tropical rain forest growth and the special characteristics of each;
2. describe the special nature of weather in the rain forest overall and at the four levels of the rain forest;
3. identify two prevalent myths about the rain forest;
4. describe specific characteristics of certain rain forest flora and fauna as well as supportive relationships that exist between selected animals and plants;
5. describe several ways that plants have adapted to life in tropical rain forests;
6. identify several continents and nations where tropical rain forests exist and locate the tropical rain forests within these nations;
7. explain how tropical rain forests differ from other types of forests, particularly the forest closest to the students' school;
8. identify common foods (banana, coffee, etc.) and products (quinine, rubber, and mahogany) that originate in tropical rain forests;
9. identify indigenous tribes who live in rain forests on different continents such as the Kayans or Penans in Borneo, the Efe in Zaire, the Lacandon Maya in Mexico, the Yanomamo and Kayapo in Brazil;
10. identify problems and consequences associated with the rapid depletion of the world's tropical rain forests;
11. provide six to ten reasons that help to explain why it is important to protect tropical rain forests;
12. identify five ways elementary and middle-school students can try to improve the health of the world's tropical rain forests.

The above objectives are relevant to environmental and global education and clearly set the stage for an active form of citizenship education, but they fall short of engaging students in a planning process related to citizenship education. This situation, however, is easily remedied. Both the *You Can Make a Difference* videotape mentioned above and the "Problems and Solutions" section of *Rain Forests: Tropical Treasures* provide well-selected citizenship projects for upper-elementary and middle-school students. Suggestions include (a) raising money to support organizations that seek to protect the world's rain forests, wildlife, and indigenous tribes; (b) making a commitment to modify consumption of wood products and food in ways that might positively influence the health of the world's rain forests; and (c) writing letters to chief executive officers and government officials in the United States, Japan, and Brazil urging these leaders to support legislation and industrial practices favorable to the tropical rain forests.

We need not elaborate further because most of the information an elementary or middle-school teacher would want is well covered in the NATURESCOPE volume and its bibliography. What is less well covered is content that would allow for selective multiculturalization of the unit; therefore, we will turn our attention to this curriculum area.

In previous chapters we used six different goals of multicultural education as guides in adapting various lessons; in this chapter we will focus on two goals, the ones that pertain to (a) expanding students' knowledge of different cultures and ethnic groups and (b) developing in students a pluralistic, open-minded attitude toward individuals and groups whose culture differs from their own. These goals are obviously related, but they are not the same. It is possible to expand students' knowledge of different cultures and ethnic groups in a manner that increases rather than diminishes ethnocentrism, and this possibility is heightened when students from technologically advanced societies, with a history of racism, study the cultures created by tribal groups who are less technologically advanced. The "multicultural" challenge for educators presenting information about the hundreds of thousands of humans who inhabit the planet's tropical rain forests is to do so in a manner that reinforces cultural pluralism while avoiding the distortion or idealization of the rain forest cultures in question.

Any unit dealing with the tropical rain forests should provide specific facts about the great diversity that exists among the indigenous people of these areas,[9] and we recommend that the teacher provide information about different tropical rain forest cultures as often as possible. This activity will extend the teacher's knowledge base and should lead to units that are progressively richer in terms of cross-cultural comparisons. Simultaneously, students should be encouraged to do individual and cooperative group research into other rain forest cultures, perhaps those that have been taught in prior years by their teacher. Although the specific rain forest culture to be presented will vary according to personal preference, we recommend that teachers consider the following criteria as they make their decisions. Where possible the indigenous group selected for study should be one that

1. has been studied by one or more anthropologists or other social scientists so that there are ethnographies (written descriptions of the culture) as well as photographs and possibly films or videos that can be used in the development and implementation of the unit;
2. takes into account the location of the class or special interests of the students. It is conceivable that students would show a bit more interest in a group located on their own continent, or in a country like Mexico that has a special relationship to the United States of America and which may be the ancestral home for a number of students in the class;
3. links to material taught earlier in class or as part of the K–8 social studies curriculum.

Finally, the indigenous group selected should be one whose special accomplishments and characteristics will highlight the skills, knowledge, and wisdom needed to survive in the tropical rain forests. Such a choice will increase the potential for students to grow in their appreciation of the sophisticated skills developed by various tribal cultures, groups who are sometimes described as "primitive" with much negative connotation loaded into the word.

With these criteria in mind, we have identified a small indigenous tribal culture, the Lacandon Maya, for study. This group lives in the Selva Lacandone in Chiapas, Mexico, the largest remaining tropical rain forest in North America, and is a good choice for an environmental multicultural unit. The group highlighted in the NATURESCOPE volume—the Efe Pygmies of the Ituri rain forest in Zaire, Africa—is interesting and suitable for a primary grade unit; however, the Lacandon Maya should interest older students in the United States of America, Canada, Brazil, and other nations for various reasons. First, it is likely that the students would have already spent some time studying the ancient Mayan civilization and its mysteries. Second, studying the past and present history of the Lacandon Maya would provide students with the opportunity to

1. review the extreme cruelty visited upon the South and Central "Native Americans" by the conquering soldiers and missionaries of Spain;
2. study the changes that occur when a relatively isolated culture begins to make contact with outside influences;
3. learn about the highly successful form of swidden (slash and burn) agriculture the Lacandon Maya have practiced for centuries;
4. increase their knowledge of the past and present of Mexico, a nation whose history and economic realities are of increasing importance to the United States and other nations.

The Lacandon Maya have been studied by several different types of social scientists, and at least three books and two films as well as assorted photographs of the tribe members are available to teachers.[10]

To facilitate the development of a unit that contains information about the Lacandon Maya, in the section below we will provide brief information about them in a question and answer format. To close the chapter, we will discuss the rationale for developing environmental multicultural units in an era when the information available to students and teachers is exploding at unprecedented rates. One estimate suggests that the information accessible in 1990 is just 3 percent of the amount that will be available in the year 2010.

THE LACANDON MAYA: BRIEF QUESTIONS AND ANSWERS

1. Who are the Lacandon Maya, where do they currently live, and where did they originate?

    The Lacandon Maya are a small group of Yucatecan-speaking Maya descendants who have lived in and around the Selva Lacandon rain forest in eastern Chiapas, Mexico, for approximately 400 years. Most authorities believe they moved into the area around Najà, Mexico, to escape persecution from Spanish soldiers and missionaries in western Guatemala, but a few others believe they are the direct descendants of the Mayans who built the temples located at Palenque and Yaxchilan in Chiapas. Today, the Lacandon Maya are one of the few remaining non-Christian Indian groups in Mexico.

2. Are the Lacandon Maya a homogeneous group?

There are two distinct groups of Lacandon Maya: the northern Lacandon—the non-Christianized Lacandon who live in Najà and Mensäbäk—and the southern Lacandon who live in Lacanha. The groups differ in customs, speak slightly different dialects of Yucatecan Maya, and rarely intermarry. The northern Lacandon have traditionally avoided the southern Lacandon because they consider them extremely violent.[11]

3. What is the origin of the term *Lacandon?*

According to R. Jon McGee, in the sixteenth century, "the Spanish used the term to refer to non-Christian Indians within a geographical area covering Chiapas and a part of the modern state of Tabasco."[12] Regarding the word's origins there are two competing theories. The first claims that *Lacandon* "is derived from lacum tun, or 'great rock,' the name of the Chol Maya fortress settlement on Lake Miramar."[13] The second theory, proposed by Robert Bruce, suggests that the word *Lacandon* was derived from the Mayan words "ah acantum," which means "to set up stone, stone pillars, or stone idols." In essence, this would be a way that Christianized Maya could refer to the non-Christianized as pagans or idolators, those who worship stones.

4. There are other contemporary Mayan descendants living in Mexico, like the Chol Maya and Tzeltal Maya (Chol and Tzeltal are Mayan dialects). What makes the Lacandon Maya worthy of study by elementary and middle-school students as well as social scientists?

The Lacandon Maya are unique in several ways. First, practically every other Mayan group in Mexico has been Christianized to some extent. The Lacandon Maya are the only contemporary group in Mexico whose daily life and rituals may approximate what peasant and religious life could have been like among the ancient Maya. They are also one of the few remaining groups who make use of "the practical environmental knowledge which accrued within the ancient Mayan civilization,"[14] and a number of contemporary social scientists believe that "aspects of Lacandon Maya subsistence and forest management systems have significance and viability for modern tropical forest production schemes."[15] Beyond this, the northern Lacandon Maya are interesting because of their continued efforts to keep their ancient religion alive even though their culture tolerates change that does not threaten the religion.

5. What are some of the key characteristics of the Lacandon Maya agricultural system?

According to James D. Nations and Ronald B. Nigh, "The Lacandon subsistence strategy centers around a multipurpose land-use system which takes advantage of a number of food-producing resource areas:

The primary forest, secondary forest growth, marshes and rivers, and lakes and streams."[16] The authors further note that "the basis for Lacandon resource management is tropical swidden agriculture (variously called shifting cultivation, slash and burn agriculture, or in Central America, the Milpa),"[17] and that the "Lacandon approach . . . centers on felling primary and secondary forest, burning the dried cuttings, and planting selected species in the clearing."[18]

The phrase *slash and burn,* which may suggest to some a careless approach to farming and natural resources, can be quite misleading. The Lacandon approach is a very patient, sensible, and long-term method of using the forest's resources in a way that does not deplete the rain forest as a source of food or as a natural habitat.

Lacandones plant and harvest a milpa for two to five consecutive years, then plant the area in tree crops and allow it to regrow with natural forest species. When regrowth reaches a height of four to seven meters (usually within five to seven years), they clear and burn the area for a second round of cultivation, or allow it to regenerate into mature secondary forest, a process which requires twenty years of fallowing. Lacandones prefer to cut milpas in regrowth areas (acahuales), and historical accounts demonstrate that this preference has long been a feature of their agricultural system.[19]

Much more can be said about the extent and sophistication of the agricultural knowledge base that has accrued within the Mayan culture, past and present. Nations and Nigh discuss

1. the Lacandon knowledge of soils, which is based on the types of trees in the area—for instance, when the Lacandones see the Ceibra tree and the breadnut ramon in abundance, they know the soil is rich and well drained;
2. the wise precautions the Lacandones take before burning rain forest to create a milpa;
3. the strategy of dispersing crops throughout the milpa to prevent large clusters of a single species;
4. planting crops like corn with a portion purposely allotted to wild mammals such as deer, squirrels, and raccoons; these animals ultimately provide the farmer with necessary meat protein;
5. maintaining the acuahal (or planted tree milpa) as a secondary source of crops, rubber, and wildlife. Nations and Nigh point out that the acuahal "is essentially a managed wildlife area."[20]

This description of the Lacandon Maya milpa agricultural system is only a thin slice of the whole picture. The intent was to show that a study of the Lacandon Maya can provide much useful information for fourth- through eighth-grade students. Learning about the Lacandon Maya will help students appreciate the depth and complexity of human cultures in general, and in this case those rain forest tribes who at first glance appear to be primitive, backward, and without wisdom that could inform the modern world. For teachers who choose to develop a rain forest unit that includes the Lacandon Maya as an example of a rain forest culture, there is much more information about Lacandon milpa agriculture in the Nations and Nigh article; R. Jon McGee has also provided a brief informative chapter on the topic as well as a thorough bibliography of resources on the Lacandon Maya.[21]

SUMMARY

This chapter has demonstrated ways to develop another type of integrated unit, one that links four pivotal but often sparsely treated curriculum areas: citizenship education, environmental education, global education, and multicultural education. The problem of omission or superficial treatment will grow rapidly as the amount of information increases geometrically in the coming decades. As a result, emphasis on teaching students to think critically and to discover and use knowledge on their own will become an overriding concern. As we grapple with these concerns, part of the solution will come from restructuring the curriculum and organizational categories that have traditionally made up the K–12 curriculum. The new combinations of knowledge and curriculum areas that should emerge will allow educators to be more creative in meeting the demands of a new era in knowledge production and consumption. As we move into this uncertain future, we believe that teachers should highlight the importance of knowledge and skills associated with the four curriculum areas stressed in this chapter. The content of a carefully designed environmental multicultural unit should influence attitudes in a way to make our future a bit more promising. For this reason we recommend that teachers give serious thought to implementing one or more environmental multicultural units per year, or find other ways to weave these curriculum areas into their ongoing curriculum.

DISCUSSION QUESTIONS

1. We conclude the chapter by saying that the content of a carefully structured environmental multicultural unit should influence student attitudes positively so as to make our future a bit more optimistic.
   a. Why do you think we have this opinion and how valid do you believe it to be?
   b. Is it the public schools' responsibility to attempt to develop in students a specific mindset toward democracy, the environment, and personal health? Is it appropriate for public school teachers and the public school curriculum to present a point of view with the hope that students will adopt it? If yes, explain your reasoning and discuss specific pitfalls or problem areas of a curriculum designed to shape attitudes. If no, explain your reasoning.
2. We have several reasons to believe that it is appropriate and practical to distinguish multicultural education from three other significant curriculum emphases (citizenship education, environmental education, and global education): first, each emphasis has its own specific domain; second, by keeping them distinct one can more easily step back to evaluate the multicultural nature of these three emphases; and finally, multicultural education is already sufficiently complicated without incorporating a set of new goals related to

these curriculum emphases. On the other hand, respected multicultural theorists such as Christine Bennett, Carl Grant, and Christine Sleeter have developed conceptions of multicultural education that incorporate one or more of them.

    a. If you were planning a workshop for pre- and in-service classroom teachers and their administrators, how would you define multicultural education?

    b. Would it be wise in your workshop to offer competing definitions of multicultural education? Why? Why not?

    c. Is there a way to define multicultural education that clarifies both its uniqueness and its connection to other curriculum emphases? What sort of visual image would be helpful in supporting this explanation?

3. We suggest that it would be valuable for fourth- through eighth-grade students, in the context of a unit that linked environmental, global, and citizenship concerns, to study the Lacandon Maya, an indigenous, relatively obscure, Mexican ethnocultural group of only about 350 people, a group that may become extinct within two to three generations.

    a. Reading into and beyond the material presented in this chapter, why do you think we believe this group is worthy of inclusion in the fourth- through eighth-grade multicultural curriculum?

    b. Based on your reading and experiences inside and outside this course, what do you think of our selection? Can you identify a better choice? Explain your reasoning.

4. Within this chapter we assert that students' knowledge of different cultures and ethnic groups can be expanded so as to increase rather than diminish ethnocentrism.

    a. From your own personal experience as a learner, can you identify school- or non-school-related learning experiences in which your exposure to a specific ethnocultural group increased rather than decreased your own ethnocentrism? If so, please describe the learning experience and its repercussions.

    b. To increase your own positive orientation to cultural pluralism, how should the material in this learning experience have been arranged?

RECOMMENDED ACTIVITIES

1. Drawing on your professor's knowledge base or your own network, identify one or more teachers with a strong reputation for teaching units that link together all or several of the curriculum areas discussed in this chapter. Observe and interview this teacher (or teachers) to discover resources and tactics that will prove useful in your own teaching.

2. Develop and prepare to implement an environmental multicultural unit that focuses on tropical rain forest issues; to the extent possible work collaboratively with one or more teachers or student teachers in an attempt to make the unit as interesting as possible.

3. Examine the instructional media center in your local school district, county or regional office of education, or university to identify specific curriculum materials that would be helpful in designing an environmental multicultural unit that revolves around pollution, overpopulation, the spread of acquired immunodeficiency syndrome (AIDS), or some other environmental/global problem area. One handbook that could be helpful as an initial source of information is *The Global Ecology Handbook: What You Can Do about the Environmental Crisis.* The book was edited by Walter H. Corson and published by Beacon Press (Boston) in 1990 with the help of the Global Tomorrow Coalition. It is a rich compendium of environmental information and can be a practical supplement to the Public Broadcasting System's series entitled "Race to Save The Planet." In addition, for teachers there are several valuable sources of information about global education. Two of the most important are the Social Science Education Consortium, Inc., 3300 Mitchell Lane, Suite 240, Boulder, Colorado, 80301-2272, phone (303) 492-8154, and the Center for Teaching International Relations, Graduate School of International Studies, University of Denver, Denver, Colorado, 80208, phone (303) 871-3106. Ten titles and brief descriptions are listed below to give you a clearer sense of the curriculum resources made available by these organizations.

a. *Global Issues in the Elementary Classroom.* Boulder, Colo.: Social Science Education Consortium, 1988.
Ideas, activities (lesson plans, student handouts), and strategies for teaching global awareness and studying human values, global systems, global issues, and global history. Includes an annotated bibliography of additional resources for teachers.

b. *Global Issues in the Intermediate Classroom: Grades 5–8.* Boulder, Colo.: Social Science Education Consortium, 1981.
Ideas, activities (lesson plans, student handouts), and strategies for teaching global awareness, global interdependence, and cross-cultural understanding. Practical, hands-on approach.

c. *Teaching about Cultural Awareness: Grades 4–12,* rev. ed. Denver, Colo.: Center for Teaching International Relations, 1985.
Lesson plans and reproducible handouts to stimulate positive attitudes about cultural differences.

d. *Teaching about World Cultures. Focus on Developing Regions, Grades 7–12.* Denver, Colo.: Center for Teaching International Relations. 1986.
Includes units on China, Japan, Southeast Asia, India, the Middle East, Africa, and Latin America.

e. *Global Issues: Activities and Resources for the High School Teacher.* Denver, Colo.: Social Science Education Consortium, 1979.
Classroom strategies and ready-to-use activities (lesson plans, student handouts) for introducing the concept of global awareness, world trade and economic interdependence, global conflict and the arms race, economic development and foreign aid, environment and technology, energy and natural resources, and human rights.

f. *The World Citizen Curriculum: Grades 7–12.* Denver, Colo.: Center for Teaching International Relations, 1987.
Intended to underscore the choices and actions that link individuals to world affairs. Includes a problem-oriented, multidisciplinary, experience-based curriculum on such topics as interdependence, cultural diversity, alternative futures, and global policy making. Volume 1 is the student resource book (concise readings to introduce the concept of world citizenship), and Volume 2 is the teacher resource guide (40 activities, 13 units, and student handouts).

g. *Teaching about the Consumer and the Global Marketplace, Grades 4–12.* Denver, Colo.: Center for Teaching International Relations, 1985.
Notes how international economic systems influence the consumer, and vice versa. Includes activities and student handouts to help students focus on the values, problems, and skills involved in becoming a more conscientious consumer.

h. *Teaching about Population Growth: Grades 6–12.* Denver, Colo.: Center for Teaching International Relations, 1981.
Lesson plans and student handouts for understanding how growth affects resources, why population is growing at an exponential rate, how populations are unevenly distributed, and how conscious decisions can affect population dynamics.

i. *Teaching about Population Issues: Grades 6–12.* Denver, Colo.: Center for Teaching International Relations, 1983.

Lesson plans, student handouts, and teaching ideas (discussion starters, simulations) on such population topics as crowding, population control, migration, and immigration.
   j. *Teaching Writing Skills: A Global Approach.* Denver, Colo.: Center for Teaching International Relations, 1986.
   Includes lesson plans and student handouts for stimulating creative writing, examining perspective, and using personal experiences to engage students actively in writing.

Journal Entry

This chapter focused on the rationale and procedure for developing units linking citizenship, global education, environmental education, and multicultural education. It would be appropriate in your journal entry to comment on the questions below as well as your own questions or feelings about this chapter.

1. Did you learn anything of value from this chapter's content, discussion questions, and recommended activities? If yes, please summarize what you have learned.
2. Has the experience of reading chapter 5 or participating in discussions or activities related to the chapter given you some new insight into multicultural education? If yes, please discuss your new insights.
3. Which, if any, of the comments made about environmental multicultural units seemed questionable or ambiguous to you?

NOTES

1. Christine L. Bennett, *Comprehensive Multicultural Education* (Boston: Allyn & Bacon, 1990).
2. Christine E. Sleeter and Carl A. Grant, *Making Choices for Multicultural Education: Five Approaches to Race, Class, and Gender* (Columbus, Ohio: Merrill, 1988), 176.
3. *Democracy's Next Generation* (Washington, D.C.: People for the American Way, 1989).
4. Jack M. Hamilton, *Main Street America and the Third World* (Washington, D.C.: Seven Locks Press, 1988).
5. In "Identifying Local Links to the World," *Educational Leadership* 48, no. 7 (April 1991), 50–52, Roselle Kline Chartok offers a very practical approach to helping students of all ages discover the links between their local communities and various nations of the world.
6. Kenneth A. Tye and Williard M. Kniep, "Global Education around the World," *Educational Leadership* 48, no. 7 (April 1991), 47–49; a similar definition appears in *Global Education: From Thought to Action,* ed. Kenneth A. Tye (Alexandria, Va.: Association for Supervision and Curriculum Development, 1990), 5.
7. Michael Weilbacher, "Education That Cannot Wait," *E: The Environmental Magazine* 2, no. 2 (March/April 1991), 30. In describing the mission of environmental education, Weilbacher drew on a direct quote from the director of Project Wild, Dr. Cheryl Charles.
8. Individual copies or the entire set of 18 volumes can be ordered by writing to the National Wildlife Federation, 1400 Sixteenth Street, N.W., Washington, D.C. 20036-2266, or by calling 1-800-245-5484. In 1992 an individual copy plus shipping cost $11.90. The entire set could be purchased for $102.95, and this price included shipping.
9. Two useful resources for learning about this diversity are the following:
   a. *People of the Tropical Rain Forest,* ed. Julie Sloan Denslow and Christine Padoch (Berkeley: University of California Press in association with the Smithsonian Institution Traveling Exhibition Service, 1988).

b. *Tropical Rain Forests: A Disappearing Treasure,* a booklet published by the Smithsonian Institution (1988) in conjunction with the exhibition Tropical Rain Forests: A Disappearing Treasure. The latter was organized by the Smithsonian Institution Traveling Exhibition Service and will travel to six different cities between 1992 and 1994. See the inside back cover of the NATURESCOPE volume on tropical rain forests for a list of the cities.

10. Each of the following three books is about the Lacandon Maya; each was written at the beginning of a recent decade: the 1970s, 1980s, and 1990s. The first book listed below, which was written by a professor of anthropology, will be most valuable for classroom teachers.

a. R. Jon McGee. *Life, Ritual, and Religion among the Lacandon Maya* (Belmont, Calif.: Wadsworth, 1990).

This should be the first book read by a teacher planning a unit on the Lacandon Maya. It focuses primarily on the religious beliefs of the Lacandon Maya but also contains several chapters that provide an excellent introduction to this group. Chapter titles include "Introduction to the Lacandon Maya," "The Conquest of the Yucatàn and Origins of the Lacandon Maya," "Social Organization in Najà" (one of the Lacandon Maya Villages), "Lacandon Subsistence and Economics," and "Lacandon Culture and the Future." The book's 10 chapters, independent of the glossary, appendices, and index, total 131 pages and can easily be read over a weekend. This book contains less photography than the two listed below.

b. Christine Price (author) and Gertrude Duby Blom (photographer), *Heirs of the Ancient Maya: A Portrait of the Lacandon Indians* (New York: Charles Schribner's Sons, 1972).

Of the books listed here, this is the oldest and briefest (56 pages) and is now out of print. When you teach the unit, this would be a good resource to have available because of its photographs and because many upper-grade students can read it on their own. In addition, it could be read to the entire class. Sections of this book could be contrasted with information in the more up-to-date McGee book to show how the Lacandon Maya are both changing and remaining the same as the pace of contact with the outer world increases.

c. Victor Perera and Robert D. Bruce, *The Lacandon Maya and the Mexican Rain Forest* (Boston: Little, Brown, 1982).

This is the longest (303 pages) and the least conventional, perhaps because one of the authors, Robert Bruce, is an atypical linguist and anthropologist. To get as close as possible to the Lacandon worldview, Bruce attempted to live the life of a Lacandon Maya to the greatest extent possible. This book, which contains many interesting observations about the Lacandon Maya, is harder to read than the McGee book. We recommend that the Perera/Bruce book be consulted after the McGee book is read. The Perera/Bruce book also contains many interesting photographs.

In addition to the above books, two ethnographic films about the Lacandon Maya, both produced by R. Jon McGee, can be rented or purchased through the California Extension Media Center in Berkeley in either ¹/₂ inch VHS or ³/₄ inch U-Matic format. Call (510) 642-0460 for further information. The films are titled *Swidden Agriculture among the Lacandon Maya* and *The Lacandon Maya Balché Ritual.*

11. McGee, *Life, Ritual, and Religion,* 1.
12. Ibid., 17.
13. Ibid., 18.
14. James D. Nations and Ronald B. Nigh, "The Evolutionary Potential of Lacandon Maya

Sustained-yield Tropical Forest Agriculture," *Journal of Anthropological Research* 36, no. 1, 2.
15. Ibid., 2.
16. Ibid., 8.
17. Ibid.
18. Ibid.
19. Ibid.
20. Ibid., 13.
21. McGee, *Life, Ritual, and Religion,* 15.

The Idea of Multicultural Education Revisited

A quick review of the preface and chapter 1 would reveal that the focus of this text is on design and implementation of multicultural education at the classroom level. There is some mention of expanding school projects to serve the local community, the different levels at which multicultural education should be taught (the school site, district and university levels), and the James Comer approach to schoolwide restructuring; much of this text, however, channels teachers' multicultural thinking into the confines of their own classrooms. This individual classroom focus, which in part derives from our belief that classroom teachers are the ultimate and critical agents of change in the multicultural restructuring process, is both a virtue and a weakness.

A CLASSROOM-FOCUSED CONCEPTION OF MULTICULTURAL EDUCATION: VIRTUE AND WEAKNESS

The classroom-focused conception is helpful because of its hands-on immediacy. This level of analysis allows us to show you clearly the many ways you can restructure the individual classroom curriculum to achieve various goals of multicultural education. This clarity and emphasis is needed for implementation. Too often a single university-level course, in attempting to deal with the full range of multicultural concepts and issues, will provide incomplete treatment of the critical classroom applications of these elements.

To attain this clarity, however, we have neglected discussing the important ways that school counselors, nutritionists, staff development specialists, principals, superintendents, parents, and community representatives can help to create a total school environment conducive to multicultural education. This is an important limitation to be aware of. As James Banks has noted, "To implement multicultural education successfully, we must think of the school as a social system in which all of its major variables are closely interrelated. . . . Thinking of a school as a social system suggests that we must formulate and initiate a change strategy that reforms the total school environment to implement multicultural education."[1]

After reading and discussing the content of this text and completing various recommended activities if you choose to become an agent of multicultural change in your classroom and school, you should realize that for you to introduce the new concepts in your classroom alone is a bit like Don Quixote jousting with windmills. Throughout the text we have suggested that for teaching to be effective, it must occur within the context of a multicultural curriculum; to that we now add the idea that *your* multicultural change efforts, to be truly meaningful for your students— whom you will most likely teach for only one year—should be part of a wider systematic change effort. This means, simply, that the umbrella of multicultural change should cover *all* aspects of education in the *entire* school district. Teachers interested in creating an effective multicultural curriculum in their own classrooms will need to work together with other like-minded teachers, administrators, school counselors, parents, and curriculum specialists to initiate school and district change. There are many ways to move toward a comprehensive schoolwide approach to multicultural education, but perhaps the most logical first step is to discuss with your fellow teachers and principal the notion of making multicultural education, in all its rich variety, a short- and long-term priority in staff development.[2] Creating integrated units with other teachers is another logical step, and planning a school-wide approach to increase parental participation in school governance is a third area worthy of exploration. Beyond this, delving into the resources listed in the appendixes should also prove helpful in preparing you to be a more knowledgeable multicultural change agent.

Finally, we hope we have encouraged you to continue your study of the emergent multicultural education literature. It is a literature of optimism; it fosters a movement that challenges teachers to enhance and extend our democracy by reaching out to all learners with enthusiasm and sensitivity. It is a movement we feel obligated and privileged to serve. We are delighted, with the help of your instructor, to have brought it to your attention.

DISCUSSION QUESTIONS

1. We acknowledge that we have ignored a critical dimension of multicultural education— the necessity of thinking comprehensively about schoolwide change when creating an effective multicultural curriculum.
   a. Based on your own readings in and beyond this course, what are some other important multicultural topics that have not been adequately addressed in this text?
   b. Are you aware of specific resources that shed light on these topics? If yes, please delineate them.
   c. What are some instructional strategies for addressing these concerns in your multicultural restructuring effort?

2. For practical reasons, we have suggested defining multicultural education in terms of its goals—what it is setting out to accomplish. Toward this end we have identified six goals for our classroom-oriented conception of multicultural education. After reviewing these goals (in chapter 1) and the planning questions they suggest (in chapters 2 and 3), discuss the adequacy or inadequacy of our conception of multicultural education. Multicultural goals delineated by other authors may help. For example, in "Multicultural Education: Characteristics and Goals" (see endnote 1), James Banks delineates a set of goals on pages 19–21, and Christine Bennett lists a different set in her text *Comprehensive Multicultural Education: Theory and Practice,* 2nd. ed. (Boston: Allyn & Bacon, 1990).

3. What is your own working definition of multicultural education? Has it changed as a result of your readings and discussions in this course? If so, how?

4. There will always be competing conceptions of multicultural education, just as there are competing theories about cooperative learning, classroom discipline, and democracy. As a result, an educator hearing about these various conceptions may comment, "Forget about this multicultural education. It's too confusing and complex, and people can't make up their minds what it is supposed to mean."

   a. How do you think we would respond to this educator?

   b. How would you respond to this educator if he or she made this comment to you after you had just presented the first hour of a three-hour workshop on multicultural education?

NOTES

1. James Banks, "Multicultural Education: Characteristics and Goals," Chapter 1 in *Multicultural Education: Issues and Perspectives,* ed. James Banks and Cherry A. McGee Banks (Boston: Allyn & Bacon, 1989), 21.

2. A helpful document for this purpose is the position statement of the National Council for the Social Studies entitled "Curriculum Guidelines for Multicultural Education," published in the September 1992 issue of *Social Education* 56, no. 5, 274–294. The primary author of this statement, which updates the 1976 position statement, is James Banks, director, Center for Multicultural Education, University of Washington. (The phone number of the center is (206) 543-3386.)

APPENDIX 1

The Typology of Multicultural Teaching

To facilitate the dissemination of information about multicultural education and multicultural teaching to cooperating (master) teachers, university supervisors, principals, and student teachers, we developed "The Typology of Multicultural Teaching" as well as a handout entitled "Key Multicultural Teacher Education Definitions." The typology was included as part of a memorandum sent to all student and cooperating teachers in the California Polytechnic (Cal Poly) teacher education program prior to the beginning of student teaching. It was also referred to at the student teaching orientation meetings held each quarter to reinforce the importance of multicultural education within the Cal Poly teacher education program. We reprint the memorandum and the typology with minor revisions.

To: Fall Quarter Six and Twelve Unit Date: September 15, 1991
Multiple Subject Student Teachers,
Cooperating Teachers, File No.: Version #7
University Supervisors

From: Leonard and Patricia Davidman

Subject: A Typology of Multicultural Teaching Designed to Help Participants Understand What the Teacher Education Program Means When It Uses the Term *Multicultural Teaching*

GENERAL REMARKS TO STUDENT TEACHERS

Multicultural instruction provides us with an exciting, significant, and sophisticated model of curriculum and instruction. The sophistication pertains to the wide range of instructional decisions that a teacher needs to make to create a comprehensive multicultural curriculum. In your first and second student teaching assignments you will be able to make some of these multicultural instruction decisions, but not others. For those you can make, it is important that you have a clear understanding of what multicultural teaching is and are prepared to incorporate elements of the model into your own teaching repertoire as soon as possible. To help you achieve these objectives, a typology of multicultural teaching with examples is provided below for your future study and discussion. As you become increasingly familiar with the six major components of the current Cal Poly conception of multicultural education, you will begin to discover other, perhaps better, examples. When you do, I would appreciate your passing them along to me or your ED 407 instructor. Finally, as you analyze these examples, please remember that effective multicultural teaching occurs during specific lessons but also before, after, and between lessons in a variety of contexts both inside and outside the classroom. It includes communication with parents and students; it affects and takes place within the entire school curriculum. At the same time that we focus on the classroom level, students should recall that multicultural education is concerned with reforming school and district-wide practices when such practices are in need of change.

GENERAL REMARKS TO COOPERATING TEACHERS

As a part of the evolution of the Cal Poly teacher education program and because of the instructional challenges facing contemporary and future educators in the state of California, the Cal Poly multiple subject program is now embracing and transmitting a conception of multicultural education that emphasizes the teacher's role in creating educational equity at the classroom level. We understand educational equity to be strongly related to (a) maximizing opportunities for the educational success of all students in a classroom and (b) analyzing the results of our educational programs to ensure that the opportunities lead to successful educational results for the wide range of students contemporary teachers work with.

Following one of the tenets of the Madeline Hunter model, which has been so influential in our region and state, we are trying to develop a common vocabulary in the area of multicultural education and teaching. This vocabulary will allow more lucid communication about multicultural teaching among professors, cooperating teachers, university supervisors, and student teachers. The typology listed below presents an incomplete list of possible teacher behaviors and is basically a communication tool. It is not a list of requirements, and it will not play a formal role in the assessment of student teachers. It is a shorthand device we are using to create a clearer vision of what multicultural teaching could look like in behavioral terms at the classroom level, and is a source of ideas for all those involved in teacher education. Finally, it is a catalyst for and an invitation to further dialogue and growth in the area of multicultural education for all concerned.

The Typology
A. Examples of Type I Multicultural (MC) Planning and Teaching
(Planning and teaching that is directly aimed at educational equity)
The teacher
1. makes sophisticated use of the elements of instruction (selecting an objective at the appropriate level of difficulty, teaching to an objective, monitoring and adjusting, using the principles of learning, etc.).
2. selects and utilizes a classroom management system that maximizes the amount of time he or she has available for individual tutoring.
3. modifies her or his oral pace and syntax to facilitate the learning of language and content material for limited English proficient students as well as other special learners, and makes use of other "sheltered English" teaching strategies.
4. allows one student to serve as a buddy tutor, interpreter, or assistant teacher to facilitate the learning of another student.
5. makes appropriate use of cooperative learning strategies.
6. uses a variety of techniques to demonstrate powerfully that in contem-

porary America men and women of all colors and ethnic groups are succeeding in a wide range of occupations, such as

   a. Friday afternoon "career awareness" interviews in which a wide range of successful Americans are interviewed by students;
   b. classroom bulletin boards;
   c. magazines such as *Ebony* that regularly contain stories about successful African Americans;
   d. book reports;
   e. visits by ethnic minority students enrolled in local colleges.

7. uses teaching techniques and curriculum materials from specially designed projects such as Project Equals and the Complex Instruction Project (Elizabeth Cohen/Stanford University).

8. promotes junior high school and high school graduation and college attendance by engaging in *follow through* and *future prediction* oral behavior, such as the following:

   a. "I want you (all) to let me know when you graduate from high school . . . or junior high school."
   b. "When you children are in high school (or college), you are going to remember this lesson."
   c. "I know that some of the children in this class will want to become classroom teachers, and I intend to make certain that that happens." An example of follow through behavior is the work of one local first-grade teacher who sends out congratulation cards to her students 10 or 11 years later when they graduate from high school.

9. engages in student, peer, and self-evaluation to monitor, assess, and perhaps modify the distribution of attention, higher-level questions and wait-time, and leadership opportunities to various individuals and groups in the class.

10. employs a flexible mastery learning model of instruction (pretest/posttest; carefully constructed teaching units; carefully prepared backup teaching strategies).

11. includes self-confidence and self-esteem building as part of the affective/cognitive curriculum.

12. seeks out and makes professional use of parent volunteers and bilingual/trilingual aides if needed.

13. makes use of informal "interest" and "learning style" inventories so as to address in classroom teaching the student's interests, learning preferences, and learning style or strengths.

14. develops a multi-ability curriculum that allows a variety of academic skills to receive classroom and teacher recognition as important.

15. makes certain that students receive their fair share of instructional resources and technology.

16. employs and models nonsexist language, such as saying "police officers" rather than "policemen."

17. creates a collaborative and supportive learning environment—"We're all

in this together; we're here to learn and grow as individuals and partners; in this class we will be responsible for each other's success."

18. examines attendance records to get an early start on implementing
plans designed to lower the absence rate of specific students.

19. collects and analyzes data from a survey of television watching to increase his or her ability to modify patterns of excessive television viewing where appropriate.

B. Examples of Type II MC Teaching
(Communication, planning, and teaching that attempts to establish a positive
and collaborative relationship between the home and school so as to (a)
place teachers in a better position to collect and use knowledge of a student's family and cultural background to provide sensitive, sensible instruction, and (b) place parents in a better position to play a meaningful role in
their child's education)

The teacher

1. meets with parents of all students early in the year to learn about
significant family concerns, values, educational objectives, changes in
the health history of the student, and so on.

2. examines the student's cumulative folder in preparation for the family
interview.

3. plans classroom social events that include as many students as possible,
or that dignify the cultural differences of a family that does not exchange birthday presents, or salute the flag, or celebrate other mainstream American holidays, and so on.

4. will manifest or allow a different pattern of communication, where
research has demonstrated that such fluency and flexibility promotes
student learning (overlapping talk in native Hawaiian students).

5. will individualize instruction to provide maximum continuity in learning for migrant learners whose family mobility annually involves an
extended stay in Mexico. This may include the development of learning
packets and cassette tapes that students can use while in Mexico.

6. modify weekend homework assignments for students who travel substantial distances to spend selected weekends with a divorced parent,
and so on.

7. will invite parents to visit and observe the class in action when the
teacher believes such visits will increase the parent's comfort level with
the public school.

8. will use parent–teacher conferences as an opportunity to
   a. manifest cultural sensitivity;
   b. elicit family cultural knowledge;
   c. develop the concept of teamwork between teachers and parents.

9. frequently communicates with parents by letters that express the idea
that "We're in this together; we need to work well together and then
learn how to cooperate even more; *our success will be your child's
success.*"

10. will remain "professionally curious" about each student throughout the course of the year and will be professionally cautious and tentative in using family and cultural background data so as to avoid making simplistic or stereotypical judgments.
11. will initiate and support schoolwide efforts to create pertinent parent education activities, such as classes in English as a second language held during school hours in the school cafeteria.
12. will initiate and support schoolwide efforts to help low-income families locate doctors who are flexible in their payment schedules.

C. Examples of Type III MC Teaching
(Teaching that attempts to foster cultural pluralism and systematically provide students with in-depth knowledge regarding a wide range of domestic and international ethnic groups and cultures)*

The teacher

1. uses the social studies and other content areas to make the student aware of the range of co-cultures and ethnic groups that interact in various ways to create the American nation and culture.
2. uses the social studies and other content areas to make the students aware of the commonalities and differences between American culture and other cultures, and the positive features of these various cultures.
3. implements units of instruction that are, in fact, historical and contemporary case studies of selected cultures.
4. teaches about cultures in a manner that encourages students to understand and appreciate the various cultures being studied rather than evaluating them exclusively in terms of mainstream American, or other, values.
5. teaches about cultures in an open-minded and flexible manner that encourages students to ask probing questions about their own culture as well as other cultures.

D. Examples of Type IV MC Teaching
(Teaching that attempts to foster intercultural, intergroup, and interethnic understanding and camaraderie within the classroom *and* multicultural appreciation, tolerance, and sensitivity in the community and larger culture)

1. Multiperspective teaching of history as well as current events (this represents movement away from a Eurocentric and Anglocentric perspective on American and world history).
2. Role-playing of dilemma stories (sociodrama and the materials developed by Fannie R. Shaftel and others).
3. Analysis and discussion of the lives and problems of true-to-life "fictional" characters.

---

* This type of multicultural teaching simultaneously aims at two of the six goals discussed in the text. The two are so closely related that for the purpose of the typology we chose to combine them into one type of teaching.

4. Student self-disclosure about cultural and/or religious background (keep in mind the supportive, we're in this together, family-like learning environment):
   a. Child of the Week Program—sometimes called Star of the Week;
   b. Autobiographical assignment in language arts.
5. Word of the Week Program with words like *tolerant, sensitive, supportive, cooperative, multicultural, open-minded, bilingual.* (Cooperation and cooperative learning are so critical to multicultural teaching that the word *cooperation* should be an ongoing word in the Word of the Week program.)
6. Teacher "witnessing" in praise of diversity:
   "Now, this looks like a very interesting and diverse classroom. Let's see, we have several students who are partially bilingual, several who . . ." or "Isn't it lovely that we have so many different plants in our community . . . or planets in the sky . . . or clouds in the sky."
7. Sister schools and sister classrooms within the same school district or county; pen pals; joint field trips; school visits, and teacher and student exchanges—the idea is to break out of segregated realities that are sometimes imposed by housing patterns, and so on.
8. Teacher recognition of and teaching about organizations that attempt to foster intergroup understanding and cooperation between diverse groups, such as the National Conference of Christians and Jews and the Anti-Defamation league of the B'nai B'rith. (The latter group, in particular, disseminates excellent intergroup instructional materials.) The idea here is to highlight positive examples of intergroup and intragroup cooperation.
9. A cooperative learning environment.
10. The teaching of American and world history to make it quite clear that the art, music, language(s), history, ethics, and political life of the nation has been decisively influenced by a wide range of individuals, cultures, and ethnic groups. (The new *California History and Social Science Framework* will be a helpful resource here.)

E. Examples of Type V MC Teaching
(Teaching that attempts to develop in teachers and students the ability and proclivity to think, act, learn, and teach with a multicultural perspective)
The teacher
1. consistently encourages students, when studying current events and specific historical periods, to wonder whether and why members of one culture or co-culture will interpret and react to one situation differently from another because of cultural differences.
2. provides independent study opportunities that pertain to the different ways representatives of various cultures communicate (both verbally and nonverbally).
3. encourages students to read autobiographical and biographical literature wherein authors discuss the ways their ethnicity and cultural background

influenced their perceptions and responses to various events, both local and distant, familial and nonfamilial.

4. gives specific lessons to show students that members of individual cultures and co-cultures perceive, interpret, and respond to reality differently because various cultures have different ways to define and create reality (e.g., categories of time, language concepts and structure, creation stories, gender role socialization, attitudes toward science, progress, family responsibilities, civic responsibilities, etc.).

APPENDIX 2

The Ethnic and Cultural Self-disclosure Inventory

Professor Davidman

Subject: Ethnic and Cultural Self-disclosure Inventory

GENERAL REMARKS

In this class many of our discussions will deal with culture and ethnicity. Your self-disclosure tonight through this inventory will assist the professor and your class-mates in preparing to listen insightfully and discuss issues sensitively. In this class it is helpful to know where the listeners and speakers are coming from and going to. Tonight, I will share my self-disclosure and then explain how you will use yours next week to introduce yourself to your cooperative learning group. In addition, in attempting to build constructive diversity into each discussion group, I will draw on the information in your written self-disclosure. Please use additional paper to complete your response where necessary.

Self-disclosure Items and Questions

1. Your name: _____

2. Where are you from? Where do you live now?

_____

_____

3. With whom do you live? (I live with friends, myself, my family, etc.) This is optional.

_____

_____

4. Which M.A. program are you in, and what do you want to do with your M.A. in the short and long term?

_____

_____

5. Please list a favorite author or book you have especially enjoyed, a significant book in your life (such as the Bible, or the Koran, or some other very meaningful book), and/or a significant learning or growth experience in your life.

_____

_____

_____

6. Do you have a favorite hobby? If so, please identify.

_____

_____

_____

7. Given our opening definition of ethnicity, ethnic group, and cultural group, would you be comfortable in describing yourself as a member of an ethnic or cultural group? If so, which groups are you a member of?

_____

_____

_____

8. Have you ever experienced interpersonal conflict because of your ethnicity or cultural group? If so, please describe.

_____

_____

_____

_____

_____

9. Do you feel your ethnicity/cultural group membership has, in any way, been a positive feature in your life? If so, briefly explain.

_____

_____

_____

_____

10. Given our course objectives, have you had any personal experiences that might help you contribute to the achievement of the specified objectives?

_____

_____

_____

11. Have specific values stemming from your ethnicity/cultural group and your family culture influenced the way you perform or feel about your chosen career? Is there some possible relationship between your ethnicity/cultural group and your choice of career?

_____

_____

12. Your phone number and address:

APPENDIX 3

Specially Designed Academic Instruction in English (Sheltered English) Observation Form

Name: _____ Teacher: _____

Date: _____ Grade/Subject: _____

School: _____

Focus: The Use of Sheltered English Instruction (Specially Designed Academic Instruction in English) to Promote Educational Equity.

1. Specifically, what did the teacher do to make her oral remarks comprehensible to the limited English proficient learners (LEP) in her class?

_____

_____

_____

_____

2. How did her oral and nonverbal communication differ from communication you have observed in other classrooms?

_____

_____

_____

_____

3. Did this teacher make use of cooperative learning groups or partners to increase student comprehension of instructions and lesson content? If yes, how did the groups or partners appear to be functioning?

_____

_____

_____

_____

_____

_____

4. How would you describe the reaction of LEP learners to this form of instruction?

_____

_____

_____

_____

5. From your interview with the teacher, what else did you learn about specially designed academic instruction in English?

_____

_____

_____

_____

APPENDIX 4

Cooperative Learning Group Observation Form

Name: _____ Teacher: _____

Date: _____ Grade/Subject: _____ School: _____

Focus: The Use of Cooperative Learning to Promote Educational Equity.

1. Does this lesson have an instructional focus, and if so, what do you think the teacher would identify as her main instructional objective(s)?

    a. _____

    _____

    _____

    b. _____

    _____

    _____

2. Was cooperative learning the main instructional strategy in this lesson or one of several that were employed? If the latter, which other strategies were employed?

    _____

    _____

    _____

3. Prior to releasing the students to work in their cooperative groups, what, if anything, did the teacher say to the students to promote effective functioning of groups? (Look for positive group interdependence, individual accountability, etc.)

    _____

    _____

    _____

4. What did the teacher do while the cooperative learning groups were functioning?

    _____

    _____

    _____

5. Were the groups in this class during this learning activity in competition with each other? If so, what effect did this appear to have on the learning?

_____

_____

6. Overall (across all groups in the class), how well did the students appear to be interacting with each other?

_____

_____

_____

7. In the one or two groups you were closely observing

a. how many of the students were consistently on task in what seemed to be a productive manner?

_____

_____

_____

b. did students have the same or different responsibilities vis-à-vis the task, or a little bit of both?

_____

_____

_____

c. did the students appear to be enjoying this learning activity?

_____

_____

8. Were the groups diversely structured in terms of gender and ethnicity?

_____

_____

9. In the group(s) you closely observed did the member(s) of one cultural (girls/boys) or ethnic (Hispanic, White, Asian, African American, etc.) group appear to dominate the interaction?

_____

_____

_____

10. Did the students in each group appear to be playing special roles at least part of the time—expert instructor, encourager, scribe, reporter, praiser, resource distributor, time keeper, etc.?

_____

_____

_____

11. What did you learn about classroom management from observing these lessons?

_____

_____

_____

12. From your observation of these lessons, what did you not understand?

_____

_____

APPENDIX 5

Position Papers by Albert Shanker

SACRIFICING ACCURACY FOR DIVERSITY*

by Albert Shanker
President of the American Federation of Teachers

We're in the midst of an important change in our school curriculum. By including the contributions of many different groups that have not previously been recognized, we're trying to make a multicultural curriculum that accurately reflects our society.

However, some groups, including the New York State Board of Regents, which has just accepted guidelines for a new social studies curriculum, may end up sacrificing accuracy for diversity. They seem to think that, in order to give kids varied points of view, it is perfectly okay to teach ideas and theories that few or no reputable scholars accept. The Regents' proposal calls this using "noncanonical knowledge and techniques" and "nondominant knowledge sources."

You can see some good examples of what's wrong with this idea in the Portland (Oregon) "African-American Baseline Essays." This mini-curriculum, made up of essays on social studies, science, language arts, mathematics, art and music, has been adopted or used as a model by school systems all over the country.

The Portland essays present ancient Egypt as an African culture that strongly influenced the development of European civilization, and this is fair enough. It's a view most reputable scholars have agreed with for 40 years, and it corrects distortions of previous historians who were inclined to ignore Egypt's contribution or to disregard the fact that Egypt was an African civilization. But the baseline essays go far beyond discussing Egypt as an African society, and they assert a number of ideas that are inconsistent with the best scholarship. For instance, they maintain that the inhabitants of ancient Egypt were black Africans.

Scholars of Egyptian history and archeology say that the evidence suggests an entirely different story. Far from being all black (or all white), ancient Egypt, they say, was a multiracial society with a variety of racial types much like that of modern Egypt. In any case, our concept of race—a relatively modern invention—would not have made much sense to ancient Egyptians, who did not look at people in terms of skin color or hair texture. So the baseline essays not only misrepresent the evidence by insisting that Egypt was a black African society; they distort the example that Egypt has to offer our own multiracial society to make a political point.

The science section of the baseline essays reveals the same preference for politics over scholarship. The ancient Egyptians' excellence in mathematics, medicine and astronomy is widely acknowledged. For example, we owe our 365-day, 12-

---

* The position papers included in this appendix are reprinted with the permission of Albert Shanker and the American Federation of Teachers. They originally were published in 1991 as part of the "Where We Stand" series of paid advertisements published under the auspices of the American Federation of Teachers.

month year to them. But kids who learn science from this baseline essay will be told that the Egyptians developed the theory of evolution (thousands of years before Darwin), understood quantum physics and flew around for business and pleasure in full-size gliders—all stuff that no serious scientist believes for a minute. We used to laugh at the Soviets for saying that baseball and everything else of any importance had been discovered or invented in the USSR. These claims for Egyptian science are no more credible, and they are equally political in nature; they are propaganda rather than science. But this is not the biggest problem.

The science baseline essay presents as science stuff that is no more scientific than the Ouija board or mediums or the horoscope in the daily newspaper. Although the essay says it is important to distinguish between science and magic, it treats magic like a legitimate part of science. Kids whose teachers follow the Portland curriculum will be told that the Egyptians could predict lucky and unlucky days with the help of "astropsychological treatises"; and they'll hear how the Egyptians' highly developed "human capabilities" allowed them to see events before they happened ("precognition") or at a distance ("remote viewing"). Ideas like these make good subjects for movies or TV series, but they have nothing to do with science. Kids who are fed this kind of thing are not getting an alternative perspective; they are being cheated.

School boards and teachers accept the legitimacy of what's said in the baseline essays because they assume that the writers have solid credentials—and the introduction to the essays plays along with this. The writer of the science essay is described as a "Research Scientist of Argonne National Laboratories, Chicago," implying that the essay was written by a top-notch scientist, perhaps with the endorsement of a federally funded lab. But it turns out that the writer is not a scientist at all. According to Argonne, he's an industrial-hygiene technician with a high school diploma whose job is collecting air samples.

We all want to improve the achievement of our students. And poor, minority children, whose performance still lags far behind that of white, middle-class kids, deserve the best education we can given them. They're not going to get it if we substitute myths for history or magic for science. Here's how Frank Snowden, a professor emeritus of classics at Howard University, puts it:

> Many students already have been misled and confused by Afrocentrists' inaccuracies and omissions in their treatment of blacks in the ancient Mediterranean world. The time has come for Afrocentrists to cease mythologizing and falsifying the past. The time has come for scholars and educators to insist upon scholarly rigor and truth in current and projected revisions of our curriculum. *Tempus fugit!*

THE DANGER OF MULTIPLE PERSPECTIVES

by Albert Shanker
President of the American Federation of Teachers

We are in the midst of a revolution in the teaching of American history. Most people would agree it's long overdue. In the past, our history has been taught as a drama in which white men had all the good roles. It was a spectacular, flag-waving saga designed to create loyalty, patriotism and sense of the rightness of everything the U.S. did—and it worked. But the picture was incomplete, and it was not honest. It ignored the contributions of women, of African-Americans, of immigrants, of the labor movement and others; it ignored important occasions on which we betrayed our ideals. I don't know anyone today who would defend that kind of patriotic saga of progress or deny that an honest treatment of our history would naturally be multicultural.

But this isn't what some people mean by multiculturalism, and certain popular ideas about the subject are very troublesome. For example, the proposal that the New York State Board of Regents recently accepted, "One Nation, Many Peoples: A Declaration of Cultural Interdependence," sounds reasonable—and certainly the racist language that characterized the "Curriculum of Inclusion," an earlier report to the Regents has disappeared. But even the latest proposal will encourage intellectual dishonesty and promote divisiveness instead of healing it.

The main point of the report is that history and social studies should be taught from the point of view of "multiple perspectives," and that this should start in the earliest grades. Now, "multiple perspectives" is an excellent phrase. It sounds open-minded, which is what the pursuit of knowledge should be. But when you put the concept into the classroom, what does it mean?

For a teacher presenting a historical event to elementary school children, using multiple perspectives probably means that the teacher turns to each child and asks the child's point of view about the event. To an African-American child this would mean, "What is the African-American point of view?" To a Jewish child, "What is the Jewish point of view?" And to an Irish child, "What is the Irish point of view?"

This is racist because it assumes that a child's point of view is determined by the group he comes from. But is there a single African-American or Jewish or Irish point of view? A child may have a point of view based on the fact that he is rich or poor or that he has read extensively or that he comes from a family of conservative Republicans or Marxists. In a society like ours, we are often, and delightfully, surprised that people do not carry with them the views that stereotypes call for. Is it a teacher's job to tell children that they are entitled to only one point of view because of the racial, religious, or ethnic group they come from? Should schools be in the business of promoting racial stereotypes and fostering differences where they may not exist?

There is another equally serious problem with the idea of "multiple perspectives" as it appears in the report to the New York State Regents. It means that the teaching of history should no longer be dominated by ideas that historians widely accept on the basis of available evidence. It urges, instead, that we open up the curriculum to diverse theories, to "noncanonical knowledge and techniques" and "nondominant knowledge sources." Again, this sounds very open-minded. But what using "noncanonical knowledge" means is that it is okay to teach theories rejected by an overwhelming majority of—and perhaps all—experts in a field because there is little or no evidence for them. It makes ethnic diversity in ideas more important than evidence of their validity.

People who worry about education standards get up in arms when some group tries to get Creationism into the biology curriculum. And they call it an act of educational courage when a school board refuses to purchase textbooks that treat

Creationism as a scientific theory. Why? Because the scientific community does not accept the validity of Creationism. Scientists say it is an attempt to pass off a religious view as science. Yet, the Regents' history report assumes that one theory is as good as another as long as the materials are "culturally inclusive." And there seems to be very little resistance on the part of people who would raise a stink if kids were being taught the phlogiston theory in chemistry or the flat-earth theory in geography.

The notion of multiple perspectives that is presented by the Regents' report sounds sensible, but it is dangerous. Schools are supposed to educate our future citizens, scholars and scientists. They should be places where youngsters learn to think and weigh evidence. But there's little chance kids will learn these basic lessons if the curriculum teaches them that the evidence for an idea is less important than the ethnic perspective of the person presenting the idea.

Schools have also, historically, been places where children of varying backgrounds learned to live together. Assigning kids different points of view based on their ethnic, racial, or religious background will exacerbate conflict or even create it when none exists. Kids who are now happy to think of themselves primarily as Americans may learn to think of themselves primarily as Hispanics or African-Americans or Jews.

Throughout the world, countries made up of different peoples are coming apart. It would be tragic if here in the U.S., where almost all feel that they are first and foremost Americans, we adopted a curriculum that would pull us apart.

APPENDIX 6

Resources for Equity-oriented Teaching

Many resources are available for teachers interested in equity-oriented teaching. The list below is quite selective and far from exhaustive. In a number of cases the selected resource has an extensive bibliography, and two of the resources are themselves annotated bibliographies. The resources are listed under the following subheadings: cooperative learning; parent–teacher communication; general multicultural education resources; sources of children's literature for multicultural education; and sources of information about new American immigrant populations.

I. Cooperative Learning
1. Cohen, Elizabeth G. *Designing Groupwork: Strategies for the Heterogeneous Classroom.* Wolfeboro, N.H.: Teachers College Press, 1986.
2. Ellis, Susan S., and Susan F. Whalen. *Cooperative Learning: Getting Started.* New York: Scholastic, 1990.
3. Johnson, David W., and Robert T. Johnson. *Learning Together and Alone: Cooperative, Competitive, and Individualistic Learning,* 2nd ed. Englewood Cliffs, N.J.: Prentice-Hall, 1987.
4. Kagan, Spencer. *Cooperative Learning: Resources for Teachers.* San Juan Capistrano, Calif.: Resources for Teachers, 1989.
   This book is an excellent resource but may not be available in your library. It can be ordered from Resources for Teachers, 27134 Pasco Espada #202, San Juan Capistrano, CA 92675 or call (713) 248-7757.
5. Kohn, Alfie. "Caring Kids: The Role of Schools," *Phi Delta Kappan* 72, no. 7 (March 1991): 496–506.
6. Slavin, Robert E. *Cooperative Learning: Theory, Research, and Practice.* Englewood Cliffs, N.J.: Prentice-Hall, 1990.
7. The December 1989/January 1990 issue of *Educational Leadership* (vol. 47, no. 4) entitled "Cooperative Learning" contains a number of interesting articles and an interview with Spencer Kagan.

II. Parent–Teacher Communication
1. Boruta, Marcia, Janet Chrispeels, and Mary Daugherty. *Communicating with Parents.* San Diego, Calif.: San Diego County Office of Education, 1988.

   In terms of providing ideas and specific examples for classroom teachers this is the best resource I have encountered. It can be ordered directly from

   > San Diego County Office of Education
   > Graphic Communications, Room 12
   > 6401 Linda Vista Road
   > San Diego, CA 92111-7399
   > Telephone: (619) 569-5391

2. Jones, Linda T. *Strategies for Involving Parents in Their Children's Education.* Bloomington, Ind.: Phi Delta Kappa, 1991.

This document is Fastback #315 in Phi Delta Kappa's excellent series on issues and innovations in education.

3. The October 1989 issue of *Educational Leadership* (vol. 47, no. 2) entitled "Strengthening Partnerships with Parents and Community" contains a number of interesting articles and an interview with Joyce Epstein, a leading researcher in this area.

4. The Family Math Project. Write Virginia Thompson, Lawrence Hall of Science, University of California, Berkeley, CA 94720 or call (415) 642-1823 to learn more about this project. Briefly, Family Math is a project of the EQUALS program of the Lawrence Hall of Science. It is designed to help parents become more involved in their children's mathematics education. Products include the following:

   a. *The Family Math Book*

   b. *We All Count in FAMILY MATH* (a film about the project)

5. The January 1991 issue of *Phi Delta Kappan* (vol. 72, no. 5) contains a special section on parent involvement with nine stimulating articles. The guest editor is Joyce Epstein.

III. General Multicultural Education Resources

1. Banks, James. *Teaching Strategies for Ethnic Studies,* 5th ed. Boston: Allyn & Bacon, 1991.

   This is the best single resource for an introduction to *multiethnic* education. The book contains 10 chapters on various American ethnic groups; each of these chapters contains a time line, historical overview, list of teaching strategies, and annotated bibliography. The appendices and remaining chapters are also quite illuminating.

2. Banks, James, and Banks, Cherry A. McGee, eds. *Multicultural Education: Issues and Perspectives.* Boston: Allyn & Bacon, 1989.

   This text is a series of essays that deal with social class and religion, gender, ethnicity and language, exceptionality, and school reform, as well as issues and concepts that clarify multicultural education.

3. Bennett, Christine L. *Comprehensive Multicultural Education,* 2nd. ed. Boston: Allyn & Bacon, 1990.

   This text provides a balance between theoretical materials and teaching strategies. The author's conception of multicultural education strongly links it to global education. Part three of the text is entitled "Strengthening Multicultural and Global Perspectives in Teaching."

4. Carrasquillo, Angela L. *Hispanic Children and Youth in the United States.* New York: Garland Publishers, 1991.

   This text is number 20 in a well-conceived and edited series of reference books pertaining to family issues. It is an excellent source for readers seeking general as well as specific information about Hispanic children and youth.

5. Froschl, Merle, and Barbara Sprung. *Resources for Educational Equity: A Guide for Grades Pre-Kindergarten–12.* New York: Garland Publishing, 1988.

   This one-of-a-kind guide will be valuable for all teachers interested in learning more about the general topic of educational equity; it is of particular value for those interested in the special equity concerns of girls and women. The guide treats equity concerns in various school-related areas and provides an annotated bibliography for each of its chapters.

6. Gollnick, Donna M., and Philip C. Chinn. *Multicultural Education in a Pluralistic Society,* 3rd ed. Columbus, Ohio: Merrill, 1990.

   This well-written and well-conceived text is primarily an introduction to the concepts that are central to a cogent understanding of multicultural education. Each of the following concepts has its own chapter in the text: culture and pluralism, socioeconomic status, ethnicity, religion, language, sex and gender, exceptionality, and age. The final chapter, "Strategies for Multicultural Education," delineates six goals for multicultural education, and seven principles for making curriculum and instruction multicultural.

7. Grossman, Herbert. *Educating Hispanic Students: Cultural Implications for Instruction, Classroom Management, Counseling, and Assessment.* Springfield, Ill.: Charles C. Thomas, 1984.

   This text is one of the best available for information on teaching Hispanic students; it is particularly valuable because of the wide range of issues it addresses.

8. Hernandez, Hilda. *Multicultural Education: A Teacher's Guide to Content and Process.* Columbus, Ohio: Merrill, 1989.

   This text provides a balance between theoretical material and specific classroom teaching strategies. It will be particularly helpful for candidates who have little or no background in anthropology. In terms of equity, several chapters in the second part of the text are particularly valuable: "Bilingualism in a Multicultural Society," "Special/Gifted Education: Multicultural Connections," and Beyond the Classroom: Home, Neighborhood, and Community."

9. Hilliard, Asa III, Lucretia Payton-Stewart, and Larry Obadele Williams, eds. *Inclusion of African and African-American Content in the School Curriculum* (Proceedings of the First National Conference on the Infusion of African and African-American Content in the School Curriculum, October, 1989). Morristown, N.J.: Aaron Press, 1990.

This illuminating series of essays will serve as a useful introduction to Afrocentric education. The book is divided into three major sections: Theory and Rationale; History, Art, and the Spread of African People in the West; Curriculum Methodology and Strategy; it also contains a suggested reading list and a delineation of curriculum aids. Sample essay titles include "The Infusion of African and African-American Content: A Question of Content and Intent," by Wade W. Nobles; "The Cultural Base in Education," by Johnnetta B. Cole; "African People on My Mind," by John Henrik Clarke; and "African Survivals in the Black Atlantic World," by Robert F. Thompson. Inquiries regarding this book should be addressed to Aaron Press, 103 Washington Street, Morristown, NJ 07960.

10. Nieto, Sonia. *Affirming Diversity: The Sociopolitical Context of Multicultural Education.* White Plains, N.Y.: Longman, 1992.

This well-written text is noteworthy because it presents an approach to education that is simultaneously multicultural and social reconstructionist; at the same time it presents informative chapters on language, linguistic diversity in the classroom, and the sociopolitical context of education. Nieto defines multicultural education in terms of antiracist education, social justice, and critical pedagogy, among other important elements. The text strikes a balance between social issues, theoretical concerns, and teaching strategies.

11. Quellmalz, Edys S., and Janita Hoskin. "Making a Difference in Arkansas: The Multicultural Reading and Thinking Project," *Educational Leadership* 45, no. 7 (April 1988): 52–55.

This article describes the background and results of a three-year project led by reading specialists in the Arkansas State Department of Education and selected Arkansas teachers. The goal of the project is to develop instructional materials that will simultaneously (a) develop the critical thinking ability of students and (b) enhance their knowledge of other cultures and specific multicultural concepts. In January 1991 the Arkansas State Department of Education published the "McRat Report"; this report, which contains more information about this well-conceived and successful project, can be obtained by writing or calling Janita J. Hoskin, Project Manager, Arkansas Department of Education, General Division, #4, Capital Mall, Little Rock, AR 72201; (501) 682-4332.

12. Sleeter, Christine E., and Carl A. Grant. *Making Choices for Multicultural Education; Five Approaches to Race, Class, and Gender,* Columbus, Ohio: Merrill, 1988.

This book describes an approach to education that is simultaneously multicultural and social reconstructionist. Several other chapters treat the human relations approach to education, multicultural education, single-group studies, and teaching the exceptional and culturally different. Although each of these chapters contains a section entitled "Recommended Practices," the book is largely conceptual and theoretical in nature. It is a valuable addition to the multicultural education literature.

13. Sleeter, Christine E., and Carl A. Grant. *Turning on Learning: Five Approaches for Multicultural Teaching Plans for Race, Class, Gender, and Disability.* Columbus, Ohio: Merrill, 1989.

    This is the companion piece to the resource listed directly above. Each of the multicultural approaches discussed in *Making Choices* is further illuminated by a thought-provoking set of before and after lessons. The before and after treatments are followed by a section that explains how the changes made the lesson better in terms of the specific approach under discussion.

14. Tiedt, Pamela, L., and Iris M. Tiedt. *Multicultural Teaching: A Handbook of Activities, Information, and Resources,* 3rd ed. Boston: Allyn & Bacon, 1990.

    This is a useful and creative collection of lessons and other resources. The handbook will complement any of the texts above that are primarily theoretical. The text contains a set of lessons on self-esteem and sets called "The First Americans," "Stereotypes, Black Americans, Hispanic Americans," "Cultures and Time," and "The Monthly Calendar." The appendix, "A Literature Base for Multicultural Education," is a valuable resource in and of itself.

15. Ramsey, Patricia G., Edwina B. Vold, and Leslie R. Williams. *Multicultural Education: A Source Book.* New York: Garland Publishing, 1989.

    This excellent source book combines illuminating essays with well-selected, richly detailed, annotated bibliographies.

16. *Multicultural Leader,* a newsletter published quarterly by Educational Materials and Services Center, P.O. Box 802, Edmonds, WA 98020 [Phone: (206) 542-4218]. The editor and publisher is Cherry A. McGee Banks.

    The newsletter has some valuable and regular features. These include essays, a book review section, a journal watch column in which essays are briefly summarized, a research review, and on occasion a look at multicultural education abroad. This newsletter is an excellent way to extend your personal network of information about multicultural issues and education.

17. *School Library Journal: The Magazine of Children's, Young Adult, and School Librarians.* For subscription information write to School Library Journal, P.O. Box 1978, Marion, OH 43305-1978, or call (800) 842-1669 in the continental United States.

This magazine, on a regular basis, will provide you with interesting articles and helpful recommendations regarding children's multicultural literature and media. For example, in 1992 the magazine published an outstanding set of reviews on cultural diversity videos. The January 1992 issue featured African Americans, and this was followed by Native Americans (May 1992), Asian Americans and Asians (September 1992), and Hispanics, Chicanos, and Latinos (December 1992).

18. *Teaching Tolerance*, a journal published twice a year by the Southern Law Poverty Center, Montgomery, Alabama. The editor's address is Editor, Teaching Tolerance, 400 Washington Avenue, Montgomery, AL 36104.

   The inaugural issue of this timely journal appeared in spring 1992. The journal will be published twice a year, and the plan as of spring 1992 is to disseminate the journal free to teachers. According to the editor, Sara Bullard, the journal "is meant to be a collection of ready-to-use ideas and strategies, . . . and a source of encouragement for the thousands of teachers who are working to build communities of understanding in their classrooms."

19. The *Resource Service Catalog of the National Women's History Project* (NWHP). The NWHP is a nonprofit educational project; its address and phone number is: 7738 Bell Road, Windsor, CA 95492; (707) 838-6000.

   The catalogue is an education in itself. Most teachers will learn something useful just from perusing the descriptions of the posters, special units, books, films, and videos that are highlighted in the catalogue. This is an organization and set of resources that every multicultural teacher should know about.

20. *Claudia's Caravan* (Multicultural-Multilingual Materials), 1992–1993. This very helpful catalogue offers a rich variety of well-selected multicultural instructional materials. These materials include dolls and artifacts, musical instruments, records/cassettes, videos, and a wide range of books dealing with various aspects of multicultural education. The catalogue can be ordered by writing to Claudia's Caravan, P.O. Box 1582, Alameda, CA 94501, or by calling (510) 521-7871.

21. The *Handbook of Research on Multicultural Education* is scheduled for publication by Macmillan in 1994. James Banks is editor and Cherry A. McGee Banks is associate editor. Guided by the editors and a distinguished editorial advisory board, this collection of articles should make a major contribution in terms of stimulating new research.

IV. Sources of Children's Literature for Multicultural Education
1. Kruse, Ginny Moore, and Kathleen T. Horning, with Merri V. Lindgren and Katherine Odahowski. *Multicultural Literature for Children and Young*

Adults: A Selected Listing of Books 1980–1990, 3rd ed. Madison: Cooperative Children's Book Center, University of Wisconsin–Madison, and Wisconsin Department of Public Instruction, 1991. This publication is available from Publication Sales, Wisconsin Department of Public Instruction, P.O. Box 7841, Madison, WI 531707-7841. Inquire about Bulletin #1923 (1-800-243-8782).

The well-conceived bibliography section includes the following among its 16 sections: Books for Babies; Books for Toddlers; Fiction for Teenagers; Folklore, Mythology, and Traditional Literature; Issues in Today's World; and Understanding Oneself and Others.

2. Tway, Eileen, ed. *Reading Ladders for Human Relations,* 6th ed. Washington, D.C.: American Council on Education, 1981.

   The primary purpose of *Ladders* is "to advance the cause of better human relations." The volume is organized around five ladders; each ladder is divided into subcategories that are grouped into age-range steps along a continuum from pre-school through high school. The five ladders are entitled Growing into Self; Relating to Wide Individual Differences; Interacting in Groups; Appreciating Different Cultures; and Coping in a Changing World.

3. Chelsea House publishes an excellent set of 75 biographies of African Americans entitled *Black Americans of Achievement.* Another set of biographies called *Hispanics of Achievement* numbered 29 as of July 1991, and a third set, *American Women of Achievement,* contained 50 stories of women's accomplishments. The catalogue of Chelsea House includes other collections that should be interesting to classroom teachers, librarians, and curriculum coordinators. The publisher's address is 95 Madison Avenue, New York, NY 10016; a catalogue can be ordered by calling 1-800-848-2665.

   In addition, please note that there is a *Black Americans of Achievement Video Collection* produced by Schlessinger Video Products and distributed by Library Video Corporation. This collection is based on the Chelsea House series and includes 30-minute videos about Jesse Jackson, Colin Powell, Martin Luther King, Malcolm X, and Jackie Robinson ($39.95 each); the address of Library Video Corporation is Box 1110, Cynwyd, PA 19004.

V. Sources of Information about Selected New American Immigrant Populations

1. *A Handbook for Teaching Cantonese-Speaking Students,* 1984, 71 pp. $4.50 each. Available from the Bureau of Publications, Sales Unit, California State Department of Education, P.O. Box 271, Sacramento, CA 95802-0271; ISBN 0-8011-0824-1. Call Sales Unit at 916-445-1260 for further information.

   This handbook is designed to assist school personnel in understanding the characteristics of Cantonese-speaking students. The publication is divided into five main sections: (1) Overview of the Cantonese Language Group, (2)

Historical and Sociocultural Factors Concerning the Group, (3) Linguistic Characteristics of the Cantonese Language, (4) Recommended Instructional and Curricular Strategies for Cantonese Language Development, and (5) Appendix of Educational and Community Resources.

2. *A Handbook for Teaching Hmong-Speaking Students,* 1988. 129 pp. $4.50 each. Available from the Southeast Asia Community Resource Center, Folsom-Cordova Unified School District, 2460 Cordova Lane, Rancho Cordova, CA 95670. Call 916-635-6815 for further information.

This handbook is designed to assist school personnel in understanding the characteristics of Hmong-speaking students. The publication is divided into five sections: (1) Overview of the Hmong Language, (2) Historical and Sociocultural Factors Concerning the Group, (3) Linguistic Characteristics of the Hmong Language, (4) Recommended Instructional and Curricular Strategies for Hmong Language Development, and (5) Appendix of Educational and Community Resources. The handbook was developed by Bruce Thowpaou Bliatout, Bruce T. Downing, Judy Lewis, and Dao Yang.

3. *A Handbook for Teaching Japanese-Speaking Students,* 1987. 124 pp. $4.50 each. Available from the California Department of Education, Bureau of Publications. ISBN 0-8011-0680-X. See note 1 for phone number and address.

This handbook is designed to assist school personnel in understanding the characteristics of Japanese-speaking students. The publication is divided into five main sections: (1) Overview of the Japanese Language Group, (2) Historical and Sociocultural Factors Concerning the Group, (3) Linguistic Characteristics of Japanese, (4) Recommended Instructional and Curricular Strategies for Japanese Language Development, and (5) Appendix of Educational and Community Resources.

4. *Handbook for Teaching Khmer-Speaking Students,* 1988. 152 pp. $5.50 each. Available from the Southeast Asia Community Resource Center, Folsom-Cordova Unified School District. See note 2 for address and phone number.

This handbook is designed to help school district personnel understand Khmer-speaking students. The publication is divided into five main sections: (1) Overview of the Khmer Language Group, (2) Historical and Sociocultural Factors Concerning the Group, (3) Linguistic Characteristics of the Khmer Language, (4) Recommended Instructional and Curricular Strategies for Khmer Language Development, and (5) Appendix of Educational and Community Resources. This handbook was developed by Mory Ouk, Franklin E. Huffman and Judy Lewis, with contributions by nine others.

5. *Handbook for Teaching Korean American Students,* 1992, $4.50 each. Available from the California Department of Education, Bureau of Publications, Sacramento, CA 95802-0271. Call 916-445-1260 for further information.

This handbook is designed to assist school personnel in understanding the characteristics of Korean-speaking students. The handbook is divided into five main sections: (1) Overview of the Korean Language Group, (2) Historical and Sociocultural Factors Concerning the Group, (3) Linguistic Characteristics of the Korean Language, (4) Recommended Instructional and Curricular Strategies for Korean Language Development, and (5) Appendix of Educational and Community Resources.

6. *A Handbook for Teaching Lao-Speaking Students,* 1989. 178 pp. $5.00 each. Available from the Southeast Asia Community Resource Center, Folsom-Cordova Unified School District. See phone number and address above.

This handbook is designed to help school district personnel understand Lao-speaking students. The handbook is divided into five main sections: (1) Overview of the Lao Language Group, (2) Historical and Sociocultural Factors Concerning Lao-speaking Peoples, (3) Linguistic Characteristics of the Lao Language, (4) Recommended Instructional and Curricular Strategies for Lao Language Development, and (5) Appendix of Educational and Community Development, and Appendix of Educational and Community Resources.

7. *A Handbook for Teaching Pilipino-Speaking Students,* 1986. 84 pp. $4.50 each. Available from the California Department of Education, Bureau of Publications. ISBN 0-8011-0291-X. See address and phone number above.

This handbook is designed to assist school personnel in understanding the characteristics of Pilipino-speaking students. The publication is divided into five main sections: (1) Overview of the Pilipino Language Group, (2) Historical and Sociocultural Factors Concerning the Group, (3) Linguistic Characteristics of Pilipino, (4) Recommended Instructional and Curricular Strategies for Native Language Development, and (5) Appendix of Educational and Community Resources.

8. *A Handbook for Teaching Portuguese-Speaking Students,* 1983. 102 pp. $4.50 each. Available from the California State Department of Education Bureau of Publications. ISBN 0-8011-0825-XS. See address and phone number above.

This handbook is designed to assist school personnel in understanding the characteristics of Portuguese-speaking students. The publication is divided into five main sections: (1) Overview of the Portuguese Language Group, (2) Historical and Sociocultural Factors Concerning the Group, (3) Linguistic Characteristics of Portuguese, (4) Recommended Instructional and Curricular Strategies for Native Language Development, and (5) Appendix of Educational and Community Resources.

9. *A Handbook for Teaching Vietnamese-American Students,* in press. Will likely be published in 1993 and will be available from the California State

Department of Education, Bureau of Publications (call 916-445-1260 for further information).

This handbook is designed to assist school personnel in understanding the characteristics of Vietnamese-speaking students. The handbook is divided into five main sections: (1) Overview of the Vietnamese Language Group, (2) Historical and Sociocultural Factors Concerning the Vietnamese-speaking Peoples, (3) Linguistic Characteristics of the Vietnamese Language, (4) Recommended Instructional and Curricular Strategies for Vietnamese Language Development, and (5) Appendix of Educational and Community Resources.

APPENDIX 7

Text Evaluation Form for Course Instructors

Name (optional): _____

Address: _____

City: _____ State: _____ Zip: _____

School: _____

Course Title: _____

Office Phone: _____

----

1. Which chapters in *Teaching with a Multicultural Perspective* did your students read?

   _____

2. For the objectives in your course, how could these chapters be improved?

   _____

   _____

3. In terms of new content, what would you add to this text to make it more useful for your course? What would you delete?

   _____

   _____

4. What did you like most about this text? Least?

   _____

   _____

   _____

5. Do you plan to continue using this text?

   _____

      Please mail to
          Leonard Davidman
          University Center for Teacher Education
          California Polytechnic State University
          San Luis Obispo, CA 93407

Index

final comments regarding, 149
generalizations, main ideas, and
     supporting information for, 138–140
introductory, selected developmental, and
     culminating activities in, 140–143
objectives for, 137–138
related main idea and facts regarding,
     148–149
statement of multicultural perspective
     for, 144

"Women as Members of Groups" (National
     Women's History Project), 93
Women in Science videotape series, 98
*Women of Mathematics: A Bibliographic
     Sourcebook* (Grinstein & Campbell),
     97
Word of the Week Program, 82–84
Workshop strategy, 10

Yiddish, 122, 123